THE PATH OF INFINITE SORROW

Dedicated to the memory of the men who served on both sides of the conflict generally known as the Kokoda campaign.

The Path of INFINITE SORROW

THE JAPANESE
on the
KOKODA TRACK

CRAIG COLLIE & HAJIME MARUTANI

ALLEN&UNWIN

First published in Australia in 2009

Maps by Ian Faulkner

Allen & Unwin
83 Alexander Street
Crows Nest NSW 2065
Australia
Phone: (61 2) 8425 0100
Fax: (61 2) 9906 2218
Email: info@allenandunwin.com
Web: www.allenandunwin.com

The Cataloguing-in-Publication entry is available from the National Library of Australia
www.librariesaustralia.nla.gov.au

ISBN 978 174175 839 9

Typeset in 12/16pt Bembo by Post Pre-press Group
Printed by Griffin Press, Adelaide

10 9 8 7 6 5 4 3 2 1

Contents

Maps

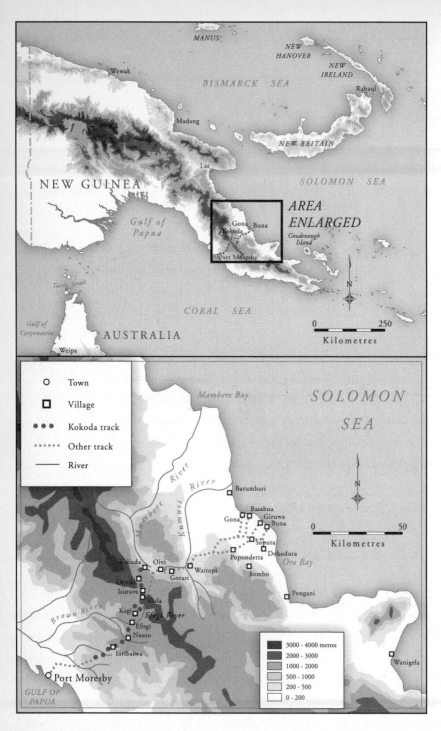

The Kokoda Track and surrounding area

Chapter I

On Ioribaiwa Ridge

The men scrambled up to a rocky peak on the Maguli Range in their brown fatigues and soggy boots, keeping low in case enemy riflemen still lurked in the vicinity, and peered over the top. What they glimpsed below fired an elation more powerful than they had ever experienced. Exhausted and starving, they didn't know they still had this emotion in them. Between gaps in the high jungle and through the mountain mist the men saw a sparkle that could only be the sun glinting off the ocean during breaks in the heavy cloud cover. It had to be the Gulf of Papua. For several days, since crossing the saddle of the Owen Stanley Range, these men had trudged and battled up and over mountain ridge after mountain ridge, expecting to see the plains and sea around Port Moresby, only to have their hopes dashed each time with yet another razorback to cross. Now, at long last, the sea lay before them. The relief was enormous. The men hugged each other and wept. Some cried, '*Tenno Heika banzai*' ('Long live the Emperor'), but not too loudly.[1]

Only 1500 of the 6000 troops who had set out on this campaign in July and August remained in good enough condition four to six weeks later to fight on.[2] Half of the soldiers who had pushed south from the beaches near Buna and Gona were now sick or wounded and had been withdrawn. Some were just behind the front line, on stretchers if they were lucky, waiting to be treated at the field hospital that would be set up in Moresby after the city had been captured.[3] Some of the men who had started out were now missing, presumed dead. Over a thousand were known to have died, many not at the hands of the enemy but victims of this majestic but inhospitable land. It had been hard, much harder than they had expected, in part because of wildly inaccurate intelligence. Those who made it this far rejoiced at the thought that, after all their sacrifice and suffering for the glory of Japan and the emperor, the success of their mission seemed imminent. The food supply line had dwindled to the barest trickle, but Port Moresby would replenish the larder.

Four days later, a little further down the track, they took Ioribaiwa Ridge from the retreating enemy. Again, the sea could be seen in the distance. At night, the men could see the searchlights of Seven Mile airfield on the outskirts of Moresby, forty-two kilometres away, their beams probing the night clouds for air attacks that no longer threatened. The moon's reflection shimmered fleetingly on the surface of the Coral Sea.[4] It was a scene of transcendent beauty, one they would never forget. Staff Sergeant Imanishi and Warrant Officer Shimada had made it to this point despite failing supply lines and an enemy who wouldn't give up. So had the machine-gunner Lieutenant Sakamoto and Seizo Okada, the war correspondent for *Asahi Shimbun*. Some of the high morale that had followed decisive victories at Guam and Rabaul had returned. Shimada's lasting memory is of finally arriving at Ioribaiwa in the highest of spirits, convinced of the success of the Moresby offensive, MO Operation.[5]

It was September 1942. These were the men of South Seas Force, or Nankai Shitai, of the Imperial Japanese Army (IJA). They had spent the last eight weeks battling an often-unseen enemy along a muddy, precipitous track worn into existence by centuries of tramping bare feet. The Kokoda Track crosses deep ravines and mountain ridges as it makes its way for some 160 kilometres over the Owen Stanley Range and adjacent ridge lines. The soldiers of Nankai Shitai had endured constant rain and frequent torrential downpours, virulent strains of malaria, dysentery, dengue fever and beriberi. They had struggled against an enemy who at any time might be no more than ten metres away in the dense New Guinea jungle, an enemy whose marksmanship was greatly feared. The enemy was Australian—just two militia battalions at first, later reinforced with battle-seasoned troops of the Australian Imperial Force (AIF) brought back from the Middle East. This was the Pacific War, as the Japanese called it to distinguish it from the preceding war they referred to as the China Incident. The principal enemy was the United States of America and the other Western imperial powers, but the Australians had been absorbed into the war as Japan secured its southern perimeter and prepared for the inevitable Allied counter-offensive.

While combat troops waited at Ioribaiwa for the order for a final assault on Port Moresby, the engineers came forward and went about consolidating the Japanese position. They dug trenches for protection from any counter-attack by the enemy and from air raids by the Australian and American warplanes that now controlled the skies of New Guinea. For more cover, they built fences around these trenches with felled trees, and cut foliage with knife or hatchet to drape as camouflage over trenches and tents. They dug latrines and they dug weapons pits. It was a campaign of endless digging with shovel and pick in the muddy mountain earth.

The Japanese positioned guns along the ridge and waited. The original timetable had had them capturing Moresby in the first week of September, but they didn't reach Ioribaiwa until the 16th. At the end of September, they were still dug in there at the end of a 200-kilometre supply line, with precious little food and scanty ammunition.

From high on a ridge overlooking the campaign objective, the fall of Port Moresby might have seemed like a foregone conclusion. A few must have known that logic said otherwise, that 1500 starving men could never prevail over who knows how many fresh combat troops waiting below. But the ordinary soldier is not trained to think about these things. His role is to take orders and carry them out to the best of his ability. All for the glory of the emperor and Japan, in the case of these men. The ordinary soldier is conditioned to follow orders without question, to believe that sheer will can overcome extreme hunger and weariness.

At Force headquarters at Mawai, a short distance behind the front line, the commander of Nankai Shitai had a different perspective. Major-General Tomitaro Horii was a stubborn man—stubborn to a fault, some would say—who had set about MO Operation ruthlessly and effectively, at least on paper, despite his doubts that such a plan was practicable. Horii's instructions now were to find a suitable defensive position behind his current HQ and hold that line until reinforcements and supplies were available.[6] He hadn't acted on those instructions, staying instead on the ridge at Ioribaiwa, but it was a forlorn hope he harboured. He and his officers knew that Japan was faring badly in the battle for Guadalcanal in the Solomon Islands and that any available reinforcements and supplies would have been diverted there. He knew also that Allied supremacy in the air was already choking supply lines. The order to withdraw, probably as far back as the northern beaches around Buna and Gona from where they'd started, was inevitable, but Horii didn't tell his troops, who were impatient to advance.

Imperial high command in Tokyo and the Seventeenth Army's commander, General Hyakutake, in Rabaul, were wavering. The men camped on Ioribaiwa Ridge knew nothing of this. They could not know that this was as near to Port Moresby as they would ever get. They could not know that from here things would sink deeper and deeper into a Stygian morass—their own real-life heart of darkness—and that all the few who survived would take out of the experience was a deep, everlasting sorrow.

How did they get to this position, and where did things go from there? That is the story of the men of South Seas Force in the Imperial Japanese Army. This is their experience of the Kokoda campaign.

Chapter 2

Empire and emperor

So where did it all begin? Perhaps as far back as the 1868 Meiji Restoration, fifteen years after America's hard-nosed Commodore Matthew Perry steamed into Edo (Tokyo) Bay and made Japan an offer it couldn't refuse, forcing it to open up to trade with the rest of the world. On his return visit, Perry was not as intimidated by a display of sumo wrestling as the Japanese had hoped. For their part, they were delighted with a ride on a demonstration railway line set up by the Americans for the occasion.[1] Economic and social upheaval from rising export prices and inexpensive foreign goods followed, leading ultimately to the collapse of the feudal Tokugawa regime, which had been dominated by the samurai. Meiji restored the emperor to centre stage in Japan some forty years before any of the men on the ridge at Ioribaiwa were born. The outcome was not only the modernisation of Japan, but a rising antagonism towards the Western colonial powers in eastern Asia and a sense of destiny for a Japanese empire. The men may have had no involvement with any of this, but it produced the environment in which their lives were now immersed.

They had grown up in the latter part of the most tumultuous period of Japanese history. Changes had taken place in virtually every thread of the country's social fabric, producing among other things a fervent nationalism. This led to fifty years of intermittent war, first against China (1894–95) and Russia (1904–05), within China against Germany (1914–15), and in Siberia after the Bolshevik Revolution (1918–22), then in Manchuria in 1931, the rest of China from 1937 and, finally, in Southeast Asia and the Pacific. All but the Siberian adventure extended Japan's overseas interests, but the last and most ambitious campaign would end in disaster for Japan and its people. Over that fifty-year period two strands wove into the national psyche, nurtured as driving impulses of twentieth-century Japan. One was the notion of a Japanese empire extending its presence into the eastern half of Asia, a pan-Asian union of sorts with Japan as its logical leader. This found particular expression in the idea of the Greater East Asia Co-prosperity Sphere. The other strand was the cult of the emperor.

The Meiji revolution transformed Japan. Railways were built, linking its cities and ports and changing Japan's relationship with the world. The major Western powers held trade concessions in various ports along the Asian seaboard. Japan wanted them too. Korea was pressured into opening three of its ports to Japanese trade. Exports to that country expanded, including European goods that had been imported into Japan, and rice and soybeans were imported from Korea. Meiji strategist Arimoto Yamagata[2] was an influential member of the political and social elites that ran Japan. He saw Korea as a 'zone of advantage' protecting Japan as a 'zone of sovereignty'.[3] The seeds of empire were sown.

In 1881, Japanese military advisers were invited by the reformist King Kojong to help modernise the Korean army. Korea had long had ties with China. Japan sought to undermine these, beginning an extended period of antagonism between the two countries that was always fought out on Chinese soil, never on Japanese. It still simmers today, more than sixty years after the end of the Pacific War supposedly brought it to a conclusion. China from time to time raises unfinished business about Japanese treatment of its people in war.

Korean popular sentiment in the late nineteenth century was frequently concerned with the influence that China and foreign powers had in its political and economic affairs. Sometimes Japan's advice and assistance was sought in dealing with this problem; sometimes Japan was seen as part of the problem. The shifting relationships between China and Japan, and between Korea's people and its rulers, came to a head on a number of occasions. An 1884 coup in Korea was quashed by two thousand Chinese troops. They were joined by crowds angry at the perceived role of Japan in the coup. Some forty Japanese advisers and residents were killed in the melee, but Japan, still rebuilding its military, let the matter go.[4]

It didn't let it go ten years later when the Tong-hak rebellion took control of much of Korea. At its core was the belief that foreigners and the nation's elite were the cause of Korea's poverty. The government again asked China to send troops, but this time Japan intervened to 'protect Japanese interests'. The 1894–95 Sino-Japanese War followed, ending in a decisive Japanese victory. Out of the peace treaty Japan won control of Formosa (as Taiwan was then called) and nearby islands, as well as the peninsula of Liaotung (Kwantung) in China.[5] It also won the right to build railways in southern Manchuria, on China's border with Russia, bringing an aggressive Japan within eyeball range of tsarist Russia.

The peace treaty following the Sino-Japanese War obliged China to pay 360 million yen in compensation. The money was spent on upgrading Japan's military and, as collateral, on shipbuilding and on modernising the iron and steel industries. The successful prosecution of a war prompted a swelling of nationalistic pride and a surge in the prestige of the armed forces, quite apart from the nascent empire it had produced. It also reinforced the maxim that force decides international affairs, something already observed with the Western colonial powers in Asia.

Since the opening of trade after Perry's visit, Japan had been constantly reminded of its second-class status in the eyes of the West. Coerced treaties granted both extraterritoriality and the right of colonial powers to set Japan's tariff rates. Extraterritoriality allowed crimes by foreigners in Japan to be tried by consular courts under foreign law, undermining Japan's national dignity. However, entrenched views were moderating.

By the end of the nineteenth century, Japan was starting to be seen by the West as a model moderniser. New treaties were negotiated ending extraterritoriality and phasing in a return of tariff autonomy to Japan.

The Japanese, for their part, saw Western institutions and technology as highly desirable, but the West itself still seemed a threat. A view was emerging within Japan that its progress depended on the development of military strength, the growth of overseas trade and emigration. By 1907, there were 65,000 Japanese resident in Hawaii (not then a state of the US) and 60,000 in the United States. The wages they sent home accounted for 3 per cent of Japan's foreign exchange.[6] As well, a population spurt from the turn of the century was changing Japan from a self-sufficient exporter of food into a nation dependent on imports of rice and raw materials. A dependence on foreign markets created a need to build up the military for expansion overseas. With limited natural resources, Japan had to trade to create wealth.

Within weeks of the signing of the Treaty of Shimonoseki, which resolved the Sino-Japanese War and ceded the lease of Liaotung to Japan, imperial Russia, backed by Germany and France, pressed for the peninsula's return to China to restore the region's balance of power. Japan complied and received another lesson in the way the major powers conducted international affairs. Russia soon secured a twenty-five-year lease on Liaotung, giving it access to the ice-free seaport of Port Arthur and to the peninsula's mineral wealth. In 1900, Russia moved troops into Manchuria ostensibly to protect its interests during China's Boxer Rebellion, but when that uprising was brought under control the troops stayed put.[7]

Japan pressured Russia to withdraw from Liaotung, but to little effect. By 1904 it had had enough. Negotiations between the two hawkish powers broke down. The Japanese navy conducted a night attack by torpedo boat on the Russian fleet in Port Arthur. Two days later Japan formally declared war, starting the eighteen-month Russo-Japanese War. The Japanese army landed in Korea, crossed the Yalu River to Liaotung and put Port Arthur under siege. The navy blockaded Port Arthur and Vladivostok. In response, Russia sent its dilapidated Baltic Fleet halfway around the world to relieve Vladivostok, only for it to be crushed off

Korea.[8] But, for all these impressive victories, Japan wasn't able to defeat the Russian army with any finality. Japan's casualties were high and its funds were running low. Russia, for its part, was in fear of revolution at home. Neither side could deal the killer blow, so the stalemate dragged on. Finally, Japan secretly persuaded US President Theodore Roosevelt to intervene. The warring parties signed the Portsmouth Treaty in September 1905, giving Japan the southern half of Sakhalin Island to its north, the lease once again on Liaotung, various railway and port concessions in Manchuria and recognition of its 'paramount interests' in Korea . . . but no financial compensation.

Japan now had mining rights in southern Manchuria and access to Korea, providing iron ore to feed its growing heavy industry. Korean leaders had used Russia to play the foreign powers off against each other, but that had unravelled with the Russo-Japanese War. The Japanese army now ran Korean foreign relations. The king, who had once invited Japanese advisers to help modernise his army, was forced to resign. The Korean army was disbanded and in 1910 Korea was annexed as a Japanese colony. The governor-general of Korea was appointed by the emperor of Japan. He held complete authority until 1945.

Having resisted Russian might, Japan was now noted as a power on the international stage, challenging the idea of white supremacy. Some hostility emerged—America decided to limit Japanese emigration—but Japan's colonies of Korea and Formosa were secure from international challenge. Japan's rulers sought to enhance its position in Asia. Overseas business interests were developed, particularly in Korea. Asia was now the frontier of expanding Japanese power and prestige. At home the elites, the political parties, the military and the press all demanded the pursuit of equality with Western imperialist powers and recognition of Japan's special interest in Asia. Japan played the international-relations game by the same apparent rules as the major colonial powers, escalating its position until it got the result it sought. British, Americans, Russians and French all ruthlessly pursued raw materials and new markets by diplomacy and negotiation, threats, gunboat diplomacy and, if all else failed, war. The Japanese saw no reason not to do likewise.

By 1914, Britain and Germany were at war. Japan joined hostilities under the Anglo-Japanese alliance, which dated back to its attempts to prise Russia out of Manchuria. Its troops took over German possessions in China's Shandong province and a number of nearby Pacific islands. The 1911 Chinese Revolution had left the country in chaos, something Japan tried to take advantage of by presenting its 'Twenty-one Demands' to the Yuan government. This ultimatum included a joint Japanese–Chinese police force in China, and Japanese political, economic and military advisers. Not surprisingly, the Chinese were outraged. The British and Americans pressed for the more extreme demands to be dropped, and a watered-down version was reluctantly signed by China. Nonetheless, Chinese popular opinion remained virulently anti-Japanese, and the US saw Japan as a competitor for its influence in China.

A perception was emerging in Japan of the American government as one that was more concerned with ends than with the means of achieving them. When the US entered the war in 1917, by the Ishii-Lansing agreement each country recognised the other's colonial possessions in Asia. Japan had a seat at the Versailles peace negotiations, where its control of Shandong was confirmed. However, it also proposed a racial equality clause in the League of Nations charter, opposed successfully by Woodrow Wilson, the US President. One of the most vociferous opponents of the clause was Australia, which was concerned about the impact on its White Australia policy, but Australia wasn't on Japan's radar then. The Japanese reaction was anger at the hypocrisy of Western governments.

Japanese war planning had followed the British model, with a strong navy to protect the home islands and support the expansion of the embryonic empire. Both the US and Japan were conscious of a naval arms race developing in the Pacific region since World War I. A series of tripartite meetings in Washington over 1921 and 1922 attempted to resolve this by setting a 5:5:3 battleship ratio for the three leading naval powers, the US, Britain and Japan. Importantly for Japan, it was also agreed that America's defence stopped at Hawaii and Britain's at Singapore.[9]

Japan did well out of the World War I. Its military involvement was minimal and often token, escorting Australian troop-ships to Gallipoli, for instance. No Japanese land forces were committed to Europe. But with Asian markets cut off from their usual European suppliers, demand grew for Japanese goods. As production increased, labour was in short supply and wages rose. The results were high inflation on the one hand and the emergence of the *narikin*, a Japanese *nouveau riche*, on the other. Japan's trade position changed dramatically. The excess of its foreign assets over its debt in 1919 (1300 million yen) reversed the balance of 1913.[10]

Japan's war boom continued after the Armistice, but by 1920 it was collapsing as the stock market and silk exports both plunged. Banks failed, workers were laid off and government spending declined. Agriculture and domestic production hit a plateau. The economy lurched through a series of crises throughout the 1920s. While Japan consolidated its dreams of empire abroad, at home there was social turmoil.

Since 1905, when the Russo-Japanese treaty's lack of compensation payments had provoked public anger, violent riots were a regular occurrence, usually with much destruction of public property and often with several people killed. These clashes might arise in response to a political stand-off or to inflation or to revelations that a senior politician was taking kickbacks. When Admiral Yamamoto resigned as prime minister in 1914, it was because of riots protesting against his relationship with the German arms manufacturer Siemens.[11] Between the world wars instability was the most consistent feature of Japanese government, which was appointed by the elites, not the parliament. Prime ministers seldom lasted more than a year or two before being overtaken by scandal, ineptitude, a deadlock on some matter of principle, inertia or assassination. Political terror was rife in the 1920s and 1930s, with attempted and successful assassinations of senior ministers and the occasional prime minister (Hara in 1921, Hamaguchi in 1930, Inukai in 1932). Show trials gave the assassins a platform to promote their views. The Japanese public found greater sympathy with the purity of their motives than with the machinations of politicians. A new mood was taking hold—or an old inclination to spirituality was finding a new context.

Everything was in transition, and the changes outside the political sphere were profound and irreversible. Traditionally, rural life had revolved around the villages, clusters of ten to seventy households with their ethic of harmony, their communal decision-making and their shrines stressing community solidarity. Almost half of all land was worked by tenant farmers.[12] Landlords were either small farmers who worked the unrented part of their land themselves or wealthy rural landholders who invested profits in the city and dabbled in politics. Their wives joined organisations like the Ladies' Patriotic Association, sent 'care packages' to Japanese troops overseas, drank tea and complained about the servants.[13] They might have been English gentlefolk. Tenant farmers lived at subsistence level, vulnerable to fluctuating prices. They were expected to routinely acknowledge their inferior social position to the landlords, from whom they could expect customary gestures of benevolence in return.

By the 1920s, a growing number of absentee landlords were being represented by estate managers who ignored the custom of benevolence. Tenant farmers began to unionise and would rent fields from several landlords so they could withhold labour from one and force the rent down. Landlords banded to fend off tenant demands or else sold their land and moved into the cities. The once harmonious rural life was becoming unstable.

City life was seeing similar change. At the turn of the century, the cities were made up of wage-earning masses and wealthy employers. Forty per cent of workers, the 'old middle class', were engaged in small family enterprises at home, but office workers and factory labourers often earned much more. A 'new middle class' emerged, educated salaried employees of corporations—*zaibatsu*, or conglomerates, like Mitsui and Mitsubishi—and the public service. In 1920, two in ten of Tokyo's employees were office workers, and they included a growing number of young women working in offices and retail stores.[14] Workers drank beer, and popular culture, through magazines, movies and bars, produced the modern boy or *mobo*, 'with Harold Lloyd glasses', and the modern girl or *moga*, with short hair, 'drinking, smoking and reading literature'.[15]

Hair salons and the permanent wave had arrived, as had radios, bathing suits and gramophone records playing popular songs like 'Is *Sake* Tears or Sighs?' Cafes, dance halls and jazz made up the new entertainment. It was called the era of *ero-guro nansensu*, exotic grotesque nonsense. Through education, traditional Japanese thought was being replaced by a culture of alienation.

The rock in all this swirling newness was the divine office of the emperor. While the prime minister might be replaced every year or two, the emperor was there to stay. In the hundred years since the Meiji restoration, only three emperors had come to the throne.

The constitution enshrined the emperor as sacred and sovereign. Meiji's Mutsohito took full advantage of that, consolidating his reign without serious challenge until his death in 1912. Proclaimed the Taisho Emperor, his son Yoshihito was of a different mould. Plagued with ill-health, he was rumoured to be mentally disturbed, so much so that his son, Crown Prince Hirohito, was made regent in 1921 and presided at official functions. Despite—or perhaps because of—the monarch's ineffectualness, it was a time of relative liberalism. Dubbed the 'Taisho democracy', it was characterised by elected politicians who were nonetheless committed to the emperor and the pursuit of empire.

Yoshihito died in 1926 and Hirohito commenced a reign named, with some irony as it would turn out, Showa, Shining Peace. He was briefed regularly by his ministers but made clear his own views, in one instance forcing Prime Minister Tanaka to resign. The military, bureaucracy, Privy Council and House of Peers (the upper house in the bicameral Diet, or parliament) were all formally accountable to and appointed by the emperor. Elder statesmen (*genro*) informally advised Hirohito, ensuring the primacy of the elites. The Diet operated on the periphery, its role being to make laws and approve the government's budget.

Back in the late nineteenth century, the statesman Yamagata had sought to quarantine the military from the press and political rhetoric of the time by setting up a military command structure directly responsible to the emperor. A cautious military was able to resist reckless popular sentiment. Now it was the military that was reckless, its enthusiasm for imperial conquests uninhibited except by infrequent murmurings from Hirohito. The Siberian Intervention was one outcome.

In 1918, Japan was persuaded by Britain and France—later joined by America—to support the fighting retreat of the pro-tsarist Czechoslovakian Corps against the Bolsheviks. Prisoners of war from the Austro-Hungarian army, the Corps had made a deal with the outgoing Russian regime. The Japanese government committed 7000 troops to the campaign, but its army unilaterally decided to send ten times that number. No reliable anti-communist government was established, and the Bolsheviks kept advancing across eastern Siberia. By 1920, the other armies had withdrawn. The Japanese army, answering only to the emperor, who remained silent on the matter, stayed on for two more years to support the counter-revolutionary government in Vladivostok. By the time Japan finally withdrew, 3000 Japanese lives had been sacrificed to this lost cause.[16] Japanese soldiers had died in a futile defence of the regime Japan had fought thirteen years earlier in the Russo-Japanese War.

The Siberian misadventure was the only stumble in Japan's growth as an imperial power and its associated play for a place on the international stage. Its two colonies, Korea and Formosa, were securely under its control. It had significant economic interests to protect in the dying Chinese empire, particularly in the north-eastern province of Manchuria. But back home, modernisation and Westernisation were putting cracks in Japan's traditional social cohesion. Government operated by deals, either shady or pragmatic, and the exercise of entrenched positions in the hierarchy. Political violence and militarism were on the rise as left and right jockeyed for ascendancy. Holding together the creaking body of an evolving society, the uneasy marriage of the old and the new, was the symbolism and consequent power of the emperor. The emperor seldom needed to exercise his power. The presumption was that he would if he needed to, so everyone acted on that basis.

Into this world had come the men who battled their way along the Kokoda Track to Ioribaiwa. All were born by the end of the 1920s. They arrived in time to see their country move into the next and ultimate stage in its imperial designs. They were there to participate in the culmination, but few would be there to witness the collapse and the subsequent rebirth.

Chapter 3

The road to total war

With the overthrow of the Ch'ing Dynasty, the last dynasty of the Chinese empire, the Chinese Nationalist Party, the Kuomintang, had grabbed a semblance of power by the 1920s, but resistance from the emerging communists and regional warlords was threatening its hold. Japanese Prime Minister Takashi Hara formed an alliance with the Western powers and the Kuomintang to safeguard his own country's interests, and this helped shore up the Nationalists. Shandong was returned to China as a gesture of goodwill. Japan, however, stopped short of supporting Chinese tariff autonomy. Giichi Tanaka was appointed prime minister in 1927, by which time Hara was long out of the picture courtesy of an assassin's bullet. Tanaka took an assertive position on Manchuria and a tougher approach to China. The predictable anti-Japanese reaction in China saw troops sent into China once again to 'protect Japanese interests'.

There had been some public concern in Japan over growing militarism since the Siberian Intervention, and about trampling the rights of Koreans and Chinese, but these were widely regarded as lesser issues. Most people were more concerned about Western imperialism, and thought Japan should lead an Asian bulwark against domination by the West. Although Japan had used the West's rhetoric to justify its colonies—talking up trade and national self-determination—when the Western powers moderated their role in China at the end of the decade, Japan was resolutely unmoved. Only the emperor had the power to rein in the military, and Hirohito, new to the throne, was either unwilling or unable to exercise it.

Chiang Kai-shek now controlled the Chinese Nationalists. Leading the Kuomintang army he united China, demanded a revision of the port treaties and threatened Japanese privileges in northern China and Manchuria. Britain and the US were prepared to renegotiate the port treaties. Japan was not. The Manchurian warlord Chang Tso-lin had set himself up as a rival to Chiang, so Japan's Kwantung Army in Manchuria supported him instead. But as the Nationalists gained ascendancy, Chang started shifting his allegiance to them and he became expendable. He was killed in 1928 by a bomb placed under his train to Mukden by a Kwantung Army officer. The finger of blame was pointed at Chang's Chinese rivals. The intention was also to force Tanaka to take an even harder line on Manchuria, but this had limited success.[1] Nonetheless, it seemed such a good idea that the army would try it again three years later.

◆ ◆ ◆

When the New York stock market crashed in 1929, Japan's economic planners and policy-makers did everything wrong. World prices dropped, the yen rose, exports fell and Japan plunged into depression. The *zaibatsu* banks sold yen for dollars, so when the government later had to abandon the gold standard and devalue the yen, the banks were able to buy back yen at considerable profit.[2] This might have been smart business, but it strengthened a widespread Japanese perception of businessmen and their political allies as greedy and selfish. The concern wasn't for the economy, however. Japan recovered from the Depression faster than Western economies and experienced a boom in demand from the US and Asia for its new and diverse range of exports. The flow of money allowed increased military spending and a return to military adventurism.

The 1920s had seen a battle for ascendancy between the political right and the left. On one side were emperor-centred radicals, driven by a spiritual fanaticism grounded in Shinto belief. Leftist intellectuals on the other side were often imperial loyalists too, pursuing the redistribution of wealth through a reframing of the political structure to unite the emperor and the people. The right prevailed, and the left went underground—if they had not already been purged. A heady mix of idealism and political violence produced a rationale for assassinations by young military officers and right-wing civilians: Prime Minister Hamaguchi was killed by a right-wing youth in 1930, and the finance minister and a Mitsui chief by a group called the Blood Brotherhood (*Ketsumeidan*) two years later. It was all part of an ultranationalist reshaping of Japanese society.

In Manchuria, the Kwantung Army saw the province in its care as a laboratory for this new social order of equality and loyalty to the state that would supplant selfish profit-seeking.[3] It had much in common with the political movements rising in Europe at the time, fascism in Italy and Spain and Nazism in Germany. Violence, if necessary, was to be used to advance ideals. The ends could always be used to justify the means, as the colonial powers had demonstrated over the previous decades.

On 18 September 1931, junior officers of the Kwantung Army blew up the Japanese-controlled railway track at Mukden in southern Manchuria and blamed the Chinese military. The commander of the Kwantung Army was aware of the plot in advance, as was General Tatekawa of Army General Staff in Tokyo. Both turned a deaf ear to what they heard. In response to the Manchurian Incident, as it was called, one of the plotters, Colonel Itagaki, led an attack on the Chinese regional armies.[4] General Honjo called out the whole Kwantung Army in support and advanced beyond the South Manchurian Railway Zone. There were assurances from the army that it would return to the Zone, but it continued to advance until all of Manchuria was under Japanese control.

The Japanese government of the time was split on the issue of Manchuria, could reach no consensus on what action to take and resigned instead. The new Prime Minister, Tsuyoshi Inukai, tried to persuade the emperor to restrain the army, to little effect, but he resisted pressure to annex Manchuria as a colony as Japan had done with Korea. A law virtually unto itself, the Kwantung Army instead installed a puppet state in 1932 with Pu-yi, the last Ch'ing emperor of China, as its titular head. The new state was called Manchukuo. It was entirely dependent on Japanese patronage for its continuing existence.

In 1933 Japan withdrew from the League of Nations after the League condemned its military adventure in Manchuria. This attracted international opprobrium but played well at home. The pugnacious activities of the Kwantung Army had the full backing of its military masters in Tokyo. More to the point, despite increased military and police surveillance throughout Japan, these events enjoyed the support of the elites, the press and the general populace. The political parties had been sidelined since the 1932 assassination of Inukai; not until after 1945 would the country again be led by a politician. A new government, dominated by the military and the bureaucrats, allowed expansionist foreign policy and the continuation of military autonomy. Monopoly corporations were set up in Manchukuo in a strategy of state-led economic development, a showcase of the new and better alternative to free-market capitalism.

While the League of Nations drafted its resolution of condemnation the military bovver boys,[5] the Kwantung Army, clashed several times with Chinese forces and annexed Jehol, in China's north. The Nationalist army was forced to withdraw from the region around Peking (Beijing) and in its place another puppet regime was set up under a local warlord. Along with Britain, the United States, already outraged by the bombing and occupation of Chinchow, was incensed by this further takeover. At the same time, American businesses were trying to invest in Manchukuo, reinforcing Japanese perceptions of US and capitalist hypocrisy.[6] Japan withdrew from the tripartite naval arms limitation agreement and began to build up its navy and army.

Japan's increasing militarism was being driven by a revolutionary right of civilian patriotic associations, like the Showa Sacred Society and various secret societies, and young army and naval officer groups. A

new officer class was being recruited from the sons of rural landowners and even peasants, instead of from the traditional samurai class, the
remnants of the old Tokugawa regime.[7] A merger of proletarian and
nationalist groups with military activists advocated violence and war as a
means of reconstructing the political framework. The two radical forces
were driven by sympathy for the plight of post-depression rural Japan
and admiration for the purity of direct action to overthrow corrupt
government.

More than 90 per cent of Japanese voters still supported the two main
political parties, Minseito and Seiyukai, but cabinet always now had a
minority of party men and the prime minister was non-party. Politicians
protected their jobs and the interests of their patrons, the *zaibatsu* and the
landowners, by cooperating with their new rulers. The Election Purifi-
cation Campaign in 1935 sought to eliminate corruption—bureaucratic
favours and vote-buying—by having elections monitored by police. The
police went so far as to sometimes interrupt election speeches critical of
the military or the bureaucracy.[8] Children were taught that Japan's political instability was caused by Western beliefs, and school lessons exalted
loyalty to the emperor and the military spirit. Through this unsteadiness
the emperor emerged as a stronger symbol but, for all the celebrations
of traditional Japanese virtues, there was no return to traditional living.
The lives of ordinary people continued to modernise, with cars, baseball
and Hollywood movies.

With the rising power of the army and, at the same time, turbulence
within the military, it became 'government by assassination'.[9] To the
military radicals and civilians of the Imperial Way faction, the *koda-ha*,
national strength came through loyalty to the emperor and spiritual
education. The Imperial Way organised the assassination of political and
business leaders as well as their opponents in the military. Showcase
trials presented their pure motives and high ideals to a sympathetic public . . . until they pushed their luck one time too many.

In February 1936, 1500 troops loyal to the Imperial Way took over
central Tokyo and sent murder squads to deal with cabinet ministers and
opponents in the military and the courts. Their call was to restore Japan's

glory: honour the emperor, defend the empire, help the common people. This time the emperor intervened, condemning their actions and ordering them to surrender. Snookered by their own ideals they obeyed the command, even though they saw the emperor's condemnation as the result of corrupt advice from his retainers. There were no show trials. The nineteen leaders of the disruption were tried and executed in secret.

These events did not damage the army, which emerged stronger and more disciplined.[10] Communist activists and leftist writers were rounded up and killed. The conflict between the political parties and the government was resolved by the appointment as prime minister of Fumimaro Konoe, who had ties with the parties, the military and business. But one month later, war with China began and Konoe was too weak to resist either the military or bellicose civilians.

◆ ◆ ◆

Major wars are generally triggered by a significant act of violence or aggression: the assassination of an archduke, an invasion of Poland, the flying of hijacked planes into corporate buildings in New York. The Pacific War of the mid-twentieth century arose from a few shots fired in China in the dead of night. On 7 June 1937, when the shots went off, Japanese troops clashed accidentally with Chinese troops at the Marco Polo Bridge (Lugouqiao) in the south of Peking. It's not known who fired the shots or even whose side they were on, and the result was nothing more than a skirmish with no casualties.[11] By August, however, the clash had built into full-scale war, authorised by Japan's cabinet. Within three months, 200,000 Japanese troops were in China. Peking and Tientsin fell quickly. The army moved south to Shanghai, where two British gunboats were bombed and the American gunboat *Panay* was sunk on the Yangtze River.[12] US and British commercial interests in the ports of Shanghai, Hangchow and Canton were also damaged. In December, Japanese troops entered Nanking, rounded up soldiers and civilians, murdered many and raped women. The extent of the 'rape of Nanking' is still hotly disputed, but the fact is not.

Why do soldiers—or why did these soldiers—resort to such violent outbursts? It is often suggested that these are part of the Japanese character, but that leaves unexplained the problem of the large number of rapes by occupation forces in postwar Japan.[13] Perhaps Nanking is better understood from the perspective of the brutalising nature of war. Although Japan's soldiers prevailed in China, the fighting had been tough. It was often hard to distinguish the Chinese soldier from the civilian. Like all militaries, Japan's was built on harsh discipline and the dehumanisation of the enemy. To Harvard historian Andrew Gordon, the fact that violence erupted in Nanking is less surprising than the fact that the Japanese high command allowed it to go on for six weeks.[14] Perhaps the intention was to bring pressure to bear on negotiations with Chiang Kai-shek and the Nationalists. If so, it didn't work.

Prime Minister Konoe tried to negotiate a settlement with Chiang, but talks stalled. Troops from both sides were constantly being moved forward so their masters would not be negotiating from a weak position. A power struggle had developed in Japan between the military and a gung-ho bureaucracy. Policies became increasingly strident, with Tokyo overturning armistices reached by armies in the field. In the end, the negotiations achieved nothing. The Nationalists retreated to Chungking, in the mountains of China's far west, and Konoe called for their 'annihilation'. The cities, roads and railway lines of China were occupied by 600,000 Japanese troops, but they never controlled its countryside. Constantly unsettled by guerrilla attacks kept going by supplies from the US and Britain, the occupation force resorted to the murder of civilians to 'pacify' the country. By the end of 1938, the conflict was at a stalemate.[15]

Japan had been trying to build up its military strength for an anticipated challenge from the Soviet Union over Manchuria when the Peking skirmishes escalated. The USSR had more troops, more planes and a more mechanised army. It was not a confrontation for which Japan held any enthusiasm, but it happened as expected. A series of border clashes with the Soviet army occurred during 1938 and 1939 north of Korea and in Nomonhan, in the Mongolian border region. Twenty thousand

Japanese soldiers died as the highly mobile Soviet forces overwhelmed the Kwantung Army, but by 1939 Russia was preoccupied with the war in Europe. A ceasefire was signed.[16]

Japan was by now getting bogged down in its own machinations and the shifting alliances of international politics. From 1938 it tried to extricate itself from the stalemate in China, but not on unfavourable terms. It wanted an alliance with Germany against Russia, but after those two nations signed a non-aggression pact that was no longer an option. Japan then tried a new direction, pursuing improved relations with the US and Great Britain, but China remained the fly in the ointment. The US public was horrified by the bombing of Chinese cities, even though the planes flew on American fuel and the bombs were made of American scrap metal.[17] America backed a policy of non-intervention, but US Secretary of State Cordell Hull was not prepared to abandon China. The negotiations got nowhere. Instead, the United States broke off its commercial treaty with Japan.

Japan announced a 'New Order in East Asia' in 1938, encompassing its territorial gains in China and Manchukuo. This was subsequently extended to the goal of Japanese hegemony over all of east Asia in what was formally called the 'Greater East Asia Co-prosperity Sphere', which would take in the rest of China and South-east Asia and ultimately perhaps eastern Siberia, India and Australia.[18] It was an imperial vision fraught with difficulties. Japan's acquisitions at the time were able to supply only part of its trading needs. The rest of its imports still came from the West and particularly the US. Japan started looking south for the resources—oil, rubber, tin—that east Asia could not supply, but in order to control these Asian markets Japan would have to replace the Western colonial powers, many of them now embroiled in the European war. To sustain its armed forces Japan still needed many commodities, especially oil and scrap iron that it got from the West.

The fall of the Netherlands and France to the German advance in 1940 created an additional fear for the Japanese. Germany might bring military control over the colonies of its conquered nations, notably French Indochina and the Dutch East Indies, interrupting development of Japan's Co-prosperity Sphere.[19] In light of the German victories and the seemingly imminent fall of Great Britain, Japan signed a Tripartite Pact with Germany and Italy. This opened the possibility of finding a diplomatic solution to the Soviet threat through Germany's new Soviet alliance and a means of stemming military aid to China's Nationalists.

The US and Britain had been supplying the Kuomintang army through Indochina (today's Vietnam, Cambodia and Laos) and Burma. Through the Tripartite Pact, France's Vichy government agreed to Japan's proposal to move troops into northern Indochina to cut off these supply lines, provoking an escalating series of US sanctions. Japan claimed it had no option now but to secure 'economic self-sufficiency', condemning American protests and sanctions as 'warmongering'.[20] The Japanese navy had said Japan could not win a war against Britain and the US—America's naval and air power ensured that—but an advance into South-east Asia wouldn't involve the navy.[21]

The administrators of the Netherlands' East Indies colony continued to refuse to trade oil, rubber or tin with Japan, even though the Netherlands itself was now under the control of an occupation force. The French Vichy government agreed to allow Japanese forces to move into the rest of Indochina to pressure the Dutch into changing their trade stand-off. Japan found instead that it had painted itself into a corner.

A furious US froze Japanese assets and imposed a complete embargo on the export of oil, scrap iron and other strategic materials to Japan. Without a supplier of oil, of which 70 per cent was imported from the US, the navy estimated Japan's reserves would last only eighteen months.[22] The only alternative source was the East Indies but they would have to be seized by force, which would inevitably draw America and Britain into the conflict. Japan tried to find a diplomatic solution while at the same time preparing for the possibility, indeed probability, of war with the US and Great Britain, which is referred to as 'total war'.[23]

This was not the cynical and considered master plan from which many people still believe Japan was working. It was a totalitarian regime without a dictator. National consensus was undermined by competing factions within the army and navy and intense animosity between the two forces. Zealots ranted from soap-box podiums, distributed pamphlets and organised protests to keep the pressure up. Japanese strategic planning was more driven by events than driving them. On every issue there seemed to be multiple positions contending for dominance. One thing was certain in the debate, however: time was a major issue. If war was inevitable, it would be to Japan's disadvantage if it were delayed. War Minister Hideki Tojo reportedly said to Prime Minister Fumimaro Konoe at the time: 'At some point during a man's lifetime, he might find it necessary to jump from the veranda of the Kiyomizu-dera temple[24] with his eyes closed.'[25]

◆ ◆ ◆

In October 1941, Konoe resigned and the hawkish general Tojo was promoted to prime minister. Negotiations with the US continued, but the new government set a deadline for itself of 1 December. If a diplomatic solution came about by that date, a hold would be put on war preparations. Otherwise, it would be total war. That was looking ominously likely. The US had stepped up its supply of arms to China and was demanding a full Japanese withdrawal. On 18 November Japan proposed a return to the two nations' pre-July positions, with Japan to withdraw initially to northern Indochina and then completely from Indochina once peace with China was restored. The US, for its part, was to lift the embargo and unfreeze Japanese assets. The response from Secretary of State Cordell Hull was that Japan had started a program of force and must take the initiative to abandon it. The Japanese government treated this response as an ultimatum—even if it wasn't one in the strictest sense, America's position was clear—and Japan decided further discussions were pointless. The decision to go to war was confirmed by the Imperial Conference on 1 December, although for security reasons no operational plans were revealed. Tojo told the conference: 'Under the circumstances, our Empire has no alternative but to begin war against the United States, Great Britain and the Netherlands in order to resolve the present crisis and ensure survival.'[26] Australia was still not on Japan's radar.

Total war began just before 8 a.m. on 7 December 1941. One hundred and eighty-nine bombers, torpedo planes and fighters from the aircraft carrier *Akagi* wreaked havoc on America's Pacific Fleet as it lay in the harbour at Pearl City, Hawaii. They first bombed and strafed Oahu's airfields, severely damaging aircraft and hangers, then, with most of the island's air defence knocked out, made torpedo attacks on battleships in the harbour unopposed. This was followed an hour later by a second wave from the carrier *Zuikaku*. By 9.30 the Japanese planes had departed, leaving seven battleships, three cruisers, two destroyers and four support vessels sunk, 188 planes destroyed and 2500 US military personnel killed. Japan had lost forty-one of its 414 aircraft as well as four midget submarines that tried to infiltrate the harbour. By good fortune, the Pacific Fleet's three aircraft carriers were not in Pearl Harbor at the time.[27] A note breaking off the current round of talks and accusing America, Britain and others of seeking domination of east Asia—to all intents and purposes a declaration of war—was delivered to Hull one hour after the attack. It was claimed that decoding problems in the Japanese Embassy in Washington had delayed the translation of the note into English.[28]

President Franklin D. Roosevelt would describe 7 December as 'a day that will live in infamy'. The Pearl Harbor attack is generally characterised as a sneak attack, but the truth is that America was asleep at the wheel. Early that year, US Ambassador Joseph Grew had reported from Tokyo that the Japanese military were believed to be planning a surprise attack on Pearl Harbor.[29] It should have been obvious that Japan might be preparing for war, given its past belligerence and the fact that the brinkmanship between it and the US was going nowhere. Western powers had praised Japan's tactic in taking Port Arthur by surprise at the beginning of the Russo-Japanese War. Why did they think Japan would not try again a move that had been so successful before? Probably the Americans didn't take the Japanese threat seriously. They were complacent and therefore ill-prepared.

Even as Japan celebrated its triumph, some of its military strategists recognised that the attack had fallen short of its primary objective.

Despite the power of newsreel pictures of tilting warships half sunk in the harbour, belching black smoke skywards, the blow struck against the more populous and better-resourced United States was not as decisive as had been hoped. The destroyed vessels were close to obsolescence anyway, and the impact was blunted further by the absence of the three aircraft carriers.[30] Pearl Harbor was neither a sneaky act nor a stunning triumph. The failure to destroy the carriers would eventually prove fatal to Japan's expansionist aims and to its operations in New Guinea, where the Allies would claw back supremacy in the air, but for now the die was cast. There was no pulling back.

On the day it dealt so devastatingly with the Pacific Fleet, Japan also attacked Kota Bharu in northern Malaya, Wake Island and Guam in the Pacific and the American colony of the Philippines. The objective was to disable the US Fleet long enough to invade and secure key areas of South-east Asia and the Pacific. Of particular importance were the oil-fields of Borneo and Sumatra in the East Indies. The Japanese knew they couldn't match American military-industrial might in a protracted war, but their hope and expectation was that the US public would have no stomach for war and would press for peace, allowing Japan to keep its expanded territory, rich in desperately needed resources.

When news of the attack on Pearl Harbor reached the US air bases in the Philippines, American fighters and bombers from Clark Field took to the air. They had landed for lunch and refuelling when, ten hours after Pearl Harbor, Japanese bombers arrived. B-17 Flying Fortresses, B-25 Mitchell bombers and Kittyhawk fighters were lined up wing to wing on the ground. There was no anti-aircraft fire or planes in the air to challenge the marauders.[31] Two days later, carrier-based planes attacked the British battleship *Prince of Wales* and the battle cruiser *Repulse* off Malaya. Both ships were without air cover and both were sunk.

The Japanese army pushed down the Malay Peninsula, driving the British out. Defensive positions were set up on Malaya's roads but the attackers outflanked them through the thick surrounding jungle, a tactic that would be used again in New Guinea in a different kind of jungle. Singapore was famously set up to repel any seaborne invasion, but

Japanese troops stormed the British island colony in February across the narrow Strait of Johor separating Singapore from Malaya. Despite a cable from Churchill instructing him to fight to the death, General Percival walked out from the Allied lines with two aides, one carrying the Union Jack, the other a white flag.[32]

By March the Americans had been driven out of the Philippines, and General Douglas MacArthur had made his famous vow to return. Contrary to Japanese expectations, MacArthur retreated to Australia. The presumption in Japan's strategic planning had been that a weakened US Navy would regroup in Hawaii to mount a counter-offensive towards the Philippines. Japan could mount raids on this route. Since MacArthur went to Brisbane, not Hawaii, and used Australia instead as the base for his 'return' Japan had to rethink its forward planning, but this seemed no more than a necessary adjustment, nothing of great concern. The total war was going too well to see any serious difficulty here. Its first phase was already completed ahead of schedule in early 1942 with the falls of Java and Rangoon, much to Japan's delight and the Allies' shock.

Back home, the Japanese people were jubilant over the succession of victories that was expanding their empire, steadily consolidating the vision of the Greater East Asia Co-prosperity Sphere. For the soldiers of the Imperial Japanese Army—most of them conscripts—it was an exhilarating time, stirring deep feelings of patriotism and purpose.

Chapter 4

From the mountains to the sea

Lying on a narrow alluvial plain between the northern mountains of the island of Shikoku and Urado Bay opening out to the Pacific, Kochi in the 1930s was a frontier town, a rough-head town based on fishing, whaling and struggling agriculture. Dour and not overly helpful, the people became boisterous at night when they drank, and sometimes got punchy. For all that, they were not unlikeable folk, with a certain rustic charm and a somewhat un-Japanese directness of manner.[1]

Flooded rice paddies shared the plain outside Kochi with fields and greenhouses growing vegetables—tomato, eggplant, cucumber, capsicum, ginger, okra—and flowers. Beyond them, among beech and pine forests on the steep hills and deep gullies of Shikoku's mountain spine, lived monkeys, wild pigs, raccoon dogs, rabbits, foxes, deer. In the centre of Kochi, wedged between its two rivers, stood the seventeenth-century castle around which the city grew and after which it was named.

As Japan readied itself for total war against the Western imperial powers, the Kagami and the Enokuchi rivers were cluttered with sampans and straw-roofed house-boats moored on their banks. A wooden bridge with paper lanterns crossed the Enokuchi. Kids jumped off it, and off the then-new concrete bridge over the Kagami. But Japan's modernisation hadn't passed the bustling town by. Women could be seen in flapper hats, pleated skirts and other Western fashions; businessmen in waistcoats dined with geishas.

Kochi town was the administrative centre of Kochi prefecture, covering most of southern Shikoku. A few kilometres away was Asakura village. Here was headquartered the Imperial Japanese Army's 44th Infantry Regiment, which drew young men from across Kochi prefecture for their compulsory military service. National service had been a fact of life since 1872; only officers were professional soldiers. The headquarters of the 44th had been processing Kochi's conscripts since Meiji times for Japan's succession of wars. Behind a grand entrance of lanterns mounted on brick piers, two-storey brick buildings marked out a square parade ground. Inside the buildings and on the parade ground a regime of harsh training, often little short of institutionalised brutality, had been producing generations of highly trained and obedient soldiers.

Sadashige Imanishi joined the 44th in January 1936. He grew up in Motoyama, a town in the Yoshino valley in mountain country behind Kochi. There he worked on the family's farm of rice paddies and vegetable plots while he went to school. His father was an avid fan of the local cock fights. This is a region that even today stages dog fights for the entertainment of its citizens.

When his mother died, the young Sadashige was unhappy with his father's plan to remarry. He went across the mountains to live with his elder sister in Ehime prefecture for a while before returning to resume his school studies.[2] In 1936 he joined other recruits of the IJA at Asakura.

Imanishi was graded 'A' in the army's physical test, an unsurprising level of health in someone used to farm work. He needed every bit of it. Recruits were subjected to any sort of physical mistreatment that took their training officers' fancy. Early-morning exercise involved brushing down their naked bodies, especially in winter. Kicking and bashing were standard practice, as were a range of capricious punishments. Any step out of line resulted in a severe beating with wooden sticks, so that complaint or rebellion quickly became unthinkable. The recruits were trained to do exactly as they were told without a murmur. Although it was a dehumanising process in many ways, it was highly pragmatic. It produced soldiers who would follow orders unquestioningly and who had no fear of fighting or of dying.[3]

Military service was a two-year obligation, and Imanishi had no particular liking for military life. After eighteen months he was happy to be allowed to return early to Motoyama to continue his school study, but his relief was short-lived. A month later, he was called up again. The Chinese Incident, as the Japanese called the undeclared war, was under way following the altercation at Marco Polo Bridge. The 44th Regiment was dispatched to China to carry out a landing operation near Shanghai in support of the Kwantung Army's push south.

The adventure started in grand style as the men of the 44th marched down the tram tracks running through the centre of Kochi. A light drizzle didn't deter the excited townsfolk from lining up under waterproofed paper umbrellas to say farewell. The Japanese media's enthusiastic reports of heroic actions by soldiers in China ensured that public support didn't waver. Flags and banners were waved on the streets and at Kochi railway station, where more crowds gathered to see the district's sons go off to fight for imperial Japan.

The landing at Shanghai, in Imanishi's recollection, was a shambles. The men had done endless training on landing operations back in Kochi, but little of it seemed to rub off in real life. This was the first action any of these troops had seen. When landing craft hit the beach, no one leapt out of the boat because enemy bullets were spraying all around. Soldiers operating the barges yelled to no avail: 'What the hell are you doing? You can't fight them if you don't get out of the boat!'

Imanishi was the first to jump into the water—not out of bravery but because a shell exploded in front of his face. The water was peppered with bullets, so he waded behind the boat and yelled, 'Jump into the water now!'

They all did as ordered and, like panicked sheep, made a rush *en masse* to the enemy positions. Bullets still spattered around them. Imanishi recalls looking back and seeing some of his fellow soldiers lying on the beach. Much of it happened in a blur.[4]

When the Japanese got up to the enemy front line, the Chinese defenders withdrew in a hurry. As the campaign unfolded this would become a pattern. An initial charge would draw fierce defensive fire, but if this didn't drive the attackers back in short time the Chinese would rapidly pull further back to a new position. Their strategy was purely defensive, with little thought of counter-attack. In response, the Japanese developed the noisy mass attack as a particularly potent tactic, especially at night and accompanied by a din of banging metal, shouting, chanting and anything else they could add to the clamour.

Imanishi recalls that much of the fighting in China was hand to hand and often with civilians, not soldiers. It was the beginnings of guerrilla warfare, but the Japanese were not trained for that and had not expected it.

The 44th Infantry Regiment fought in China for three years, part of the Japanese probe into southern China that, successful at first, eventually bogged down in stalemate. The return home was subdued, with none of the excitement of the departure. Soldiers were taken directly to Asakura railway station, past Kochi, and they marched in double file the short distance from there to the regimental headquarters entrance. Whitewood boxes holding bones of their fallen comrades were cradled in white slings across the men's chests. Watched silently by villagers in white cloaks, the troops disappeared between the imposing square columns and into the base.

◆　◆　◆

On the northern shore of Japan's Inland Sea sits Fukuyama City. It was a small fishing village on the delta of the Ashida River before Fukuyama Castle, built in the seventeenth century, provided a focus for growth. By the 1930s it had become a busy commercial port, with a forest of fishing-boat masts in front of steep wooded hills. Wooden fishermen's houses clustered along the shore. Net fishing for sea bream (*taiami*) in the Inland Sea was and still is a major occupation for the port's boats. Located in the prefecture of Hiroshima, Fukuyama developed as the administrative centre for the surrounding region, which produced twill and cotton cloth and reed matting as well as rice. The hills and Chugoku-sanchi mountains around it protect the city in the typhoon season, creating a mild Inland Sea climate.

Since Meiji times, the 41st Infantry Regiment had been based in Fukuyama City, its headquarters standing behind solid square columns very much like those that guarded the entrance to Kochi's regimental base.[5] Yori-ichi Yokoyama joined the 41st as a conscript in April 1940. Until then, he had worked on the production line for the textile and fibre manufacturer Teijin. Coming from a poor family, his education had not progressed beyond primary school. Yokoyama's first instruction was in basic military and survival skills. He became a good marksman, a talent he would make remarkably little use of in the next five years of active service. After completing the basics, Yokoyama moved on to Fukuyama Army Hospital, adjacent to the regimental base, for specialist training as a medic. In fact it wasn't very specialised, being limited to first aid and battlefield medicine. Private Yokoyama's predominant memories of this time are of the brutal training regime and the regularity with which he was beaten up as part of it.[6]

The regiment was committed first to occupied Shanghai, to help consolidate Japan's control of its military gains in southern China. It then moved into French Indochina as a quasi-occupation force after Japan's deal with the Vichy government.[7] As a medic in an occupation force rather than in an attack operation, he found the tour relatively uneventful.

◆　◆　◆

The 44th Infantry Regiment at Kochi was reorganised as 144th Regiment in August 1940, under the direct control of Imperial Headquarters in Tokyo and not within the command structure of any of the army divisions. The regiment's commander was to be Colonel Masao Kusunose. It was made up of three battalions, commanded by Lieutenant-Colonel Hatsuo Tsukamoto, Major Tadashi Horie and Lieutenant-Colonel Gen'ichiro Kuwada, respectively. The 3500 troops that the regiment had gathered up from Kochi prefecture were a mix of new conscripts and veterans of the China campaign. They didn't know it at the time, but they were part of Japan's fall-back strategy in case a diplomatic solution could not be found to its growing difficulties on the international stage.

The ordinary soldiers who were the engine of the 144th were drawn from the mountains, plains, towns and coastal villages of Shikoku. Mostly from farming or fishing communities, they would have to be moulded to the needs of the IJA. They were a mixed bag. Yuki Shimada was a rice seller from the port town of Usa, a whaling and fishing centre.[8] Jiro Okino was working in an artificial silk factory in Osaka when he was called up in 1938. He trained in the Horse Transport Section, but after being hospitalised with a venereal disease he returned to civilian life and the silk factory. In 1941, he was recalled to the army.[9] Taro Yamamoto worked with a fisherman after leaving school until he got a job at an artificial silk factory in northern Shikoku. He entered the army in 1941 and was assigned to Kuwada Unit.[10]

Kokichi Nishimura had lived in Kochi town with his widowed mother and grandmother until he was eleven, when the family moved to Tokyo. There, he worked in a factory and studied technical drawing at night, eventually finding a job in a Tokyo foundry. In 1940, when he turned twenty, Nishimura was required to take a train back to his home town and undergo the army medical examination. In April the follow-ing year he joined the other Kochi recruits at Asakura.[11]

Yukiharu Yamasaki had joined the army in January 1939. It had seemed inevitable to him that he would be going to war, so he volun-teered a year earlier than the conscription age. 'Photos of many men of my age who died on the China front line were in the newspapers every day,' he explains. 'That made me think I would also have to sacrifice myself for the country.'[12]

After China, Sadashige Imanishi had returned again to civilian life. He taught at the local school in Motoyama, but before long he was called up for the third time and resumed training with a number of new recruits. Veterans of the Chinese campaign like Imanishi, now a sergeant in Tsukamoto Unit, helped relate the training to the realities of battle.

Landing exercises were a particular obsession of the trainers. A model ship was built in the middle of the parade ground, and recruits had to jump down rope ladders slung from the side into small boats sitting on the grass.[13] Then, for greater realism, further landing exercises were conducted on the grey sands of the public beach at Katsurahama, by the mouth of Urado Bay, and on the dry shingle alongside the Niyoda River, a few kilometres further on from Asakura.

The training also addressed skills thought necessary in any coming war in Asian (or Pacific) jungle regions: fighting at night using blindfolds; protecting a gun while swimming or wading; rope-walking over gullies in the mountains; moving silently. They did sleep-deprivation exercises; they did weekly shooting on a 600-metre range set up on the training field; and they were made to go on long runs wearing full kit, with beatings for those who didn't perform up to expectations. The harsh treatment and brutality that had characterised earlier training continued. Men were slapped in the face daily and constantly bruised. Officers gave them impossible instructions, and beatings for failing to carry them out. No questioning of the training was permitted. Recruits would often be found crying in lavatories.[14]

'We were just told to move automatically without thinking because everything had to be done quickly,' says Nishimura. 'Even a tiny second's delay could get us in trouble. So however hard we tried, we never got appreciated, just beaten up. Literally, we were expected to move fast enough to dodge bullets.'[15]

◆　◆　◆

Imperial General Headquarters, in preparing for the possibility of war in the Pacific, planned to use Truk atoll in the Caroline Islands as a major forward base for the Japanese Combined Fleet. The Carolines, along with the Mariana and Marshall Islands, had become a Japanese Mandated Territory following World War I, having previously been German colonial possessions. Guam, in American hands since 1899, was on the southern end of the Marianas and would need to be wrested from US control. More importantly, in a war with the United States and Britain, Imperial HQ was concerned that Truk would be vulnerable to air attack from Allied bases in Rabaul, on the island of New Britain, particularly by the new Boeing B-17 bomber. The capture of Rabaul, capital of the Australian Mandated Territory of New Guinea, was necessary to ensure the safety of the fleet base at Truk.

The response to these concerns was the formation of South Seas Force (Nankai Shitai)[16] under the command of Major-General Tomitaro Horii. Horii was from Hyogo prefecture, around Kobe, in the south-western end of Japan's main island, Honshu. A graduate of the Army Military College, he was assigned to the headquarters of the Shanghai Expeditionary Army in 1932 before being put in command of 55th Infantry Division.[17] A bluff, dedicated soldier, unusually plain-spoken by his country's standards, Horii is often described as 'short, pudgy and bespectacled' in Australian commentaries, drawn from sources who would never have set eyes on him. He was none of these: fifty years old by the time he got to Kokoda, he was of average height and did not wear glasses.

Horii's South Seas Force was based initially on 144th Regiment and various support units drawn from 55th Division, including artillery, signals, transport and medical units. The nominal strength of the force was 5000 men, 1000 horses and 100 vehicles. Orders for mobilisation of South Seas Force were issued on 27 September 1941. Within a week the elements were brought together at Marugame, on the northern side of Shikoku.

Horii wanted to make sure this integrated force was aware of the standards he expected it to keep. Late in 1941, perhaps prompted by his experience in China, he issued a *Guide to Soldiers in the South Seas* to curb atrocities by his troops. It contained five simple statements:

1. Do not needlessly kill or injure local inhabitants.
2. Behaviour such as looting and violating women is strictly forbidden.
3. Buildings and property in enemy territory must not be burned without permission.
4. Scrupulously keep secrets and maintain security.
5. Treat ammunition carefully and keep waste to a minimum.[18]

The 144th Regiment left Kochi in late September, but this time there was no parade through the town. Their departure was to be kept secret. They were told to pull down shutters in the windows of the train that would take them away. They were not to let their families visit, but many people gathered along the railway line anyway. The rumour mill had been working feverishly. Many had a five-*sen* coin stitched into a stomach band by their mothers as a lucky charm.

Sitting in the train, Yamasaki thought, 'I will never come back alive.'

The train took the troops over Shikoku's mountains to Marugame. Eight weeks later, they boarded nine transport ships in nearby Sakaide Harbour. The men had not been told what their destination was, but on a stopover in Osaka they were issued with summer clothing and sunglasses. It seemed they were heading south, but to where? Imanishi and his mates discussed the possibilities. 'We were trying to guess. If our ship headed east we would fight against Americans and if it's west, we would be landing in China. Then the ship headed east.'[19]

Once the ships were at sea many of the troops got seasick from the high swell, but eventually they docked at Haha Jima in the Ogasawara (Bonin) Islands, about a thousand kilometres south of Tokyo. Here, horses were hoisted from the ships on slings and the soldiers conducted exercises in night landing. Their stay was short; on 4 December—three days before Pearl Harbor—they set sail again on the nine troop-ships, escorted by Fourth Fleet.

At sea, they heard the news that Japan had declared war. They were told they were heading for Omiya Island, which no one had ever heard of.

Before dawn on the 10th, the fleet arrived at what the men would eventually recognise as Guam. The battle plan was to land in three different bays in conjunction with naval landing forces. A strong wind was blowing, creating a swell, so the transports anchored well out from shore and barges ferried the soldiers through heavy seas to the beach. When all were landed they began marching inland, attacking Apra Harbour from the rear and occupying the capital, Agana, without much opposition. Key areas were under Japanese control by mid-morning.

One member of the Japanese advance party brought back three American soldiers with water bottles and a small dog. The men had been off duty and exploring the island, seemingly unaware of the attack on Pearl Harbor two days before or air raids on Agana across the island. One came up to the platoon commander, Lieutenant Inoue, with a smile and offered his hand.

'Who are you guys?' the American asked through an English-speaking Japanese soldier. 'Why are you here?'

'We are the Japanese army. We are in the middle of a war and you have been captured.'

'No way! You're kidding. It's just a drill, right? OK, that's enough. Now, let us go.'

They said they'd run out of cigarettes and asked the Japanese if they could spare some. Some of the invaders started laughing. It was hard to feel hostility towards the friendly, disbelieving Americans, but they were taken prisoner just the same.[20] They were three spirited boys three days out of date on world history.

◆ ◆ ◆

With the invasion completed Guam was handed over to the Japanese navy, but South Seas Force remained on the island for another month training for its next operation, the capture of Rabaul.

Chapter 5

Forward base Rabaul

The Australian administrators in Rabaul had been advised that Japanese forces were coming. Soon after Pearl Harbor, all Japanese living in the town were interned and later shipped to Australia. European women and children were evacuated, but the pleas of Chinese men for their women and children to be relocated at the same time were ignored.[1] The administration took a very colonial view of the people under its wing.

While the men of South Seas Force trained in Guam for the Rabaul offensive they were told, for once, about the objective and their role in the operational plan. There would be three sets of landings. Kusunose Unit would invade Rabaul along a road from the ocean coast, the main force of the 144th would attack Lakunai airstrip on the eastern edge of the town, and Kuwada Unit would land at Keravia Bay and occupy Vunakanau airstrip, south-west of Rabaul. Rabaul was defended by Lark Force, an AIF battalion under Major Bill Owen, and a militia force of local men, the New Guinea Volunteer Rifles. Ten Wirraway fighter-trainers and four Hudson bombers made up the local RAAF squadron, having arrived in December on the declaration of war.

This was different terrain from the tropical paradise the 144th were enjoying. The region around Rabaul was made up of mountains and

deep valleys, covered with dense jungle. The plains flooded frequently
with heavy rains. Boggy marshland covered much of the low-lying areas.
Disease was rife: malaria, dysentery and tropical fevers. The Japanese soldiers knew none of this.

Rabaul had been put through a softening process with regular aerial
bombing of its key installations since early January. A major attack on the
20th destroyed oil tanks and several aircraft. A follow-up raid the next
day drew a feeble air response. It seemed that Rabaul's air defences were
seriously depleted, and so they proved to be.

Troop-ships had left Guam on the 14th carrying South Seas Force.
They were to rendezvous with a naval landing force coming from Truk.
The navy's objective was New Ireland; Nankai Shitai's was New Britain,
to the south and east. One soldier's diary described conditions in his
transport, *Venice Maru*, as cramped and uncomfortable. A newspaperman
on *Yokohama Maru* wrote that the decks were scorching and the cabins
felt like steam baths.

As the convoy steamed towards its destination, the warship *Tsugaru*
spotted a sailing ship which its officers convinced themselves was the
American general MacArthur fleeing from the Philippines. *Tsugaru*
gave chase, only to find it was a Japanese fishing boat whose crew, in
turn, believed they were being pursued by a US destroyer. After the
untroubled landing on Guam, the reality of war had not yet taken hold.
Relieved to find their fears unfounded, the fishermen gave tuna to the
warship crew and shouted '*Banzai!*'

Meanwhile, an Allied flying boat reported Japanese cruisers heading
towards Rabaul. The Australian commander in New Britain, Colonel
John Scanlan, readied his troops for an imminent enemy landing. Following a radio message that Kavieng in New Ireland was under attack,
he ordered the evacuation of Rabaul's airfields and sabotage of their
runways. Other military facilities were also destroyed. Rabaul was evacuated, troops going to Keravia Bay, south of the town's Simpson Harbour,
where Scanlan expected the main enemy force to land. Civilians headed
towards the southern end of the island. The evacuation of the capital, in
haste and quiet panic, was completed by midday.

The 22nd dawned cloudy. Amid frequent sudden showers the Japanese invasion fleet anchored off the ocean coast, nowhere near where Scanlan's defenders were waiting. (This was the point where German troops had landed in World War I; history wasn't going to repeat itself this time.) On board one of the troop-ships Sergeant Imanishi smoked, watching Zero fighters circling above and waiting for the planned night landing. He thought, 'If I were not a Japanese man, I would never be able to see such a moment as this. I'll never forget the powerful feeling I have now.' It was a transcendent moment of national pride mixed with romance, but he experienced also the first stirrings of a lingering uncertainty about where Japan could go from here. He wasn't sure he could foresee an outcome to this enterprise.[2]

A strong afternoon breeze blew the clouds away, then dropped as night fell. Under a moonless but clear sky, twelve-metre landing craft skimmed over still ocean waters under the light of Very flares, each barge with up to seventy men on board. The mainland was pitch black, but light from the erupting Matupi volcano and some buildings burning in Rabaul helped guide the craft to shore. The men were alert and confident, on guard to the potential threat but with every reason to expect this assault to be like Guam, the still weather and pools of light adding a Hollywood touch. Nordup beach, said by intelligence to be a good place to land, turned out to be an earth cliff two or three metres high, but no one was around to challenge the men as they clambered up it. It took another thirty minutes or more of searching the dense shoreline forest to find a road over the saddle. There, the attacking force overwhelmed a small group of Australian soldiers left to defend the administrator's house on the road down to Rabaul. By dawn the Japanese were occupying the house, its residents having left with the town's other evacuees.

While the first unit attacked Rabaul from the ocean side to the east, the second unit landed an advance party to disable the ten artillery pieces identified by intelligence and to occupy Lakunai airfield. The party found two large anti-aircraft guns destroyed by earlier bombing, but no amount of searching could uncover the other eight. The intelligence, to put it bluntly, was wrong.

The main force of the second unit landed at dawn and moved on the township. Private Nishimura was given a sabre and pistol for the morning to replace his rifle. He was told he was to lead his platoon's advance into the town. He would appear to be an officer and thus act as a decoy if armed men still lurked among the buildings. Told he was leading because of his athletic skills—of which he talked frequently—he was to fire his pistol if he sensed anybody in front of the advancing troops. They patrolled through deserted streets, looking in every house, down every alley. Nishimura's heart was in his mouth. Rabaul was eerily empty; there wasn't even a cat to be seen. The entire town was searched without incident and, when it was declared to be clear, Nishimura sat down, breathing heavily with relief. The tension had been nearly unbearable, but his pride hadn't allowed him to show it.

It's not easy to determine what the purpose was in setting up the private as a potential sitting duck.[3] Was it an officer finding someone to take the risk for him? Or had Nishimura's comrades tired of hearing about his fitness and decided to put him in his place?

The third unit of the Japanese landing force, Kuwada Unit, was to land on Vulcan Beach and move inland to capture the second airfield. Unfortunately for them, this was the place the Australian commander had expected the main force to attack, so Colonel Kuwada's men faced the only significant resistance in the operation. To add to their difficulties, a path had to be cut through the jungle to reach the airfield. The company deployed to provide cover landed on the wrong side of Vulcan Crater, with no landmarks to guide them, and found barbed-wire entanglements and enemy defenders. Progress was slow, unlike the other two incident-free landings, but troops could be freed from elsewhere and were ferried across Simpson Harbour to assist.

Yamasaki, now a sergeant in Kuwada's battalion, found himself landing in the pre-dawn under heavy fire from Australian rifles and machine-guns behind coconut-palm log barriers. Initially driven back, the Japanese moved in the space under their own artillery trajectories and pursued a retreating enemy. By afternoon they reached Vunakanau airfield, with its cratered surface and no aircraft. Yamasaki's lasting memory of this day is finding that all the sandbags forming the defensive positions were filled with sugar.[4]

By 7 a.m., Major Owen had given the order for the AIF to retreat. Colonel Scanlan could see no value in further loss of life and issued a general order of 'every man for himself', so by afternoon the Australian survivors were fleeing in disarray as heavy rain set in. Soldiers and civilians split into small groups and withdrew through the jungle. They had no preplanned escape routes, no assembly points, no emergency supply dumps.[5] Only the RAAF had a plan. Flying boats picked up 120 airmen at a prearranged point down the eastern coast of New Britain. For the rest, they rushed through the bushes in pandemonium in trucks and cars, one truck overturning on a sharp bend. Vehicles were abandoned when the road became unserviceable. Soldiers dismantled their Lewis guns, too heavy to carry in retreat, and threw them away. They were running, but often with little idea of where they were running to. They became exhausted, got lost, were struck down with tropical disease or simply gave up. Within two weeks, more than half the fleeing Australians had surrendered or been captured. Some were betrayed by native New Guineans who sensed a change in the local winds of fortune.[6]

Rabaul was now securely in Japanese hands—'a nice little town built by Germans', houses enclosed by green hedges spotted with hibiscus.[7] Army engineers began repairing and upgrading the damaged airfields. The more remote Vunakanau was uneven and on soft ground, but Lakunai, next to the town, offered better potential. By the 25th it was suitable for fighters, and by mid-February was able to be used by medium bombers.

The Japanese field command in Rabaul could start to focus on the Australians on the run south from the capital. Leaflets were air-dropped announcing:

To the Officers and Soldiers of this Island! SURRENDER AT ONCE! And we will guarantee your life, treating you as war prisoners. Those who RESIST US WILL BE KILLED ONE AND ALL. Consider seriously. You can find neither food nor way of escape in this island and

you will only die of hunger unless you surrender. January 23rd 1942.
Japanese Commander in Chief.[8]

Patrols were sent after the retreating enemy, resulting in a series of
unsavoury incidents in which Japanese soldiers covered themselves with
anything but glory. Followed down the coast on both sides, on the west
coast to Ataliklikun Bay and on the east to Wide Bay, the escapees waited
for swollen rivers to subside before they could continue. Japanese pursuit
was slowed by mud, fallen bamboo and rotting trees, and continued by
boat when swamps impeded. Frustration set in. Nishimura was with the
pursuit force on the western coast. He recalls they captured a number of
soldiers, killing them somewhere in the jungle. They couldn't fit all the
captives in the boats, nor could they let them go to fight another day.[9]
In the euphemism used by both sides in the New Guinea war, they were
'dealt with'.

Following intelligence that enemy forces were accumulating in
the forest north of Wide Bay Japanese troops set out in pursuit from
Kokopo, on the north coast. Few would be prepared to confess after
the war to being involved in the events that followed, the subject of a
war crimes tribunal, although many of the soldiers who were not there
admit to knowing of the events. Lieutenant Yananose, a company leader
in Kuwada (3rd) Battalion, acknowledged his 8th Company was there
but claimed his second-in-command, Lieutenant Noda, was leading the
patrol on that mission. Noda died in action during the war.[10] A New
Guinean guide who was with the patrol has said military police (*kempeitai*) were part of the group.[11] *Kempeitai* brutality was feared by Japanese
soldier and New Guinea native alike.

As best the events of the 'Tol plantation massacres', as they have come
to be known, can be reconstructed from fragmentary accounts, five Japanese Daihatsu barges arrived at 7 a.m. on 3 February and swept Tol
plantation, about ninety kilometres due south of Rabaul, with machine-
gun fire. Some of the seventy troops holed up in plantation houses tried
to escape and were captured. A group of twenty-two came out holding a piece of white material, probably a singlet or underpants, and

waited. The Japanese lined up the Australians without any struggle, and rounded up others from nearby Waitavalo plantation. The prisoners were tied together and marched into a hut overnight.[12]

The next morning, eighty prisoners were brought out with their hands tied behind their back and marched with guards into the bush. The twenty-two who'd surrendered had already been separated out. Gunfire was heard, and the guards returned with blood-covered binding rope but no prisoners. It's not clear why the guards felt a need to retrieve the rope; the reason is possibly as mundane as the need to account for store items issued.[13] At other times when prisoners were taken into the bush there was no gunfire, but blood-curdling screams were heard and the guards returned with blood on their bayonets.[14] Clearly some, and possibly many, of the Australians were bayoneted while tied. This is not inconsistent with Japanese military training. Kure Naval Station's *Notes for Unit Commanders* recommends forcing raw recruits to bayonet prisoners to cure any apprehensiveness they might have about doing it in actual combat.[15] Cold-blooded perhaps, but very pragmatic. Military training is not for the squeamish; he who hesitates in hand-to-hand fighting is lost.

The number of people killed at Tol is usually reckoned at about 150. The wartime propaganda version has all captured Australians tied to coconut trees and bayoneted, which raises the question: how do we know? In fact, not all were killed and there were witnesses apart from the unacknowledged Japanese present. Bernard Yamasta and Vincent Madero, both from Rabaul, were taken on patrol and have described the day in much the same terms as the account above. Major Owen had arrived at Tol on the 2nd with two other soldiers and gone on to Kalai Mission across the bay to find food. They returned to see, unobserved from across a river, Japanese soldiers taking captured Australians into the bush one by one. They heard gunfire and screams, and saw Japanese return without prisoners.[16] Backing off undetected, they eventually got back to Australia.

Left for dead with bayonet or gunshot wounds, six of the captured Australians survived and were eventually evacuated. Private Cook was a medic who had his Red Cross armband ripped off and his medical supplies trodden into the ground. Given a choice of being bayoneted or shot he chose shooting, but was bayoneted anyway. After several thrusts, he was assumed to be dead by departing Japanese. Cook crawled until he met other retreating Australians.[17] Private Robinson successfully dashed for freedom from a bend in the track on the march into the bush. He wandered for three days, hands still tied behind him, until he was found by other Australians.[18]

The explanation usually offered for this behaviour is that the Japanese didn't have barge space for all their prisoners, so 'dealt with' the overflow. As it happened, the twenty-two surrendered prisoners were taken back to Rabaul as prisoners of war. On the way back, the barges stopped at Adler Bay and picked up more soldiers under a white flag.[19] Unfortunately, they were among the 800 being transported to Japan in mid-1942 on the freighter *Montevideo Maru* when it was sunk off the Philippines by the US submarine *Sturgeon*.

There's no question Tol was an act of barbarity. Japanese military training included indoctrination that the expected enemy in the Pacific War was a racist, colonial oppressor bent on subjugation of the Asian races, in the same way that Australian military training of the time proposed all Japanese were small, short-sighted, buck-toothed and less than human. In both cases, it makes the enemy easier to kill. Additionally, Japanese soldiers were trained in the belief that the Allies would kill all prisoners taken—indeed, that allowing yourself to be taken prisoner would bring shame on you and your family.

As a postscript to this affair, a Japanese reconnaissance plane had crashed on Vulcan Crater shortly before the landing at Rabaul, killing both pilots. Japanese authorities found later that the bodies had been buried with dignity and issued an instruction for Australian captives to be treated with similar respect.[20]

One consideration that has not been advanced is the degree to which disease played a part in the abhorrent behaviour at Tol. There was a violent outbreak of malaria during the clean-up of Rabaul and among the pursuing patrols, particularly those operating from Kokopo. Antimalarial clothing and drugs were issued but medics had initial difficulty in diagnosing the disease, and the majority of soldiers, with no experience of tropical warfare, were complacent. Malaria had been absent in Guam. Not all patients with fever could be taken to hospital; some drifted into delirium after several days and some died.[21]

Malaria outbreak notwithstanding, the occupation forces busied themselves expanding the colonial backwater capital into an operational base for Fourth Fleet. In addition to repairing airfields, Rabaul was extended with a flurry of building and renamed Nankai City by its new administrators. Twenty-nine sawmills were set up to service this activity. The town had 330 buildings when it was invaded. The Japanese trebled that figure during their occupation,[22] supplementing their own construction units with POWs brought from other parts of East Asia as well as those taken in New Guinea. The local Chinese population was ordered to live in designated areas outside Rabaul, but worked as labourers along with Chinese POWs brought to New Britain.[23]

The Japanese mostly didn't interfere with local women, and officers were very strict about transgressions. This might have had more to do with racial attitudes than decency. There have been claims that some women and girls were forced to work as 'comfort women' but, since local Chinese girls had been operating as prostitutes for Australian soldiers before the occupation,[24] it is more likely this was just a switch of clientele. As they settled into New Britain life, the Japanese began importing Japanese, Korean and Chinese 'comfort women' from elsewhere.[25]

Rabaul's native population had mixed experiences of Japanese occupation. Some remained pro-Australian; others turned pro-Japanese for survival and sometimes for 'payback' against rivals.[26] According to the diary of Lieutenant Moji of Kure 3rd Special Naval Landing Party (SNLP), the Japanese were impressed by Rabaul's quiet bay, coconut trees and houses with red galvanised iron roofs but not with its local people, with their black skins, red loincloths and teeth stained red from chewing betel nut.[27] Impressions grew more positive over time but the Japanese remained largely indifferent to the New Guineans, even though many have recollections of bartering with friendly villagers, exchanging Japanese cigarettes for local produce.[28]

Danks Tomila remembers soldiers entering his school in a village outside Rabaul, cutting down photos of King George, tearing up the Australian flag with bayonets and damaging school equipment. However, he says, they were friendly to villagers and did not interfere with their houses or gardens. The Japanese opened schools in Rabaul and Kokopo, teaching rice-paper making, carpentry and *sake*-distilling and selecting some students for military training. Some ex-pupils can still speak a few Japanese words and sing Japanese songs. One recollection is of being taught to say 'Japan Number One! America and Australia Number Ten!' and of shaking hands with the Japanese. If the children didn't recite this, their faces were slapped.[29] Villagers were paid for their produce, until the Japanese cut down their coconut trees some months later and told them they no longer owned the gardens. The villagers simply moved into the bush to make new gardens.

Over time, relationships between occupants and locals became more strained. As food grew scarce stealing increased and punishment was harsh, ranging from severe beating to execution. Often the harshest treatment came from the *kempeitai*, who would torture and sometimes execute villagers suspected of spying. One villager was flogged for walking in front of *kempeitai* headquarters.[30] On the other hand mainland New Guineans, who had been plantation workers, were used as 'kempei boys', indigenous military police. Without local roots, they too were feared by villagers. But the serious deterioration of relationships mostly took place when Japan's war and its dreams of empire were unravelling, after Nankai Shitai had moved on to its campaign on the New Guinea mainland.

◆ ◆ ◆

The first stage of the Japanese war plan had been completed ahead of schedule. Although it wasn't actually expected until 1943, Tokyo began to focus on Phase 2 in anticipation of an Allied counter-offensive. With General MacArthur relocated to Brisbane, this now seemed more likely to come from Australia than Hawaii. Japan's strategy was to blockade the supply route between the US and Australia. The master plan was

FS Operation, the occupation of New Caledonia, Fiji and Samoa. As Rabaul was pivotal to this operation, it was proposed to occupy Port Moresby in Papua to consolidate protection of the Rabaul base.

In preparation for future operations, soldiers in Rabaul spent days marching with sacks stuffed with volcanic ash in their backpacks.[31] Sergeant Imanishi's men did landing exercises on Matupi Island, in Rabaul Harbour, and practised advancing from the beach to attack a target. They were also taught how to cook rice with coconut milk because of the difficulty of finding clean water in the jungle. Imanishi was not persuaded. 'Rice cooked with coconut milk was too sweet to eat. It makes you feel sick,' he says.[32] But most of this instruction helped prepare them for actions to come. Some of the soldiers would soon get an opportunity to put it into practice.

Airstrips at Lae, Salamaua and Wau, on the northern coast of New Guinea, were being used as forward bases for Allied bombers from Townsville and Cairns, operating via Port Moresby. Orders for a Japanese joint army–navy offensive were delayed by a US carrier-based air attack on Rabaul and Fourth Fleet, but on 5 March an invasion force set out from Simpson Harbour. It was armed *inter alia* with boxes of specially printed currency in familiar denominations of shilling and half shilling (not sixpence) to pay for local labour. The 2nd Battalion of the 144th, under Major Horie (not to be confused with General Horii), was to attack Salamaua, and Kure 3SNLP was to land at Lae after air raids had softened up both targets. The invasion force had more difficulty getting to its destination than occupying it. Sailing through a succession of tropical storms for two days, it anchored off Salamaua in poor visibility and violent weather. Horie's men landed after midnight, unopposed despite signal flares giving notice of their arrival, and occupied the airfield by 3 a.m.

The troops had approached the airfield cautiously, crawling on hands and knees, Private Nishimura among them. In the stormy darkness, he came across a cord attached to a smooth ball of some weight. Asking his mate to guard it while he reported it to their platoon leader, Nishimura turned back when he heard his friend laughing. The 'bomb' turned out to be a watermelon. The privates feasted on it, then resumed their unchallenged invasion.[33] Australian troops had withdrawn south to Wau. Most locals had evacuated to Wau or Port Moresby in expectation of the attack. Japanese forces occupied the towns of Salamaua and Kela by dawn.

That morning, B-17 Flying Fortress bombers attacked the still-undeparted transport ships, killing three people. Two days later, Allied bombing at Lae and Salamaua sank four ships, killing 129. Although ten Allied planes were brought down, it was the first large-scale damage inflicted by Allied counter-attack since the start of the war, but in the euphoria of yet another victory the victors did not give the implications of this much thought.[34] Horie Battalion handed over the garrison at Salamaua to the navy, as planned, and returned to Rabaul.

◆　◆　◆

While the Japanese military developed its plans for Port Moresby, the army and navy continued their mutual sniping over future operations. The army's focus was on China and Burma, and on guarding against an attack from Soviet Russia. An Allied counter-attack in the South Pacific was the navy's responsibility. Middle-ranking naval staff in Tokyo proposed an invasion of Australia to prevent its use as a base for the anticipated counter-offensive. The case was put by Admiral Yamamoto in March 1942 to Japan's military planning group, and Admiral Nagano claimed that three divisions of the Japanese army could occupy key centres on the continent.[35] The army was singularly unimpressed and opposed the proposition forcefully. Its counter-argument was that it was still at war with China and fully occupied securing the Pacific and USSR perimeters, that strong local resistance could be expected in Australia and that shipping troops and their support would be at the expense of resources supply for the war effort as a whole. The IJA estimated the dubious exercise would require twelve divisions and 1.5 million tons of transport shipping. The proposal was rejected, never to surface again.[36]

Not surprisingly, Australia's military also addressed the prospect of a possible Japanese invasion of Australia. Its Chiefs of Staff regarded the loss of the 'Malay border' as the first stage. In March, Cabinet was advised by the military of anticipated landings around Darwin in April and on the east coast the following month. A map depicting a Japanese invasion via Western Australia and Darwin had been given to the Australian legation in Chungking by China's Director of Military Intelligence, but neither the Chinese nor the Australian military regarded the map as genuine. Nonetheless, Prime Minister John Curtin showed it to journalists, with the predictable outcome of headline hysteria.

At the same time, MacArthur was telling the Advisory War Committee that he doubted Japan would invade Australia, although his reason—that there wasn't enough in Australia to be worth the risk—wouldn't have endeared him to his temporary hosts. Neither Churchill nor Roosevelt thought invasion likely, but advised Curtin in the context of a debate about bringing Australian forces in the Middle East back to defend their homeland. Though Curtin was advised after military intercepts of the Japanese decision not to invade, it wasn't until well into 1943, when the Kokoda campaign had been clearly won, that he would concede invasion was unlikely. In that time, there had been a panic reaction in the Australian press and public from government advertising and propaganda. 'He's coming south' posters had proliferated. Military historian Peter Stanley speculates that Curtin's claim of an invasion plan might have been made for electoral advantage or to mobilise the Australian people or to cover the success of Allied code-breaking, but concludes it probably arose from the pressure of responsibility as prime minister. Not only did Curtin not save Australia from a real threat, Stanley suggests, he gave it a legacy of bogus invasion-plan stories.[37]

◆ ◆ ◆

By April, Allied air attacks were causing extensive damage to Japanese air capacity and the Allies were beginning to take control of the war in the air. General Horii expressed concern to Imperial HQ about growing Allied air superiority and wanted thought given to paratrooper forces occupying airfields before an invasion. Tokyo demurred on that but assigned a high-speed anti-aircraft ship, *Asakayama Maru*, to South

Seas Force. B–26 Marauder bombing raids on Lae and Rabaul in April had severely limited Japanese air capacity, but the installation of the elite Tainan Air Corps in Rabaul soon after had the potential to rectify that. The eleven Zero fighters in Lae flew missions over the Owen Stanley Range to attack Port Moresby and they were able to intercept Allied air attacks on Japanese bases. Neither side had established air superiority at that time.

An invasion of Port Moresby (MO Operation) and a showdown with the US Pacific Fleet at Midway Island had been in planning since early 1942. The timetable was sped up after surprise American air raids on Japanese cities on 18 April. They had minimal military impact but a strong psychological effect on Japan's public and its Imperial command. They didn't make much impression, however, on South Seas Force in Rabaul, which set out on the MO invasion on 2 May with high optimism. These were the soldiers who had occupied both Guam and Rabaul within a day. Here, they had a protective fleet in support and air cover supplied by the light aircraft carrier *Shoho*, to be joined by two more carriers, *Shokaku* and *Zuikaku*, coming from Truk atoll. But the Japanese were unaware that US cryptologists had broken their naval code and that, as a result, two American carriers and accompanying warships were steaming towards them.

Kure 3SNLP landed on Tulagi in the Solomon Islands without incident and set up a refuelling base for the operation. That was short-lived. The next day, the US carrier *Yorktown* launched three strikes against shipping and aircraft at Tulagi, sinking a destroyer and crippling its seaplane reconnaissance capability. The operation, under the overall command of Admiral Inoue, was now notified of the presence of *Yorktown* in the vicinity. Carriers from both sides spent the next day searching fruitlessly for each other in cloudy weather. The fleets were little more than a hundred kilometres apart but didn't know it. Inside the gloomy, cramped belly of *Asakayama Maru*, the landing troops of Nankai Shitai sat anxiously, inclement weather bashing against the ship's outer shell.

The 7th of May was the first of the two days of the Battle of the Coral Sea, history's first naval battle in which the opposing fleets never set eyes on each other. It was a battle of carrier-based aircraft in which blunders played a significant role. A US oiler had been incorrectly identified by planes from the *Shoho* as a carrier and sunk. Realising their mistake they returned to their own carrier, which by then had been spotted by the enemy. Planes from both American carriers attacked *Shoho* and sunk it while it turned into the wind so it could launch its Zeros.

The Allied force, meanwhile, had detached six warships under Australian Rear-Admiral John Crace to block the transport ships heading for Port Moresby. It was a risky strategy without air cover and, predictably, the ships were attacked by Japanese torpedo bombers. Minutes later they were attacked again, this time by American B-17s by mistake. Crace commented wryly about the second attack: 'Fortunately their bombing in comparison to that of the Japanese formation minutes earlier, was disgraceful.'[38]

In fact, neither side's planes had inflicted much damage on Crace's ships, but Japanese planes returned to Rabaul and reported sinking three ships anyway. The locations of each side's ships were getting increasingly uncertain. The Port Moresby invasion fleet was ordered to reverse course until the situation could be clarified. On board, soldiers had heard the deep thud of two waves of air-dropped ordnance but had no idea what direction the battle was taking. They could detect their vessel turning around, but no one was telling them why. They relied for morale on their highly drilled belief in their cause.

Planes from *Zuikaku* returned as darkness was falling, their pilots exhausted after flying long hours through foul weather with poor visibility. They mistakenly lined up to land on a US carrier, pulling out only at the last minute. No guns were fired, so the Americans must not have noticed the error either.[39]

On the second day of the battle, the main fleets located each other at first light and launched raids. *Shokaku* was bombed three times, making its deck unserviceable for landing. *Yorktown* and *Lexington*, the two American carriers, were hit by bombs and torpedoes, and *Lexington* had to be abandoned and sunk to prevent its falling into Japanese hands. Only *Zuikaku* remained undetected in the rain. Although some of its planes had to be pushed off the deck to allow the *Shokaku* planes to land, it was now the only carrier left in the battle. Crace's fleet, without air cover, was all that stood between the MO invasion force and Port Moresby, but Inoue was misled by flyers' reports on Allied strength. He recalled the invasion fleet at 9 a.m. Admiral Yamamoto, on hearing of his junior's order, reversed it and called on his air arm to 'destroy the remaining enemy force'. By then, any search for *Yorktown* was in vain. The carrier was already well on its way back to Pearl Harbor. By afternoon, General Horii was advised that the Moresby operation was postponed and the convoy was returning to Rabaul. 'First, I offer my deepest congratulations for such an unprecedented victory. Secondly, I confirm that I understand we will return to Rabaul,' was Horii's sarcastic reply.[40]

Both sides claimed the upper hand in the Battle of the Coral Sea, and each could provide some justification for its claim. Japan had lighter shipping loss. Its sunk carrier, *Shoho*, was considerably smaller than *Lexington*. However, the object of the operation, the invasion of Port Moresby, was abandoned, probably prematurely, and a dent had been put in the Japanese navy's aura of invincibility. One lesson learnt by the Allies in the encounter was the futility of high-altitude bombing of moving targets. Both sergeants Yamasaki and Imanishi were in the transport ship, and both remarked on the number of bombs dropped without hitting the target while it was taking evasive action. Nerve-racking, perhaps, but they survived to return to Rabaul. A second attempt at the seaborne invasion of Port Moresby was scheduled for July.

The Midway Island operation was the opportunity for Japan's navy to reverse the minor setback in the Coral Sea. It did anything but that. The army was initially opposed to invasion of the mid-Pacific island, but the navy was prepared to go it alone. This was to be the confrontation that would break the US Pacific Fleet's back. Unfortunately, Allied code-breaking had alerted the enemy to the coming attack and a fleet was waiting. The element of surprise completely lost, four Japanese carriers were sunk: *Akagi*, *Kaga*, *Soryu* and *Hiryu*. Japan's defeat in the 4–7 June Battle of Midway also meant the loss of its Pacific supremacy. FS

Operation, the plan to isolate Australia by taking Fiji and Samoa, was postponed for two months, then until December. Effectively, by then, FS Operation was cancelled.

◆　◆　◆

General Hyakutake of Seventeenth Army delayed his return to Davao, in the Philippines, so that Staff Officer Imoto of Imperial HQ could brief him on developments after the crushing defeat at Midway. 'FS Operation has been postponed,' said Imoto, 'due to the setback at Midway.' No one talked about defeat or retreat in the Imperial Japanese Army. 'The plan instead is for an overland attack on Port Moresby as a joint army–navy operation.'

The postponement of FS Operation made sense. After Midway, Japan's reduced naval strength would not be able to support it. The attack on Port Moresby was harder to fathom. Overland via what?

Research in Manila had unearthed an English explorer's account of his travels around the northern side of New Guinea. The book indicated the existence of a road to Port Moresby. Was it a road or a track or a four-lane highway? The exact nature of the route got lost in translation. The Englishman was reporting something he had been told; he wasn't concerned about its capacity to service an invasion force moving across the mountains. The military proceeded as if it had found a surveyor's map. A report following air reconnaissance claimed to confirm the likelihood of a road to the Papuan capital. A serviceable road, it said, ran from Buna on the coast to Kokoda in the northern foothills of the Owen Stanley Range, with a serviceable bridge across the Kumusi River. A road ran up to thick jungle but couldn't be seen through it. It was assumed it continued under the jungle canopy, but when troops got to New Guinea they found that the road—such as it was—stopped at the jungle. A route from Kokoda to Isurava, further south, was judged to be serviceable before it disappeared in the clouds. No other roads were detected.[41]

The reconnaissance observer was Lieutenant Rinzo Kanemoto. It was his first time ever in a plane and he lost his sense of direction. At 2000 metres, he couldn't tell the width or the condition of the ribbon-like

road far below him, apparently winding in and out of the jungle. Several
Lockheed P-38 fighters in the vicinity added to Kanemoto's confusion,
which was reflected in his report.[42] Evidence of a road over the mountains was clearly inconclusive, but the military judged that a vehicular
road was available for supply from Buna to Kokoda. They expected an
engineer regiment and Formosan labourers would be required to repair
the road and construct further roads. They needed that and more. The
Imperial army had seriously miscalculated.

A sceptical General Horii was far from persuaded that a supply line
could be maintained for troops advancing along the Kokoda Track, in
whatever state that would prove to be. His chief of staff, the bookish
Lieutenant-Colonel Toyonari Tanaka, did the necessary calculations
and presented the results to Seventeenth Army HQ. Buna to Port
Moresby was a 360-kilometre march with, given the expected terrain,
260 kilometres of it just trudging. Without a vehicular road—and that
possibility seemed very remote—the force would need to be supplied
by packhorses or, if the ruggedness precluded that, human carriers.
With a front line of 5000 men, each with a daily food requirement of
600 grams, the daily needs of South Seas Force were estimated to be
three tonnes of provisions. By the time the front line got to the Owen
Stanley saddle, about halfway to Moresby, Tanaka estimated that 230
carriers would be required daily for a twenty-day round trip, that is,
4600 carriers in total. Once the front moved to Port Moresby, 32,000
carriers would be required. Munitions and other supplies would add
to the load but, since 32,000 men was already out of the question, that
no longer mattered.[43]

Horii was less circumspect than most of his countrymen, so his pes-
simism about the high risk of failure provoked a degree of caution in the
forward planners of Davao and Tokyo. It was decided the new attack plan
for Port Moresby should be preceded by a feasibility study, designated
Ri Operation Study. This would determine if an overland operation
could indeed be advanced over the route known locally as the Kokoda
Track and, if so, how best to achieve it. On 1 July a new order was issued
for an advance force to land on the northern beaches of Papua, secure

the region, including capture of Kokoda's airstrip, and advance only as far as the saddle of the Owen Stanley Range in order to evaluate the suitability of the 'road' to Port Moresby for a full-scale operation.

An advance force was put together under Colonel Yosuke Yokoyama, commander of 15th Independent Engineer Regiment. It was to be made up of Yokoyama's regiment, 1st Battalion of 144th Regiment under Lieutenant-Colonel Tsukamoto, a mountain artillery company and other support units. The navy released 500 of its Formosan (the Takasago Volunteers) and Korean labourers to South Seas Force for the operation. Two thousand local men from Rabaul were coopted as additional labour, a move of questionable advantage to the broad effort. The local populace reacted badly to the use of its people as indentured labourers outside New Britain, undermining the program of pacification being pursued by the occupying administration.[44]

Yokoyama Advance Party was to advance to a line on the western side of the Owen Stanley Range and occupy it—but to go no further than that. It was to assess the condition and quality of the roads and the need for improvement of the Buna–Kokoda road. It was to look at the roads along the Kumusi and Mambare rivers, and at the road that ran from Kokoda to Port Moresby. It was to assess those two rivers for the possibility of transport by barge. Roads on the northern side of the mountains were to be repaired to accommodate motor transport, ideally heavy army vehicles; on the southern slopes the road was to be made suitable for packhorses. A base would be constructed at Buna as a support centre for MO Operation, were it to go ahead. Food was to be stockpiled, including for horses, in an area as near to the front line as possible.[45] Attention to detail; thoroughness in preparation. Yokoyama Advance Party was preparing for the overland attack as much as for its assessment, but Imperial HQ in Tokyo was still waiting for that assessment to arrive from Colonel Yokoyama, the senior engineer of the advance party, before ordering the full advance.

Some thought it might not have been a bad thing that Midway had knocked the wind out of their sails—it was only the navy anyway—since the restraint being exercised would reduce the risk of going headlong into an action that closer examination might show could never succeed. The caution was commendable, but it would all come unstuck with one rash call from one individual that started South Seas Force on its fatefully misjudged expedition.

Chapter 6

The taking of Kokoda

He blew into Seventeenth Army headquarters like a tropical squall that lifted papers off desks where they weren't properly weighted. Self-confident, with an air of supreme authority, Lieutenant-Colonel Masanobu Tsuji had arrived in Davao, and he was there to make things happen. Acclaimed as a strategist in the Malaya campaign and author of a pamphlet of 'paternal homilies'[1] giving advice to men at the front, he had drawn both critics and admirers with his zeal. He was now a staff officer at Imperial Headquarters, but Tsuji had known Seventeenth Army chief of staff Major-General Futami when both were at Army General Staff. Although they had not been close, Tsuji made much of their past association. Notwithstanding his rank Futami was polite to his former colleague, as is the Japanese way, but he remained cautious in his dealings with him. Well he might be. Moon-faced and with a shaven head, the bespectacled Tsuji was a mover and shaker. Finding female typists working in army administration at Davao, he recommended their immediate repatriation to Japan.[2]

The main purpose of Colonel Tsuji's visit, however, was not to maintain the army as a male preserve. He was in Davao to deliver the order made four days before officially cancelling FS Operation, the tactical manoeuvre to capture Fiji and Samoa, and by so doing disrupt MacArthur's supply from the US. An overland assault on Port Moresby would now be the main thrust of Japan's South Pacific strategy. Tsuji arrived on 15 July, a week before Yokoyama Advance Party was due to leave Rabaul for New Guinea to assess the suitability of the Kokoda Track as an invasion route. He brought a counter-instruction from Imperial Headquarters.

'If we're going to have an effective air war of attrition against eastern New Guinea,' Tsuji advised, 'Port Moresby has to be attacked as soon as possible. It's imperative. Even the Emperor is concerned about this. So, without waiting for the results of the Ri Operation Study, Imperial HQ is ordering Seventeenth Army to attack Port Moresby.'[3]

As unexpected as this change of plan was, it came with the imprimatur of the Emperor and therefore had to be carried out. That same afternoon, Seventeenth Army drew up new operational plans.

Three days later, Seventeenth Army HQ issued orders for the Moresby offensive. South Seas Force was to land near Buna, advance along the Kokoda 'road' and capture Port Moresby's airfields. Ryuto Unit—made up of engineering, road and bridge construction, motor transport, communications and military police units—was to land at Buna and set up a supply and administrative base near Kokoda. An anti-aircraft artillery battalion was earmarked for the air defence of Buna and for building bridges over the Kumusi, the river that had to be crossed to get to Kokoda. Army Signals Unit would set up a communications base in Rabaul for the campaign.

While the overland assault was under way, 35th Infantry Brigade was to prepare for operations at Milne Bay and the Louisiade Archipelago at the far eastern end of New Guinea. Their objective was to set up an operational base for another attempted seaborne landing at Port Moresby in support of and coinciding with the main attack via the Kokoda Track.

Finally, General Hyakutake and his HQ were to relocate from Davao to Rabaul.[4] The stakes had been raised significantly, and a full-scale offensive was off and running. There would be no considered evaluation now. Instead, the advance party was to set up base as a combined army–navy operation and advance to Kokoda. The main attack force would join them two weeks later and push across the Owen Stanley Range to Port Moresby.

Masanobu Tsuji was not a man to let the grass grow under his feet. He lined up two Mitsui Corporation freighters as transport ships, and escort destroyers from the Imperial Japanese Navy. He also organised four packhorse companies and four bridge construction companies, but vetoed Seventeenth Army's request to strengthen 15th Engineer Regiment. They'd sensed Tsuji was a 'can-do' man, but he was not going to let them think he was a soft touch. He would pull the strings and he would decide which strings were to be pulled. On the 22nd General Hyakutake transferred to Rabaul, and Tsuji went with him.

Tsuji's leadership was positive and it was prompt, but it would turn out to be unauthorised. Evidence was available in various military communications, but no one connected the dots. The navy's Fourth Fleet planned for Sasebo 5th Special Naval Landing Party (SNLP), or Kaigun Rikusentai—akin to American marines—to accompany Yokoyama Advance Party to Buna and establish a landing outpost and airbase. Even if the Moresby attack was deemed too difficult, there would still be a need for advance airbases near Buna. Curiously, the navy continued to refer to Ri Operation Study rather than the full offensive, now called MO Operation by the army. As well, Imperial HQ's communications seemed ambiguous on the current state of operational commitment. It was curious, but no one paid it too much attention at the time. In the continual bitter rivalry between the two services, the navy's being a bit out of touch would be seen as evidence of Tokyo's fading favour towards it.

◆ ◆ ◆

Preparation by Yokoyama Advance Party took on an air of urgency as Day X approached.[5] Day X in this instance was 20 July. Tension rose with the order to follow the landing at Buna with preparations for a confirmed advance on Port Moresby. The offensive was no longer just a possibility. It was now going ahead without the prior assessment of its feasibility, with all the dangers and challenges that such a military action would entail. Adrenaline-charged soldiers in Rabaul saw aircraft—about forty Zero fighters and attack planes—taking off and returning from sorties on Port Moresby's airfields on the 18th and 20th. There was a buzz of expectation through the ranks. Morale was high from the successful campaigns at Guam and Rabaul: a feeling of invincibility.

On the afternoon of the 20th, the docks at Rabaul's Simpson Harbour were a hive of activity. Men, horses, vehicles and supplies were all stowed in the holds of the two high-speed freighters *Ryoyo Maru* and *Ayatosan Maru*. It took the whole afternoon, with the invasion force boarding last. Soldiers of the advance party assembled in the early evening, along with Sasebo 5SNLP and naval base units. The two services operated under separate commands that were expected to coordinate their actions—and mostly did—but the enmity, especially at senior levels, ensured that an integrated force for a particular campaign was never contemplated.

The procedure was workmanlike and efficient. These were highly trained soldiers at the peak of their performance. The tension of anticipation could be felt, but there was no sense of dread. Although the Japanese navy might have suffered recent setbacks, Nankai Shitai had enjoyed nothing but success. The offensive against Port Moresby was a bigger operation, they all knew that, but they had every reason to feel confident. Had the navy prevailed in the Coral Sea, they might already be there. In any case, they were only an advance party, to be joined by the main force after the Kokoda airfield was secured. Then the offensive on the Papuan capital itself would commence.

The convoy—two destroyers, two cruisers and the two transports— left Rabaul's Simpson Harbour at 8 p.m. and headed out into rough seas. Talk was difficult in the cacophony inside the ship's hold, which the men shared with supplies secured for the voyage. The roar of the ship's engines, the crashing of heavy seas against their metal shell, the groaning of ropes and machinery; the possibility of air or submarine attack during the journey; the incessant movement to and fro imposed by the sea—all combined to plunge the soldiers into their own thoughts. Cramped in an ominous gloom under low ceilings they waited, preparing their minds to meet a new enemy, a confrontation in which they would kill or be killed.

On board *Ayatosan Maru* the soldiers of Yokoyama Advance Party, in their brown cotton-drill tunics, contemplated the coming campaign. They had encountered Australian troops before, but the assault on Rabaul had been completed almost as soon as it started. What they had heard suggested these might be tougher opponents than that action had led them to think. Fellow soldiers who had come up against the Australians in Lae and Salamaua said they were skilled marksmen, more dangerous than the Americans. They made good use of cover and were effective with grenades. The vast majority of the men inside these vessels would never have met an Australian, and knew nothing about the country, its culture or its people. Sadashige Imanishi, crouching in the half-light of the belly of *Ayatosan Maru*, pondered this with his comrades-in-arms. 'We said Australia is the destination of British criminals,' he recalls, 'so they must be very cruel and we have to be very careful.'

The Japanese soldiers believed their fighting spirit and mental power would prevail in any confrontation with this rough convict stock, but they had no illusions about how hard it might be. 'I also had this premonition that the battle we were going to might be something very tough, like we would eat soil in the ground. It was exactly as I expected.'[6]

Despite the troops' apprehension, the convoy was not challenged by enemy aircraft or submarines on the uncomfortable voyage to the Buna coast. At 7 p.m. the following evening *Ayatosan Maru* mistakenly arrived at Gona, some fifteen kilometres west along the coast from Buna. The intention had been to land at nearby Basabua, avoiding the reefs off the Buna coast, but that had not eventuated. *Ryoyo Maru*, with its load of marines, horses and motor vehicles, had gone on as planned to Giruwa, nearer Buna.

On arrival, Japanese destroyers shelled the beaches of both Buna and Gona. Papuans and the handful of European civilians in the area later spoke of the formidable sight of immense warships on the horizon in the late afternoon, and of their further dismay when the ships began shooting soon after. The move had the intended impact on the people it was meant to impress.[7] A platoon of Australian observers at Buna and a smaller party at Gona withdrew before the Japanese landed.

As darkness fell the landing party began disembarking, a host of peaked tropical field caps, each with its sun curtain of four strips at the back. Two thousand troops and support personnel slid down ropes hung over the ships' sides and onto waiting barges. Once filled, the barges glided across the water in the moonless night. No one spoke except when an instruction was given, the dominant sound the whirring of motors driving the barges in formation towards shore. Normally Japanese soldiers were chatterboxes; now there was silence, with everyone alert. Barges hit the shore in succession, each with a grating thud. Men leapt out with their knapsacks, splashing through the last metre or two of the ocean journey and up the black sand of Gona beach, well-drilled in the landing procedure that had dominated their recent training.

Nine hundred infantrymen from Tsukamoto Battalion of the 144th were on Gona beach by the end of the night, along with 100 Formosans and Koreans and 400 carriers indentured in Rabaul. Engineers and artillery units were also landed. There had been no sign of the enemy, here or at Buna beach, where 430 troops of Sasebo 5SNLP landed with various support units.

With the morning came bad weather, hampering the final stages of transfer of supplies and equipment. The fifty-two horses on *Ryoyo Maru* had yet to be brought to shore when the landing operation's good fortune deserted it further. Japanese Zeros had been unable to provide air cover because of stormy weather at take-off in Rabaul, but the opposition coming from the south managed to find its way through. Wave after wave totalling about 100 Australian warplanes—bombers and P-400 Airacobras—attacked the Gona anchorage.[8] Personnel on land headed for cover; those still on board got out of sight and hoped their destroyer's artillery could deal with the intruders. It couldn't. Shells and bombs landed around and sometimes on moored ships, a terrifying experience in powerlessness for anyone still on board. *Ayatosan Maru* was hit by a bomb and burst into flames. The destroyer *Uzuki* was damaged and turned around to return to Rabaul.

Ayatosan Maru was clearly a doomed vessel, its loss an early contribution by the Mitsui Corporation to the Japanese war effort. The ship was abandoned and foundered off the beach at Gona where it remained, half-submerged, for the duration of the Kokoda campaign. *Ryoyo Maru* was ordered to return to Rabaul without unloading its cargo of horses.[9]

◆ ◆ ◆

Lieutenant-Colonel Hatsuo Tsukamoto was of the old school of Japanese military. A martinet inclined to find fault with everyone and everything, he was also a heavy *sake* drinker. However, love him or loathe him—and it was mostly the latter—the 900 soldiers of 1st Battalion of the 144th had him as their leader. As soon as necessary supplies had been landed at Gona the troops were ordered to move inland, pushing through the coastal strip of jungle to find their way blocked by extensive swamps. Stumbling about on the edge of these miry ponds, they eventually found tracks to get them further inland. Designated forward units moved quickly along the road to Kokoda, in trucks until the road became unsuitable for motor transport. They marched from that point. The remainder of the battalion went to Buna in the morning with Tsukamoto, to advance later to Kokoda and reconnoitre the promised 'yellow brick road' to Port Moresby.

Scouting the area around Gona, a party led by Lieutenant Ida came across a Western-style building among the sago palms. Pushing the door open with his foot, the lieutenant entered cautiously. The first thing that struck him was the delicate fragrance of perfume. Torchlight revealed no one in the room, although a young woman's clothes lay there. On the kitchen table were two coffee cups. He held them and they were still warm. Whoever was here had only just left. It seemed that women, maybe two of them, lived here.

'They can't be far,' he said to his men. 'Look for them.'

The phone rang, and when he picked up the handset a flustered voice said in English, 'Head for Kokoda immediately!'

They combed the house to see if the occupants had hidden themselves and searched outside in the foliage.[10] It seemed that the two residents had made good their escape.

That afternoon, the Japanese forward party made its first contact with opposing forces. It came across a scouting party from the Papuan Infantry Battalion (PIB) stationed nearby at Awala, a force made up of native Papuans with Australian officers. After a brief exchange of fire, the PIB soldiers quickly scattered.

At Giruwa, as at Gona, unloading and transfer to shore had continued through the night of the 21st. The beachhead was secured by dawn and the village of Buna occupied by the marines of Sasebo 5SNLP, the villagers having fled as soon as ship's artillery started firing in their direction. All through the day of the 22nd Buna was a scene of constant, well-drilled activity, as if a movie shoot or a circus had come to town. Japanese troops and support labour went about constructing an operational base. Unit headquarters were built, fortified bunkers dug and anti-aircraft guns installed along the coast. Work began on an airbase at Buna, to be constructed in haste by expanding and improving the existing airfield. A wharf was built to land supplies and reinforcements and was later used to evacuate the sick and wounded. Another base was built at Sanananda, at what before the war had been a shipping terminal for the Sangara rubber plantation. Giruwa became the site of the main Japanese hospital. In short time, a military town rose out of the swamps and jungle among the coconut and sago palms.

Road-building squads worked swiftly on a remarkable feat of improvised highway engineering. The Transport Battalion established a vehicle base at Soputa, about ten kilometres inland, and cleared a track to the base in two days. Trucks could drive on the coastal roads and in to Soputa, but movement through the jungle and grassland beyond them was made difficult by rivers and steep gullies. Roads were improved with 'corduroy' logging, in which logs were embedded across the compacted earth track so it would hold firm under continually passing trucks. However, persistent rain and the ever-present mud meant vehicles still often bogged on these roads. Whenever that happened, they were abandoned and men took over carrying the supplies. Road repairs enabled vehicles to get sixty kilometres from the coast to Sanbo, where munitions and supplies stockpiles were set up. The road beyond Sanbo was suitable only for packhorses, forcing a rethink of the original plan to stockpile at Kokoda.

The Allies had stationed a company of militia at Kokoda in early July. The 39th Battalion was made up of reservists who had been intended to operate as a home guard but were brought to New Guinea on the somewhat specious argument that it was 'Australian soil', in many cases without being told their destination. They were denigrated by the regulars as 'chockos' (from *The Chocolate Soldier*, a well-known prewar musical[11]), soldiers who would melt in the heat of battle. Nonetheless, they were brought over the Kokoda Track in expectation of a Japanese landing. They would have to deal with that as best they could. No one seriously believed that Japan would attempt to move an assault force along the track.

The Australian command, alerted to the Japanese landing by coastal observers in radio contact, ordered the balance of 39th Battalion to get to Kokoda as swiftly as possible. They started flying across from Moresby on the 24th, including the new battalion commander, Lieutenant-Colonel Owen, the same Bill Owen who as a major had watched the Tol plantation incident unobserved six months before.

Meanwhile, as frenetic construction activity continued around Buna, the Japanese forward party of Tsukamoto Battalion pressed on towards Kokoda. Captain Sam Templeton, the company commander in Kokoda, sent two of his three platoons forward to meet the approaching enemy at Awala, where they linked with the main force of the Papuan Infantry Battalion stationed there. They were encircled by the Japanese with a speed and agility that astonished them. Australian and local soldiers, recognising that their cause in Awala was lost, withdrew. Most of the sixty-odd PIB members there deserted, although some made their way back to Kokoda with the Australians. In many cases, the Papuans had been pressed into joining the military by an authoritarian administration. They had little heart for it. The war with Japan, after all, was Australia's business. The Japanese were just another group of strangers intruding in their country.

Into the early morning after the Awala withdrawal and while the bulk of their forward troops returned to Kokoda, an Australian patrol remained alongside the Kumusi River where it could be crossed at

Wairopi (Pidgin for wire-rope bridge). When a signal came to pull back to Kokoda, they did so after slashing support cables and sending the bridge crashing into the river. A group of about twenty men stayed hidden on the western bank of the Kumusi.

It was still the dry season. The Kumusi was relatively low and could be waded to the other side. When the Japanese forward unit arrived at the river, they did that—and walked into an Australian ambush. Fifteen men of the forward party were killed in the exchange of fire, an early indication of how hard this campaign might be and the troops' first taste of Australian marksmanship.[12] The toll would have made sobering thinking if the Japanese had had the luxury of thought. In this situation, all mental energy goes into mobilising an effective response. Their riflemen returned fire and the Australians retreated to join the rest of their company at Oivi, east of Kokoda.

The main force of Yokoyama Advance Party, advancing after the forward units, was now starting to trickle through to join them at the enemy's front line at Oivi. Japanese troops pressed in on the defenders with a frontal attack. It seemed only a matter of time before the Australians would be driven back. Templeton knew another platoon had just flown in to Kokoda and was coming to Oivi in support. Realising this was now futile, he decided they should be headed off before they got into unnecessary trouble. Instead of sending a runner, the company commander made the fatal mistake of going back himself, alone. Sam Templeton was an older officer, a veteran of World War I and something of a father figure to the poorly trained and inexperienced militia under his command. They called him Uncle Sam. He tended to take on tasks himself rather than delegate. Here was yet another instance, his last. He was never seen again by the Australians, and his fate had long been a mystery.

The Japanese at Oivi executed a flanking movement, trapping the defenders in a clearing, but the Australians held them off as dusk turned to night. The attack under dark followed a scenario that had worked in China and would unnerve defenders here. Men would hack through the scrub, banging mess tins and shouting orders in English. It was a tactic that sowed confusion, and the retreating Australians would see much more of it in the coming stages of the campaign. This time, however, the Japanese found the defenders' clearing empty. A Papuan police boy who had been with the Australians had guided them after dark along Oivi Creek, the cacophony covering the sounds of their departure. By the time the attack was made on the empty clearing, their quarry was well down the path back to Kokoda.

All their quarry that is, except for six Australian militiamen caught behind the flanking movement. They found their retreat path blocked by Japanese medics attending to the wounded. Outnumbered, they resolved to bluff their way past.

Private Charles Pyke, one of the group, recalls: 'We said we will go through, but we won't draw attention, we will just keep going. If we get challenged, just open up with everything from the hip and keep going, that's our only hope.' They walked straight past the Japanese, hearts pumping, rifles held tightly, each side behaving as if the other wasn't there. 'They were fixing up their wounded,' Pike says. 'They were yabbering. They didn't challenge us. I don't know why, I don't know if they were that confused, we weren't even challenged.' The six got back to Kokoda.[13] The Japanese probably didn't challenge them because they were all either non-combatants or wounded, but in any case they were conscripts: trained to fight when ordered, but mostly reluctant to fight when it was unnecessary.

On the other hand, Sam Templeton did run foul of Japanese troops on his way back to Kokoda. Wounded and left on the ground, he was found later by Lieutenant-Colonel Yanagisawa, a medical officer from the Engineer Regiment. Thinking, 'I am a doctor as well as a soldier,' Yanagisawa took him back to the Japanese positions and applied first aid to his wounds. The first words Templeton said were: 'My name is Templeton.'

The wounded enemy officer was questioned by Colonel Tsukamoto about the number and location of Australian troops. Laughing, Templeton replied, 'In our rear position, 80,000 Allied troops have gathered for our support. I wonder how many of you guys will actually get out of here alive. I'll be counting.'[14]

The Japanese battalion commander was infuriated by the Australian's fearlessness and his mocking tone. He wouldn't abide such insolence from his own troops, some of whom were looking on; why should he take it from an enemy prisoner? Something in Tsukamoto snapped. He drew his officer's sabre and thrust it deep into the Australian's belly. There was almost no sound.

◆ ◆ ◆

By 28 July, a week after the landings at Buna and Gona, Yokoyama Advance Party was grouping for its first major assault. The airfield at Kokoda was the main objective, but coupled with it was a strategic need to drive the Australians out of the village of Kokoda, which sat on a plateau above the grass landing strip. Troops continued to come forward to join the main force, bringing supplies, munitions and other necessities. Drizzle had become persistent, the roads more muddy. The frequency of air attacks forced the advance party to move mostly at night. Bridges over the Kumusi were in a never-ending cycle of bombardment and rebuilding. There were delays as soldiers camped on the river bank waiting for engineers to rig new bridges.

The Japanese had carried hundreds of bicycles with them on the landing barges. Most were abandoned when the road became rough and muddy, although sick soldiers would still get about on them in the Buna–Gona area. Sergeant Imanishi carried his bicycle as far as Oivi, even holding it above his head as he waded across the Kumusi.

'I was hoping to get on it on a flat area and put some bags on it,' he says. 'I carried the bicycle and climbed up a steep hill. I was so thirsty. Then someone said, "Look at that! He carried his bicycle to here."'

Feeling embarrassed, Imanishi dumped his bicycle in the bush. 'But after Oivi the road was flat. I regretted it so much.'[15] It would have been a short-lived triumph. The track starts to climb after Kokoda and from that point offered nothing to cyclists.

◆ ◆ ◆

The mystery of Colonel Tsuji's instruction to Seventeenth Army command was resolved on 25 July when a telegram reached Rabaul from

Colonel Hattoni of Operations Sector in Tokyo. Pointing out that Imperial HQ was still waiting for results of the feasibility study, Hattoni asked what progress had been made. With Yokoyama Advance Party already in New Guinea, the gap between Hattoni's understanding and Tsuji's instruction was embarrassingly wide. Reversal of the MO Operation order would create the possibility of un-reversing it a few days later if Yokoyama's report was positive. The solution: a face-saving response. General Hyakutake telegraphed back that in Colonel Yokoyama's assessment the overland attack on Port Moresby was indeed practical, and that the main force of Nankai Shitai was preparing to land soon in Papua and commence MO Operation.

'The original instruction was clearly an independent judgement of Lieutenant-Colonel Tsuji,' recalled Imperial HQ senior staff officer Imoto after the war. 'It wasn't recognised as particularly problematic at the time, though I think some people felt slightly awkward. Personally, I had reservations about whether it would be a good thing in the end, but I didn't have the confidence to argue against it or present an alternative.'[16]

Tsuji had actually been sent to Davao to make a decision on the overland offensive once Yokoyama's report arrived, not to pre-empt that report. On the day the Tokyo telegram reached Rabaul, he had left the town for Buna with the final group of the advance party. He had known Yosuke Yokoyama from the Malaya campaign and planned to offer him encouragement for his mission and to inspect the roads to Kokoda. Unfortunately for the emissary from Tokyo HQ, his run of good fortune had come to a temporary end. Two days out at sea and approaching Buna, the convoy came under intense fire from Allied aircraft. Superstructure in the destroyer in which Tsuji travelled was hit, hurling pieces of metal through the air. One of them struck him in the throat and he had to be repatriated to Rabaul.

Tsuji was soon back on his feet and on the warpath, complaining to Imperial HQ that the enemy had gained air superiority in the Buna area. The navy's air strength was insufficient for the needs of that sector of the war, he said, but the navy was not telling army command that. Tsuji might have been trying to lend support to the army in its ongoing rivalry with the navy, but he got no thanks from General Hyakutake. Tsuji was a nuisance who had already compromised him over the Hattoni telegram. He complained to Chief of Staff Futami about the difficulties the interloper was causing him, saying the army might be better off if he was sent back to Tokyo. Futami counselled against forcing the issue. He explained in his memoirs: 'I felt that if he was made to return this time, then his influence on future events would perhaps be quite significant.'[17]

Japanese are not in the habit of calling a spade a spade and Akisaburo Futami was no exception. The general knew, nonetheless, what he was referring to. Tsuji might have his detractors, but he also had influential connections in the Tokyo military's world of intrigue. Pressing the matter could rebound. Hyakutake took his chief of staff's advice.

◆ ◆ ◆

After burning some of the huts with their stores on the night of the 26th, Colonel Owen had withdrawn his defenders from Kokoda back up the track to Deniki, leaving behind blankets and groundsheets. His reasoning was that it was easier to hold off the Japanese advance on the track than in the wider, more open ground of the village and its northern approaches. He may also have thought there was unlikely to be any Japanese plan to go beyond Kokoda, so he was moving himself and his men out of harm's way. However, when told the next day that the Japanese hadn't occupied the vacated village, he had a change of heart and returned his men to Kokoda. Another day passed, and the Japanese forces remained on Oivi hill. The Australians were positioned, tense and waiting, around the edge of the tongue-shaped plateau on which the village and its rubber plantation stood.

At 2 a.m. on the 29th, after peppering the defenders from dusk with mortar fire from across the river, about 180 Japanese troops advanced up the short, steep slope to the plateau. With the full moon shining eerily through a thin grey mist and a repeat of the shouting and chanting developed in night attacks in China, the assault had the atmosphere of a large-scale theatrical performance. Defenders responded with machine-gun and rifle fire. They were well positioned to throw grenades down the slope, but the oncoming Japanese were relentless. Within an hour they were attacking from the rear as well.

Lieutenant Matsuoka, one of the platoon leaders, had said, chatting before the attack, 'If I was commanding at the very front, I would be much more useful.'

Tsukamoto overheard that remark and chipped in, 'Well then, you go there.'

Matsuoka didn't have any experience of war, having just graduated from Officer School. He kept screaming 'Charge!' as he climbed up the slope but soon he was shot and killed, a pointless sacrifice to his own greenness.[18]

On the other side Colonel Owen, who had kept his head down at Tol, wasn't smart enough to do the same at Kokoda. Despite warnings, he patrolled around 'to show his leadership' and was felled by a sniper's bullet in the forehead.[19] He died that evening.

Imanishi's 2nd Company was kept in reserve, within earshot of the attack. 'We could hear soldiers' voices. Someone shouted "Charge!", then sounds of hand grenades and gunshots continued after that. It stopped sometimes, but again you hear sounds of twenty or thirty shots and then someone screams "Move and charge!"'[20] The sounds of attack were all the more overpowering because of the quiet that preceded them, unnerving when the jungle was known to be full of enemy soldiers.

The confrontation at Kokoda developed into one of hand-to-hand fighting and close rifle fire in the ghostly half-light, as trails of thickening mist drifted through the rubber trees and out over the rim of the plateau. Shouting continued, mixed with bursts of gunfire. It was often difficult to distinguish friend from foe. Eventually the Japanese broke through at several points and it became clear that the defenders could not hold out. The Australians withdrew to Deniki, taking with them what weapons they could carry.

By morning, the Japanese had occupied Kokoda and the grass airstrip below. They had taken possession of a number of weapons left behind: 180 grenades, 1850 rifle rounds and five machine-guns. These troops carried five-shot bolt-action Arisaka Type 38s, often too long for short soldiers, who found it difficult to reach the bolt when the rifle was shouldered for firing and a poor match for automatic weapons like the Bren and Lewis guns. The Japanese grenades had to be struck on the ground at forty-five degrees to activate their four- or five-second fuse. Both rifles and grenades dated from the Russo-Japanese War. The Japanese light machine-guns didn't work very well either. Troops eventually used captured machine-guns for fighting, as long as they could find ammunition. On the other hand, two weapons that performed devastatingly well for the Japanese on Kokoda were the wheel-mounted Model 41 mountain artillery gun and the Juki heavy machine-gun (Model 92). The newer Juki was known by Allied troops as the 'woodpecker' for its tat-tat-tat sound.

There had been gains of weapons and territory, including an airstrip the Japanese would never use, but the price paid in casualties was not cheap. Lieutenant Hirano, whose platoon had been carrying provisions to the front line, heard that over twenty men had been killed or wounded in taking Kokoda, including a company commander, Lieutenant Ogama. 'It left me dazed for a while,' he wrote. Returning to his company, Hirano prayed for the dead and consoled the wounded. He then went back to carrier duties.[21]

Small niggles were starting to surface in different sections of the advance party, but being small they caused little concern and were seen as isolated and unconnected. A signals-unit diary notes that food was running short and that a requisition was made for yams. Meals had been reduced to two a day.[22] But for most of the soldiers the campaign had started too well to let a few setbacks discourage them.

On 2 August, Allied planes bombed and strafed Japanese positions at Kokoda. A village hut was burnt along with a platoon leader's gear and a store of potatoes, which were eaten charred. Nonetheless, Tsukamoto thought Kokoda was secure from ground attack and moved most of his troops forward in the jungle to outflank the Australians at Deniki, leaving just a handful of soldiers guarding the airstrip.

The Australians launched a counter-attack with three companies on

8 August to try to recapture Kokoda. One attempted an ambush around
a disused track but was met and driven back. Another company came
under intense fire from mountain guns and rifles between Deniki and
Kokoda. Frustrated, the Australians charged down the valley into Japanese fire. In their surprise the defenders drew back temporarily, but
they eventually reversed the tide. Lieutenant Hirano's platoon, taken
off carrier duties and put into combat, was in the Japanese pursuit of
retreating enemy that afternoon. A reconnaissance party overshot the
Australian lines, moving close to Deniki, where two of its scouts were
killed. Hirano's men collected the bodies and returned to the main
force.[23]

The third Australian company, to everyone's amazement, entered
Kokoda unopposed through the rubber trees at the back of the village. They had come down a secondary track that was unknown to the
Japanese. The few soldiers guarding the airfield below withdrew into
the jungle, giving the attackers time to dig in defensive lines around the
plateau rim on the approach from Oivi and in the rubber trees behind.
The Australians were back where they'd been ten days earlier, this time
behind the Japanese main force, which would have to come back to deal
with them.

The next day, Colonel Tsukamoto ordered a counter-offensive in
driving rain. After reconnaissance of the rubber plantation, troops with
mud-smeared faces and foliage tied to their clothing for camouflage
tried to dislodge the new occupants of Kokoda but were driven back
from well-set positions. With torrential rain adding to their difficulties
the Japanese made a series of attacks throughout the day, probing the
defences to ascertain the enemy's positions.

Hirano's platoon had advanced to within seventy metres of the
Australians in the dusk attack but were unable to charge from there,
having got their formation wrong in the downpour and the darkness.
Later in the night, after moving closer on hands and knees in the mud
and slush, they got to the enemy guard under the rubber trees. One
Australian was killed by bayonet before machine-gun fire forced the
attackers back. The Japanese platoon scattered and couldn't reassemble

in the dark, preventing a repeat charge. Hirano went to the rear with two soldiers in an attempt to assemble his men, but took a wrong turn in the dark and found himself within range of an enemy soldier throwing hand grenades. He speedily retreated, ending a night of failure. As the platoon rested, struggling to ignore cold and hunger, Hirano recorded in his diary his 'tears of bitterness' for the men they had lost.[24]

Sergeant Imanishi had been participating in the attack on Deniki when his platoon too was ordered back to help regain Kokoda. In China he and his comrades had experienced little counter-attack—hence Tsukamoto's light defence of Kokoda and its airstrip—but it was becoming clear that here they were dealing with a different enemy. Imanishi began to worry about more rearguard sorties by the enemy and found he was looking anxiously behind himself as well as at the known Australian positions in front. The campaign, despite its progress, was growing more dangerous and uncertain. And having seen the slouch hat for the first time, Imanishi wondered what it said about the enemy he was about to do battle with. He recalls: 'Sometimes I saw Australian soldiers wearing a hat with a wide brim. I wondered if they could really fight the war with a hat like that.'

On the 10th, two days after the Australian reoccupation of Kokoda, the Japanese advanced into heavy gunfire. They responded with grenade launchers and machine-guns but were pushed back. A second attack about noon was not able to break through either. Waiting until dusk, when the predictable drizzle would begin, Tsukamoto's men charged under the cover of smoke candles and the proven tactic of cacophony, which joined with the crack of bullets in an eerie symphony. The Japanese were not repelled this time—although Hirano managed to catch his foot on a fallen tree and sprawl flat on his face—and they breached the Australian defences. But once again the enemy had withdrawn during the charge.[25]

Next morning, soldiers of Yokoyama Advance Party collected their dead and cleaned up the battle area. The mood was a strange combination of sombreness and exhilaration. The fighting in the rain over the previous two days had been bloody and arduous, but these men had prevailed. Then came the sound of Allied aircraft, and apprehensiveness turned to joyful surprise. Unaware that Kokoda had been reoccupied, the planes made a supply drop over the airstrip—into the hands of the waiting Japanese. Imanishi was in the clean-up detail that enjoyed this unexpected bonus, which included food and cigarettes. The food was much better than the rations they had, but the men enjoyed the cigarettes most of all.

The Australians had clearly recognised their mistake. A few hours later more planes appeared, this time on the attack. The men in Kokoda ducked for cover, but many of their fellow troops were already rejoining the Japanese attack on Deniki. After a series of strikes on their positions 39th Battalion pulled back to Isurava, the next village on the Kokoda Track.

Yokoyama Advance Party's mission was completed. They now had to await the arrival of the main body of South Seas Force, due to land at Buna in a few days. Tsukamoto, as the leader of the combat troops, had become the effective commander of this part of the operation. Yokoyama was a mere army engineer, responsible for a feasibility study that had long dropped off the agenda. He had slipped into the background. Tsukamoto reasoned that if only a tiny Australian force was defending a key objective like Kokoda, there was not likely to be strong opposition on the Track. He was not to know that the Allies were busy strengthening the garrison at Port Moresby. Already bolstered to 22,000 troops—infantry brigades, Australian and American air units, anti-aircraft units, engineers and support staff—it would soon number 28,000.[26]

The opposing forces at and around Isurava sat waiting, each hidden from the other but knowing the other was there. The pristine silence of the mountains hung over them like a veil, broken only by the sound of rain when it fell. No birds, no insects. Ears straining, nostrils filled with the reek of churned mud and vegetation and the heavy, sweet aroma of the rainforest, they waited.

Chapter 7

The fateful delay

On 17 August at 9.20 a.m. the balance of South Seas Force paraded at Rabaul's Simpson Harbour, bowed twice towards Tokyo and the Imperial Palace and boarded the merchant ships *Ryoyo Maru* and *Kazuura Maru*.[1] They steamed towards Buna under the protection not of Fourth Fleet but of Eighth, under Vice-Admiral Mikawa. Fourth Fleet had been replaced in the South Pacific after fumbling the pass in the Coral Sea. Bad weather and a high swell made the crossing rough, and the three planes providing air cover were forced to withdraw. The convoy arrived at Basabua late the next afternoon, without sighting any enemy aircraft. That might have been partly on account of the weather, but in any case the Allies were probably preoccupied with Guadalcanal.

Ten days before, landings at Guadalcanal and Tulagi in the Solomon Islands had heralded the start of the much-anticipated Allied counter-offensive. The Japanese responded with confidence, but were having difficulty recovering ground they had lost in the initial Allied assault. The arm-wrestle over Guadalcanal would increasingly draw Japanese attention and supplies away from New Guinea. More immediately, General Horii was continuing to have reservations about the viability of MO Operation. He advised the Rabaul chief of staff, Major-General Futami, that prisoner-of-war interrogation had revealed there were 20,000 Allied troops now stationed in Port Moresby. Futami, in reply, remarked on Horii's lack of confidence that he could defeat 20,000 enemy and suggested that the figure was an overestimate anyway. Horii was also concerned about the supply plan. He didn't believe there were sufficient carriers to get the attack force to Moresby and was counting on supplementing supplied provisions with whatever could be gleaned from local villages, abandoned army camps and from Port Moresby when they reached it. He warned Army HQ in Tokyo of this calculated risk but got no meaningful response.[2]

A few days before the combat force left Rabaul, 3000 non-combatants had landed at Basabua after surviving a heavy enemy air attack. Construction soldiers and labourers in that group strengthened the airstrip so that by the 16th a reduced fighter unit of six Zeros was operating at Buna. On the morning the convoy set out, Japanese fighters and bombers attacked Port Moresby's Seven Mile airfield and struck gold. Allied transport planes had been parked alongside the landing strip, waiting to air-drop supplies to reinforcement troops making their way along the Kokoda Track. All the aircraft were damaged or destroyed in the raid. The timing was particularly good for the Japanese because Lieutenant-General Rowell, the new Allied commander in New Guinea, had arrived in Moresby only the day before and ordered that the exposed transports be dispersed and camouflaged.[3] The planes were put out of action before this was acted on.

Among the newly arrived non-combatants were three journalists from the newspaper *Asahi Shimbun*: Okada, Sato and a photographer, Katayama. They had assembled at the Army Department in Tokyo with a mix of opportunists and idealists: brothel-keepers from Osaka and Tokyo sending prostitutes to the China and Burma fronts, Shinto and Buddhist priests, café-keepers, teachers, shampooers, welders. All were excited, either because it was their first trip abroad or because they were expecting to profit from the journey.[4]

After they landed in New Guinea the newspapermen left their radio set at Soputa, having taken four days to cover the twelve kilometres from

Buna on the newly built road. They left an assistant in Kokoda with a portable transmitter and made their way up the track.[5]

◆　◆　◆

For the troops already in Papua and waiting for the main strength of South Seas Force to arrive life was mostly humdrum, but there was the odd minor skirmish to remind them that they were in the middle of a war. Lieutenant Hirano, a platoon leader in Tsukamoto Unit, recorded 12 August in his diary as a beautiful day with birds singing, just like a Japanese spring, although spring is nonexistent in equatorial New Guinea. On the 14th, he noted, they advanced to attack Deniki but the enemy wasn't there; the next day, patrolling near Isurava, they were met by enemy fire out of jungle cover, detoured and withdrew, only to find some of their men missing. Returning to look for them, they were hit with automatic-rifle fire that killed three men and wounded one. That night, Hirano wrote, his heart was filled with pity and his food was tasteless. On the 16th, the weather was clear and there were a few cases of diarrhoea and malaria. The next day, Corporal Fujioka and his guard team accidentally 'let natives escape', and Colonel Tsukamoto threatened them with court martial.[6] And on it went, daily life in a lull between battles.

Sergeant Imanishi's platoon too played the waiting game near Isurava. Its leader was shot on a scouting patrol and Imanishi took his place, still trying to determine Australian defensive positions. 'I climbed up a hill with binoculars to find the retreated enemy. I saw smoke in the distant jungle and thought, "There you are!"'

Further scouting parties tested the Australian placements and found the enemy reluctant to retreat from them. In one patrol, Imanishi and Sergeant Ohara went ahead with a small group. One of the men said, 'An enemy soldier is behind the big tree,' and the Australian was shot before he'd spotted them. Ohara and a few of the men climbed a hill to observe the enemy's main positions there but they didn't come back. In the silence, there was no hint of movement from the man they had shot or from any other enemy troops. The air was still and calm. The men

waited. Then—the cracks of gunshots and a grenade explosion. Imanishi, nerves on edge, climbed the hill, fired his rifle and screamed,
'Ohara, come back here!'

He knew the enemy was listening for any sound from him but he
couldn't stop himself. Warrant Officer Matsuo, in charge, said they
should return to base now that they'd located the Australian positions,
but Imanishi didn't want to leave his friend behind. A few minutes later,
the observation group returned without Ohara. They had been attacked,
they said, and he had been shot in the chest. Imanishi and these men followed the trodden grass back up the hill and found Ohara lying on his
knapsack. He said, 'I cannot breathe well.' Imanishi returned to his patrol,
made a simple wooden stretcher and came back with four soldiers. They
brought Ohara in to the unit, bleeding profusely. He died soon after.[7]

◆　◆　◆

Two battalions of the 144th and a mountain artillery battalion were the
mainstay of the first wave of the force landing at Basabua to reinforce
Yokoyama Advance Party. Over the next two days motorised barges
ferried them to Buna, from where they were to advance to join the
front-line troops near Isurava. The wet season had started and, after the
brief respite, there was a deluge almost every afternoon and into the
night.

Each soldier landed with fifteen days' rations, made up of fifteen
kilograms of rice, miso (soybean paste), powdered shoyu (soy) sauce and
salt, which was to be supplemented by whatever they could find on the
land. The kit also included a Meiji-era rifle, sixty rounds of ammunition,
two hand grenades, a water bottle, a spare uniform, a steel helmet and a
camouflage net. Back in Rabaul, all the soldiers had made woodmen's
carrying racks for their loads, which they now bore on their backs 'like
pilgrims with portable shrines'.[8] Each man also had in his kit a *hinomaru
yosegaki* (Rising Sun autograph) flag with messages written on it by
friends and neighbours. Presented to him before leaving to bring luck
when carried into battle, it reminded the soldier to do his duty and
bring honour to his family.

There were variations to the standard kit according to need, function and rank. Officers, for instance, carried swords. The disassembled Juki heavy machine-guns were carried by a crew of eight, along with four boxes of ammunition each holding 600 rounds. The grenadier, Nishimura, carried a ten-kilogram grenade launcher and ammunition instead of a rifle. Sergeant Yamasaki had anti-tank landmines and a gas mask in a kit weighing over fifty kilograms. As it was forbidden to throw ammunition away, he jettisoned some of his rice.[9]

South Seas Force was expanded with 41st Infantry Regiment from Fukuyama, which was brought to Rabaul on 16 August and landed at Basabua on the night of the 21st. First Battalion was held back in Rabaul, while the other two battalions were transferred to Papua cramped inside the troopships *Kiyokawa Maru* and *Myoko Maru*. Under low ship ceilings, two men to a *tatami* (floor mat), the men played *hanafuda*, a gambling game with cards, all the way to the Buna coast. The engine noise was almost deafening, but they had got used to the din when relocating from Malaya to Banguo in the Philippines.

On the declaration of war the 41st had joined the Malaya campaign against the British and Indian armies, during which they also encountered Australian soldiers. They respected the Australians as fighters but weren't daunted by them, having defeated them at Gemas (Malaya) and Bukit Timah (Singapore).

Medic Private Yokoyama remembers English soldiers coming across him in Malaya while he was taking care of Japanese wounded. They had the chance to kill him, but chose not to. Yokoyama believes the red cross on his bag saved his life on that occasion, the first of several close calls that have him convinced luck was a key factor in his war.[10]

As their ships reached Basabua on the New Guinea coast the men of the 41st Infantry jumped into waist-deep water, thirty-kilogram packs balanced on their backs. They followed the other recently landed combat troops to Kokoda, gingerly ferried across the Kumusi River, now swollen 100 metres wide by the torrential downpours that marked the beginning of the wet season. Nearby ground would often flood, and some troops were drowned overnight after setting up camp in a river-bed. This country's weather patterns were dangerously different from anything they knew. Bridges built across the Kumusi didn't last long. Those not destroyed by heavy logs careering downstream in the torrent were smashed by Allied bombing. Engineers had set up a rope-and-pulley system to enable night crossings by boat.

The transport of logistic units to the Papuan coast was completed by 2 September. Three hundred horses had been brought in and the force of labourers from Formosa, Korea and New Britain boosted. Three hundred tonnes of supplies had been warehoused at Buna and were being taken the twenty kilometres to Sonbo by truck, then by packhorse or human carrier to Kokoda.

Combat troops from the 144th and 41st had already arrived at Kokoda, along with General Horii and the 144th Regiment commander Colonel Kusunose. They conferred with Colonel Yokoyama, who had been there since the outset, and determined that the 144th would attack Isurava within a day or two. The 41st, under Colonel Kiyoshi Yazawa, would be held in reserve, guarding the rear and assisting with transport of supplies. Only 2nd Battalion, under Major Mitsuo Koiwai, had been moved up the track. Kobayashi (3rd) Battalion, including medical corpsman Yokoyama, remained on the coast at Giruwa under the command of Colonel Tomita, who was in charge of logistics units at Force headquarters.

The 41st's Yazawa had already built a difficult relationship with his 2nd Battalion commander. Koiwai had objected to the regimental chief's demand that the soldiers march a second consecutive night in heavy rain with full packs. Yazawa was a strict taskmaster; Koiwai fancied himself as a philosopher-soldier with an instinctive feel for battle. It was a personality clash that would dog the 41st throughout the campaign.

Horii's tactical pattern for MO Operation would be a unit attacking entrenched enemy positions from the front while the main force moved around to charge the enemy's flanks and rear. Where feasible, charges would be made at night under cover of fog or rain. The advance party's experience suggested they could expect quite a fight from the Australians. Even though weak resistance had been reported from around Isurava, Horii and his senior officers were not going to take any chances.

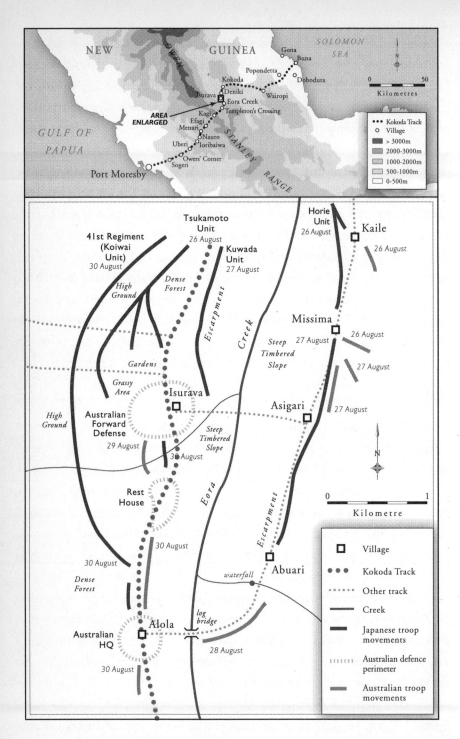

The battle of Isurava, August 1942

After Kokoda, the track moves onto mountainous slopes covered with dense matted rainforest and meanders along precipitous ridges. Even when repaired, it was barely traversable by horse. Many of the animals the Japanese had brought would be killed, slipping off the path and crashing down the steep incline. Before long they were abandoned, left behind to find their way about the coastal lowlands and be put to occasional use there. The horses gone, each soldier plodded on, step by step, walking stick in hand, up muddy slopes, down into deep valleys, carrying his own supplies and assigned load in the direction of Port Moresby. There was less undergrowth in the mountain forests than there had been in the lowland ones, but here appeared new obstacles: giant fallen trees and, as the soldiers approached Australian front lines, limited visibility. The Japanese soldiers couldn't see the enemy, reputed to be excellent marksmen, even though they might be no more than ten metres away. Often the first sign of them was rifle shots. The men of South Seas Force would continue to be spooked by the hidden enemy, just as the Australians would be spooked by them.

◆　◆　◆

Isurava village sat on a flat clearing between two creeks, way above Kokoda plateau. To its left, from the Japanese perspective, was a deep chasm in which Eora Creek tumbled far below; to the right, higher ground covered with dense mountain jungle. Six hundred metres behind the village, on the lip of the escarpment overlooking the Eora valley, was a government rest house. The Australian defenders were dug in around a clearing of long grass behind an overgrown garden, with a clear view of the track coming from Deniki and Kokoda. General Horii's plan for the assault on Isurava was to make the predictable frontal charge up the track, but only as a feint for twin flanking movements that would enable attacks on the enemy sides and rear. They would be unanticipated with the seeming impenetrability of the jungle.

On the night of 25 August, South Seas Force began its advance on Isurava. It was raining, as usual, and the nights were getting chillier as they moved higher into the Owen Stanley Range. Vegetation was tied onto the soldiers' clothing as camouflage and they crawled carefully and noiselessly forward, one group up the Naro Ridge above the village and Australian positions, another towards Abuari waterfall on the other side of Eora gorge, and a third up the track from Deniki. Tsukamoto (1st) Battalion and Horie (2nd) Battalion pushed through the rainforest in the slush of its muddy, moss-covered floor. Horii was holding Kuwada (3rd) Battalion and 41st Regiment in reserve.

At dawn, the village was bombarded with mortar and mountain-gun fire, immediately followed by the first wave of charging, shouting Japanese, striving for positions on higher ridgelines so as to thrust from above. The defenders targeted return fire on breaks in jungle cover on the slopes. Providing artillery cover for the attacking force was not easy from within the thick vegetation. Oppressive heat, caused by high humidity under low continuous cloud cover, was sapping their energy. Australians were often holding their fire until their assailants were at point-blank range, giving them little opportunity to locate defensive positions.

The Japanese movements were causing as much confusion within their own ranks as they were for the enemy. The troops found it difficult to stay on course and keep contact with each other in the jungle. Sergeant Imanishi's platoon was in the frontal attack. It had crawled well forward down a slope and found itself under fire from behind. In the adrenaline charge of battle, no one could tell if this was enemy or friendly fire until someone blew a bugle. The firing ceased. Another attacking company had moved to the top of the hill and had unwittingly been firing on them.[11] At the same time, Lieutenant Hirano's platoon had forded the front village creek and encountered unexpected enemy fire. Another platoon detoured to a hilltop while Hirano's men continued to snipe at the Australians.[12] Was one of these groups firing on Imanishi's men? No one knows. The soldiers had no time to exchange notes; they had to press on regardless.

While the hard grind of frontal assault was being carried on by some of Tsukamoto's troops the rest of his battalion were making their way slowly, sweating from the heavy humidity, into the country above Isurava, so thickly forested they sometimes had to hack their way through entwined vegetation. On the other side of Eora Creek, Horie's men had set out the previous night along the eastern track between Deniki and Alola, where it joined the Kokoda Track behind Isurava. Private Nishimura was among these troops. A unit of the battalion ambushed an Australian militia patrol near Kaile and drove it back towards its base at Alola.[13] The withdrawing militia found to their dismay that the main force of Horie Unit had meanwhile captured Missima village, part-way back to Alola, killing or scattering the signalmen there and smashing their radio. The Australians had to divert and try to find their way back to friendly territory, a daunting task with their extremely limited jungle experience.

The next day, a second militia patrol went looking for the missing one, encountered the Japanese at Missima and was decimated. By afternoon, a third patrol was out searching for the first two. It too came in contact with the Japanese and was dispersed into the jungle. Horie's men moved forward and dug in near the waterfall at Abuari, about a kilometre short of Alola—which, unknown to the Japanese, was by then sparsely defended. Had they proceeded to Alola Horie might possibly have mounted a decisive rear attack on the Australian positions, shortening the battle for Isurava by a couple of days. That might have had a substantial impact on the outcome of MO Operation, as it turned out, but it was not to be. Instead, the troops brought Juki heavy machine-guns up to Abuari and shelled the Australian brigade HQ across Eora Creek at Alola.

On the night of the 26th, in pitch darkness and soaking rain, the frontal attacking force skirted around two Australian platoons forward of the village and successfully stormed the native garden. It was a small gain for a day's work, but the flanking troops were still advancing towards the rear of the Australian positions. The Australians, for their part, had recognised during the day that they couldn't hold out much longer. One of them, Bert Fry, says their commander told them, 'If the 2/14th don't get here within hours, we're gone.'[14]

The 2/14th was one of the battalions of Australian Imperial Force (AIF) regulars brought back to Australia from the Middle East and sent to the front line of the Kokoda campaign. The only way for them to get to Kokoda now was by walking the track from Moresby. They started arriving during that day, tired from several days' march on the precipitous path. They had been in battles before, but in nothing like these conditions. Troops continued to reach Isurava in small groups, adding to its defences and enabling the garrison to hold out a crucial few days longer.

Colonel Kusunose of the 144th brought his Kuwada Unit out of reserve and into the fray the next morning. They moved into attack positions, testing the defences and concluding that they'd been reinforced. It was relatively quiet until mid-afternoon, when mortar and machine-gun fire peppered the Australian positions, followed by a new frontal attack with the fresh troops. Sergeant Yamasaki was one of those fresh troops in this, his first taste of action in Papua. His platoon had gone down into a valley when they came under intense automatic-rifle fire. He'd never encountered automatic rifles before, but he soon learnt to hit the ground the instant shots rang out.

Sweeping fiercely across the front creek, the Japanese sliced through their opponents' right flank and swarmed over their positions from behind. As the breach widened, more troops poured in—and were met with Bren gun and Tommy gun, bayonet and grenade. Fighting was vicious, hand-to-hand, both sides using boots, fists and rifle butts. Once, an Australian chaplain moved into bushland to retrieve a wounded sergeant. There was no Japanese fire while he did so, but as soon as he got to cover the firing started again. For Kuwada's men the day appeared close to won, but two counter-attacks eventually forced them back and the Australian line held.[15]

While the defenders were occupied with the frontal charge, part of Kuwada Battalion skirted down into the creek valley and around the eastern flank, targeting Isurava village and the rest house. Progress was extremely difficult as men picked their way through matted vegetation on the steep bank and across huge boulders piled high in the fast-running creek, all the while subjected to machine-gun fire from above. By afternoon, they had a foothold on the side of the river but were exposed and suffered continuing casualties. The thrust on the eastern flank was brought to a halt. On the opposite bank of Eora Creek one of Horie's patrols had continued up the track to Abuari waterfall, to be stopped by a reinforced troop of Australians coming through in search of the missing patrols. Hand-to-hand fighting with grenade exchanges didn't resolve the issue. Both sides backed off and held their positions.

The rest of Kuwada's men attacked from the higher ground on the other side of the Isurava defences. Though the fighting often involved one-on-one struggles, it did not seem personal. Charging, screaming, slashing and swinging, the men were on automatic pilot much of the time, with a dream-like sense of reality. 'I saw some Australian dead bodies,' Yamasaki recalls. 'They were covered with grass. Accidentally, I sat on one of the bodies without recognising it.'

Heavy rain fell throughout the night, making sleep even more unlikely. The Japanese probed the defenders' lines with bayonets rather than rifle fire, ensuring the Australians too remained hyper-alert. Yamasaki's unit was about to launch a night attack when he realised the light-machine-gunner had disappeared. In military parlance, he had gone to the rear without permission. In ordinary terms, he had deserted out of fright. Yamasaki fought as a light-machine-gunner the next day, but his new role would be short-lived.

Dawn on the 28th brought a fire fight. The Japanese probed the lower flank of the forward arc, again seeking weaknesses in the Australian defences, then switched to the other side, where they could emerge from the bush screeching like the crows that are heard everywhere in Kochi. The Australians continued to be tested all day, but though the Japanese broke through briefly in mid-afternoon a counter-attack soon restored their position. They were being gradually outflanked but resisting fiercely: casualties among the Japanese were high.

The night of the 28th was clear for a change. At dawn a Japanese artillery barrage launched the struggle all over again, with ferocious attacks on the Australian forward arc. Once again, the Japanese breached the front line and poured through the gap, and once again they were stopped. But this time the pause was only temporary. They continued to press their advantage through the afternoon, especially on the right flank, where they attacked from cover on the higher ground. Yamasaki and his comrades had learnt to hit the ground when automatic gunfire started, but the Australian grenades lobbed on them caused many casualties.

In one sortie, Yamasaki saw an enemy soldier's helmet between the trees and shot at it. Moving forward, he saw more helmets on a crest, so he and his fellows charged. A grenade exploded right in front of Yamasaki, throwing his rifle some ten metres. He ran back to retrieve it but couldn't grab hold. Only then did he notice he couldn't feel his hand. It wasn't bleeding, just numb. He looked down and saw that half the hand had been blown off. Returning to base, Sergeant Yamasaki was ordered back to Kokoda. His war was over.

As the Australian vanguard was gradually enveloped by the succession of Japanese charges, its hold on Isurava grew tenuous. The only possible line of retreat was the main track, increasingly vulnerable—along with supply lines of food and ammunition—as the attack closed in. By dusk, under heavy fire, the Australian front-line troops began to withdraw the kilometre or so to the area around the rest house. There, they dug in.

Despite their own progress and the defenders' slow loss of ground, the Japanese were suffering high casualties. After a few days of unrelenting attack and dogged resistance, doubt was creeping into the troops' minds. Small things started to loom large. When the men weren't trying to keep ants away from the food, they were on guard for leeches. They had to be obsessive about caring for their weapons. With the frustration starting to fray nerves, Horii deployed units from the 41st for the first time. He needed to keep his attack force refreshed.

As it turned out, 30 August was the final day of the battle for Isurava. For much of that day the Japanese made repeated bayonet charges into enemy gunfire. In the mayhem, numbers prevailed. The best the Australians could do was to hold off the attackers while their own units withdrew. Afternoon saw the start of three days of pouring rain. Water streamed everywhere, filling every nook and hollow, cascading into abandoned weapons pits and soaking the clothes of all the troops on both sides as the sweltering humidity had done before the rain fell. In the deluge, Horii brought in Koiwai Unit of the 41st to make a wide detour through the jungle high on the enemy's western flank and reinforce the attack on the Australian rear on that side. This advance brought them by evening onto the Kokoda Track, but no Australian soldiers could be seen. In the morning they moved 800 metres further down the track and found themselves in the village of Alola, now abandoned.

Food was starting to run low. It was ten days since the 41st had landed at Basabua with their issue of rations; thirteen days since the main force of the 144th had landed. Yokoyama Advance Party had now been in Papua for six weeks, and the feast from the mistaken Allied air-drop at Kokoda was already long forgotten. Supplies coming from Rabaul were suffering innumerable delays: some were rerouted to Guadalcanal, where the recovery effort was going badly, and Allied air attacks were also sharply reducing consignments to New Guinea. When the supplies were landed, the difficulties only continued. Provisions had to be transported over the swollen Kumusi River. Keeping up carrier numbers was a growing problem. There were difficulties with Korean labourers, and increasing desertion by indentured workers from Rabaul and Orokaivan tribesmen from the local villages—those who hadn't headed for the hills when the invasion force arrived.

Relief from the growing hunger came unexpectedly, in an undignified chain of events that exposed the tension and desperation that had built up in these soldiers during five days of grim struggle. With the enemy withdrawn down the track, troops of the 144th moved forward over a high point at the back of Isurava rest house. The next village, Alola, sat alongside the junction with the track that ran down the eastern side of Eora Creek and its gorge. Soldiers of the 41st's Koiwai Battalion were already in Alola, scouting the village. Word flew on the bush telegraph that a large store of rations had been found, left behind by the Australians. They had gone in a hurry rather than be closed in completely by the circling Japanese. As well as food they had left ammunition: 25,000 rifle cartridges, 1500 Tommy-gun rounds and 500 grenades.

As men crossed the peak they saw, in the village below, troops of the 41st swarming excitedly. They broke into a run, down the slope towards the huts. Behind them, soldiers exhausted from lack of sleep and the aftermath of battle suddenly found the strength to rush up the slope and over the top. Seizo Okada, the journalist, was with the 144th and ran with the rest on autopilot. He knew he was making an exhibition of himself and felt ashamed as they all swooped on the cluster of huts like a pack of wolves on their quarry, but nothing could hold him back. He was desperately hungry—and he hadn't even been fighting.

As he ran into the village, he passed soldiers milling about on the forest fringe or sitting on logs beside the track like dogs with a bone. Their mouths were filled with foods of different sorts, unidentifiable as they chomped voraciously, their faces lit with ecstasy. Men chewed, they didn't talk. Their pockets bulged, their arms were laden with cans, but no one spoke.

Okada pushed his way through the crowd to an open area in front of a tall, thatched Papuan hut. Excited soldiers pushed and jostled, scrambling through the door or bustling out with armfuls of booty. It was like the entrance to a giant anthill. Okada moved into the hut with other ants. Inside was a vision splendid, a shrine to the gods of hunger. Mountains of cans were piled up: cans of butter, of cheese, milk, corned beef and of many things these men had never seen before. The earth floor was littered with cans that had fallen off the once-tidy piles or been pushed off by rummaging soldiers. Conspicuous in this cornucopia were a number of large tins of Arnott's biscuits.

'What a feast all these things were to us,' Okada recalled. 'It seemed as though we had suddenly landed in fairyland. We had run out of the meagre rice ration long before, and had trudged on day and night eating only tasteless army crackers which we call *kammempo*, with occasional wild potatoes and papayas.'[16]

The soldiers of Nankai Shitai were mostly from farming and fishing villages in Shikoku. Much of this was food they had not seen or tasted before. They filled up with the familiar items and threw away half-opened cans of corned beef with deep suspicion. Okada feasted on Arnott's biscuits and butter. He had not tasted anything so fine since well before the Pacific War started.

'Here in the Papuan mountains the standard of living was higher than in Japan! I thought I saw something of the appalling power of Anglo-American civilisation that Japan had so recklessly challenged,' he later wrote.[17]

In the maniacal scramble for food, men were loading up more than they would be able to carry when the march resumed along on the track to Port Moresby. Sanity seeped in slowly, and they began to restrict themselves to what could be carried with the rest of the gear in their backpacks. They began to chat again. Then a piercing cry brought them fully back to their senses.

'Enemy plane!'

Men dashed everywhere—out of the storehouse, across the open space, into the jungle. A US Navy fighter came in low over the treetops, ran a stream of fire over the clearing, banked and machine-gunned the hut. Any men still in it darted out in all directions between the raking lines of bullets. Some made it to safety; some were thrown to the ground, cans tumbling out onto the dirt in front of them and rolling a short distance until they, like their erstwhile possessor, came to a stop. Some men never got out of the hut. The plane made a second strafing run at the hut then flew away, come and gone in five minutes.

Men came rushing back out of the jungle and resumed scooping up cans. Some attended to the wounded and dead on the ground; some took charge of the unfortunate ones' dropped cans. Some warned that the plane could come back, but no one took any notice. They were too busy looking after themselves, dehumanised by their hunger and the unexpected riches they'd stumbled across. The storehouse was cleaned out well before rearguard and support troops got to it.

◆　◆　◆

The Japanese wounded faced a one-day stretcher journey downhill to the field hospital at Kokoda, but there were few stretcher-bearers. Many of the Papuans, and New Guineans brought from Rabaul, became too ill to work or deserted. Increasingly, the army was relying on volunteer Formosans, Korean labourers or Japanese troops to carry supplies to the front and the wounded to the rear. Only those who might recover were treated or evacuated; the seriously hurt were left to die. Vines were used to lash the injured to their stretchers and fresh branches were placed over their heads for shade. They were carried along the edges of sheer escarpments and down into and out of valleys, and lined up next to native huts at each night's staging post like timber in a yard.

Yokoyama was a corpsman, a medic working behind the battle lines on the track. He had tincture of iodine, gauze, scissors and a surgical knife in his medical bag, but no morphine. After a while, he ran out of quinine for malaria. He could provide basic first aid either to enable soldiers with minor wounds to get back into the fray, or to tide over those with more serious injuries until Formosan stretcher-bearers could get them back to Kokoda.

Akiyoshi Hisaeda was a transport soldier in 55th Division 1st Field Hospital. In his diary he wrote that Kokoda's hospital was a cheerless sight as they approached it across a river ten metres wide. In front, a metre-high sign in black ink on wood announced: Field Hospital Entrance. The embankment nearby was covered with grave markers cut from saplings and painted white. Inside, numerous small wards were lined up like livestock pens, the walls constructed from thin poles, the wounded and sick packed tightly inside. The roof was made of blackened banana leaves and constantly dripped with water from surrounding trees. The floor was spread with green leaves and thin saplings. Patients lay on them in blood-stained, blackened uniforms. There were no blankets. 'The hospital, where not a word was uttered, had sunk to the pit of a deathly silence,' Hisaeda wrote.[18]

Back in the now-occupied village of Isurava a pile of gear and weapons was laid out under a long tent, belongings of the men killed in the fighting just concluded. Casualties of battle and losses through sickness—malaria and dysentery were still a major problem—were high. Companies of some 180 men had been reduced to fifty or sixty. The troops lit funeral pyres to burn the dead so their ashes could be transported back to families in Japan. Australian mortars, attracted by the fires, lobbed in the middle of this ceremony, killing a few more.

In the late afternoon Imanishi's company commander, Lieutenant

Hamada, started announcing awards for soldiers in the battle. It was a time of reflection for the sergeant. 'Each time the commander called a soldier's name, one by one, like, "Private so-and-so", as the staff-sergeant I had to report, "He was killed in action." As I reported, I could not stop my tears coming out so badly. I saw so much of the dead soldiers' equipment in the long tents and I thought of them and realised how cruel the war was.'

Its unpleasantness ran at many levels. During the battle for Isurava Imanishi had sent one of his men, Private Tanigaki, to battalion headquarters to get orders for the coming day. The private returned angry and upset, saying, 'Our battalion commander is drunk!' Imanishi's heart sank. He and Colonel Tsukamoto had both fought in China, so he knew Tsukamoto had a drinking problem. On one occasion in that campaign he had got aggressively drunk on *sake* and set fire to the officers' residence. Imanishi had hoped he'd left his problem behind in China, but it appeared that in New Guinea the colonel had had his private supply of *sake* brought up by carrier along with the rest of the force's supplies.[19]

What made this worse in Imanishi's eyes was that Tsukamoto was a career soldier, not a conscript. The quality of officers in New Guinea, he says, was far lower than in China. In the earlier campaign officers would pitch in on hard tasks, like the occasional scouting patrol. Here, on the Kokoda Track, they were more inclined to stand back and give orders, seldom joining the troops in their assigned tasks.

It's a criticism levelled mainly at middle-ranking officers. Imanishi excludes Colonel Kusunose from this judgment: he was widely respected both as a soldier and for his even-tempered manner. Others who were in the field with Kusunose agree.[20] General Horii also seems to have had the respect of his troops. A soldier with a refreshing directness and a common touch, he kept his campaign headquarters near to the Japanese front line—though he did not ride a white stallion along the track, as many Australian veterans have fancifully suggested.

Many of the Japanese veterans are very critical of the quality of their own firearms. For Yamasaki, the forty-year-old Arisaka Type 38 rifle was not up to jungle combat. It was a single-action weapon, up against the

Allies' automatic rifles. The Juki heavy machine-gun, the 'woodpecker', seems to be the only weapon the Japanese held in high regard. Imanishi believes it was even a mistake to bring heavy mountain guns onto terrain so difficult to traverse. Soldiers who were in a target zone, however, would probably dispute this. The long-range howitzer was capable of causing considerable havoc and was often quite damaging to the Australian troops.

Nishimura had a knee mortar but didn't use it at all. The shell was too easily exploded by overhanging branches, making it more of a danger to Nishimura than to the enemy. When it was fired under an extensive tree canopy, the canopy tended to suffer most of the damage. Then again, the canopy was also good protection against aerial bombardment.

In the brief respite between the end of the Isurava battle and the return to the track, the soldiers part-way up the Owen Stanley Range had time to reflect on the shift in their fortunes. Isurava is an oddity in modern warfare for its close fighting with guns and grenades and hand-to-hand combat with bayonets. The Japanese had prevailed in this particular battle, but at considerable cost. In a few short days after their exhilarating succession of quick victories, the war had got much, much harder. The arithmetic of Isurava did not bode well. Even if the lower ranks couldn't work it out, their commanders certainly would have done so. The overland invasion of Port Moresby was predicated on a speedy crossing of the Owen Stanley Range. It didn't allow for five days at Isurava trying to dislodge stubborn defenders. The delay would prove a fateful one.

The exhausted Australians had withdrawn to the next settlement, Eora Creek. The Japanese forward movement recommenced, 'an endless serpentine movement of infantry, artillery, transport unit, infantry again, first-aid station, field hospital, signal unit and engineers, deep into the Owen Stanley Range'.[21] General Horii might have been behind schedule, but a second Japanese thrust on Port Moresby was under way to spread the burden of attack. The navy had landed at Milne Bay, on the eastern tip of Papua, to secure the Allied airstrip there and use it as a support base for a sea assault on Moresby to coincide with Nankai Shitai's arrival in force off the Kokoda Track.

Chapter 8

Milne Bay

Milne Bay was not a place you'd choose to go for a holiday.[1] Sitting at the eastern end of New Guinea, it was cut off from the rest of the island and could be reached only by sea or air. Surrounded on three sides by jungle-clad mountains, with mangrove and sago swamps running along the coast and with its climate of torrential rains and oppressive humidity, it was a most inhospitable part of the world. Coconut and rubber plantations had been abandoned by their Australian owners in early 1942. The drainage set up for malaria control had fallen into disrepair, and the disease was rampant. Nonetheless, a plan had been devised for a second attempt at attacking the Papuan capital by sea to coincide with the overland assault. A base would be needed to launch the new invasion. The Japanese navy decided to land at Samarai, an inhabited island without military presence just around from the southern head of Milne Bay, and set up a seaplane base. This would be near very uninviting country, but it was a convenient staging point for invasion and no one would be there to threaten them. Or so the military thought.

After the Coral Sea battle, MacArthur decided to build an Allied airbase on the tip of Papua. It would patrol against any further incursions by sea on Port Moresby and allow raids on Rabaul without the risk of flying over the cloud-covered Owen Stanley Range. Milne Force was established under the Australian Major-General Cyril Clowes. US Engineers were to construct three airstrips at the bottom of Milne Bay; Australian infantry and artillery would provide protection. Two RAAF squadrons of Curtiss P-40 Kittyhawks arrived to operate out of the newly built airbase. Allied troop numbers increased by stages from July and by late August there were 9000 in the area: 5000 infantry, the rest non-combatants.

On 3 August, Japanese aerial surveillance discovered for the first time an unwelcome airfield near Rabi on Milne Bay as well as jetties nearby, clearly a serious impediment to the planned Moresby attack. The reconnaissance plane reported forty-six Kittyhawks on or around the runway.[2] Without capture of that airfield, the planned invasion of Port Moresby faced a serious risk of failure. The second airfield there was never sighted, nor was the third strip, then about to be bulldozed. It was decided to deal with the newly found airfield immediately. The entire strength of Tainan Air Corps and much of Fourth Air Corps staged a major air attack on Rabi the day the Allies landed at Guadalcanal. There's no record of the Japanese assessment of this raid, but as they continued to conduct raids throughout August it is clear they did not think they had put the Rabi base out of commission. Some raids were thwarted by bad weather. Some pilots reported intense anti-aircraft fire, but also claimed they'd shot down significant numbers of the P-39s and P-40s they encountered. Japanese air losses were reportedly light. Still, Rabi continued to provide highly effective opposition to their air missions.

The Japanese navy had been victorious in a second battle of the Solomon Sea. Although the Ichiki Detachment Advance Party had been beaten back from its landing there, planners were confident that a combination of the main force of Ichiki Detachment with Kawaguchi Detachment would be sufficient to retake Guadalcanal. Attention could now return to the Allied base at Rabi. An attack would take place posthaste. The intention was no longer to build a Japanese base at Samarai but to drive the enemy off its existing Rabi base and use that to support the Port Moresby operation. The Japanese still had no knowledge of the number of Allied troops at Milne Bay, but they saw no reason to expect many. It was a new airbase that would have men to service that operation, but it was hard to see what purpose a garrison could serve. Nonetheless, unbeknown to the Japanese, one was there.

The navy and army had argued about which service should carry out the attack. The army was concerned about the exposure of its landing barges as Allied air superiority continued to grow. The outcome was that it would be a navy operation. Kure 5th Special Naval Landing Party (SNLP), led by Commander Shojiro Hayashi, and some of Sasebo 5SNLP were to land east of Rabi. The landing party would include 350 men of 10th Establishment Unit, engineers to repair the airfield. In addition, the main force of Sasebo 5SNLP, some 350 men under Commander Torashige Tsukioka, were to come from Buna on Daihatsu motorised barges and land at Taupota, on the ocean coast directly above Rabi. This unit would cross overland and attack the base's rear while the main force came from the east. Sasebo 5SNLP had been part of the original landing force at Buna, along with Yokoyama Advance Party.

On the morning of the 24th, a convoy left Rabaul with 800 combat troops and the engineers. Planes from Buna base were to provide surveillance for the convoy, but that didn't eventuate. A P-39 Airacobra attack on Buna airstrip that morning left it with only six serviceable Zeros. By the following afternoon, the convoy was being bombed and strafed by Allied aircraft. Although it suffered some damage, it stuck to its task and at sunset the planes had to withdraw. Tsukioka Unit, coming from Buna at about the same time, was not so lucky. It had beached at Goodenough Island when ten Kittyhawks swooped on the barges, destroying all seven as well as the unit's radio. The prevailing conditions had cooperated with the Allies. After waiting all morning, their planes had been able to take off in the afternoon during a break in the weather. Tsukioka Unit was now marooned on the island, without communication and unable to participate in the Rabi operation. It would take two months for those men to get back to Rabaul.

♦ ♦ ♦

In what was named RE Operation, the troops landed overnight in pouring rain at Waga Waga, on the northern shore of Milne Bay, further east than they had planned but still within striking range of Rabi. They pushed back a militia company defending the eastern outpost, but there wasn't much space to operate in. A pebble beach, a line of vegetation and a narrow muddy track were all that separated the bay from thick matted jungle spreading up the coastal high ground and into the Stirling Range behind. A small jetty constructed out of sandbags was used to land supplies from barges: rations, ammunition, fuel and two Type 95 Ha-Go light tanks. Time was precious. Drums of fuel were thrown off barges close to shore and left to drift in. Just before sunrise the convoy headed out of the bay to the safety of open sea, leaving the landing barges pulled up on the pebble beach.[3]

That same morning, Airacobras had again attacked fighters operating out of Buna as they took off to provide cover for the landing force. Sergeant Kazuo Tsunoda flew one of seven Zeros brought in to replace those lost the day before. Three of the planes were cut down as they took off, just before Tsunoda did. 'The P-39 is equipped with a 39-mm gun,' he explains. 'Once you get shot by that gun you become a fireball. All of my men became fireballs and exploded.'

Tsunoda managed to get airborne in a steep climb, only to be attacked by enemy planes. His engine severely damaged, he was forced to land almost as soon as he had got into the air. The plane couldn't be repaired so Tsunoda was returned to Rabaul, leaving his wrecked Zero on Buna airfield.

Other support aircraft left Rabaul that day, but bad weather on the way forced them to return. The only planes to make it to the landing site were Kittyhawks coming from Rabi's two operational airfields. Within minutes of taking off, they were strafing barges and equipment scattered along the beach at Waga Waga. The result was havoc for the Japanese operation. The destruction of the landing barges meant there was now no chance of moving equipment and men down the coast and nearer to the airfield objective. The assault force's advance would have to be restricted largely to night-time, and progress would be slow. Rations had been dramatically reduced by the morning's raid as well.[4] It was a devastating early blow, reversing the optimism with which the Japanese landed. 'The feeling that if we went on we would certainly succeed had completely disappeared. We sat on fallen trees and remained silent,' recalled Lieutenant Moji, who was there with Kure 5SNLP.[5]

The invasion force moved west, keeping to the bushy fringes of the spongy coastal track. Clouds were leaden and low, the rain alternating between drizzle and downpour. It stayed that way for most of the time the attack force was at Milne Bay. The two tanks moved at the front of the advance, alert for air attack and leap-frogging the lead. High-turreted and lightly armoured, with two machine-guns and a turret gun, the three-man tanks were deadly against infantry. They were even more lethal at night, when their reflector lights could pick out soldiers. It was near impossible to fire a rifle directly at the light source, which was sunk into the tanks' outer shell. Asbestos-lined to reduce interior heat, the tanks could get up to forty kilometres an hour with their Mitsubishi diesel engines, but for those inside it was still a pretty rough ride.

Soldiers advanced on foot just behind the tanks, under cover of the adjacent jungle. When enemy patrols were encountered the Japanese tried a tactic that had been useful at Kokoda, calling out in English 'Give up!' amid the volleys of rifle and tank-gun fire. For them, a level of theatricality was part of the intensity of battle. For the more prosaic Australian militiamen, most of whom were facing action for the first time, it was a frightening and confusing experience.

The landing force encountered only pockets of resistance until the late afternoon when it approached KB Mission, about halfway to Rabi. There it met company-strength opposition moving across the mission's coconut plantation with minimal air support. The RAAF's Kittyhawks had been concentrating on the Japanese landing site at Waga Waga. Only now did they turn their attention to troops moving along the coast, but dusk was falling and diving through rainclouds and low over the tops of coconut palms was risky. They had little impact on the advancing Japanese, whose firepower overwhelmed the defenders, now reinforced with a second company. The most serious setback was when one of the tanks, making its way across a narrow log bridge over the mission's front creek, ran into the shallow water.[6] Eventually, however, it steered itself back onto the track.

Night fell quickly, and the Australians withdrew in the rain to a new defensive position by a second creek. It was a wide, swampy area with boggy ground underfoot, but it overlooked a clearing. The Japanese, trained in night assault and with the threat of air attack gone in the dark, followed and ambushed the Australians before they could settle into their new positions. Meanwhile, under cover of night, non-combatants back at Waga Waga were sorting through the remnants of their wooden cases of supplies to see what was salvageable after the day's shelling. The answer: not a great deal. A signal to the convoy brought the destroyer *Tenryu* back into Milne Bay, slipping in to land new rations. The dry *kammempo* biscuits were all that could be offered. *Tenryu* left before dawn could bring another day of air attack, after taking on board the wounded and some non-combatants.

At ten o'clock that night, a full-scale frontal attack was launched at KB Mission with machine-guns and flame-throwers. At the same time, troops waded into the bay or the jungle and around the defenders. For the inexperienced militiamen, indecision reigned supreme in pitch darkness made worse by constant rain, slushy ground and thick vegetation. Some of the attackers ordered a withdrawal in sufficiently good English for the Australians to unwittingly obey. Worse for them, word of the 'withdrawal' was passed around. The defenders congregated at command HQ in the mission itself, where the withdrawal was halted temporarily by Captain Bicks, commander of the Allied eastern defences at Milne Bay. With the Japanese following and circling, defence of the site became untenable. Bicks withdrew his entire force across the Gama River in the hope that the wider, fast-flowing barrier might stall the Japanese advance. By then, however, dawn was approaching and the attack force, conscious of the potential for renewed Allied air attack, disappeared like a tribe of vampires to congregate unseen in the jungle at the back of KB Mission. After its shaky start the day had progressed well enough for the naval landing party, but it was still completely unaware of the degree to which the Allied garrison outnumbered it at Milne Bay.

As soon as the sun had risen on the 27th seven Zeros from Buna and eight carrier-based bombers attacked the No. 1 Strip near Gili Gili, one of the two airfields operating in the area, inflicting limited damage. They came under such intense anti-aircraft fire that four of the Zeros and two of the bombers were lost, curtailing air activities for some days. On the other hand, one of the light tanks near KB Mission was spotted by a local Kittyhawk in the afternoon, but it brought the plane down as it dived from over the bay.

Meanwhile, the Allies had moved an AIF battalion forward from north of Gili Gili. The 2/10th were veterans of Tobruk, but this was a totally different battleground. The AIF passed the militia at Gama River and moved into the mission grounds in the late afternoon to set up defensive positions. Japanese patrols watched from the shadows as mortars were sited on the perimeter.

Night fell, pitch black as usual apart from moments of dim moonlight. The moon was hidden behind low rain clouds most of the time. The Japanese had lain low for the day at the back of the mission to escape the enemy Kittyhawks. Now the vampires stirred. Disturbed insects chittered, then silence fell. A tank growled towards the mission, followed by the other tank. In intermittent rain, troops assembling behind in the jungle chanted and shrieked like a demonic choir to unnerve the soldiers who'd just moved into the area and to fire their own spirits for the coming conflict. The choral overture ended, the night's performance began. As the Japanese troops charged, there was rifle fire and occasional hand-to-hand fighting with bayonets. When the opportunity presented itself, boots, rifle butts and fists were used as well. Even for these experienced Australian soldiers the unearthly cacophony of voices, gunfire and machine noises was unlike anything they had ever experienced, and they were quite unprepared for it. Machine-gun fire into the treetops shook coconuts down onto them, causing further disorientation. The tanks backed off, and each in turn beamed its headlights through the pouring rain towards the defenders. When a position was lit up, it would be sprayed with machine-gun fire from the tank. Then the light would be turned off and infantry would come forward, again firing machine-guns.

The succession of dazzling light and complete darkness added another layer to the confusion. The tanks operated like tag wrestlers, each coming forward while the other withdrew to reload its guns.[7]

In less than an hour, front and middle positions had been overrun. Surviving defenders scattered in all directions, using the dark night for cover along with the thick bush that had served the Japanese so well. Knowing they would be facing tanks, the Australians had brought 'sticky bombs' with them, grenades with adhesive coating designed to blow holes in tank armour. As the assault edged relentlessly forward attempts were made to disable the tanks with these devices, but in the tropical humidity the sticky bombs wouldn't stick. Sometimes the Japanese advance was brought to a halt by stiff resistance, but it was only ever temporary. In fits and starts the attackers kept coming, always with tanks leading the infantry. One by one, the pockets of defenders were scattered into the night to make their way back as best they could by whatever circuitous route they could find.

The Australians started withdrawing before midnight, a move that poor communication turned into a shemozzle. The Japanese set fire to a mission hut, adding a Wagnerian touch, with men from both sides darting in all directions under flickering orange light. When the fighting subsided, Japanese troops assembled behind their tanks near the blazing hut, confident they had won a decisive battle in RE Operation against the mainstay of the Allied defence at Milne Bay. Under the cover of darkness, they moved forward briskly behind the tanks towards what they believed to be Rabi's only airfield. Now, however, the tanks struggled to maintain marching pace as they got repeatedly bogged in the sodden track, their engines showing signs of strain after pushing all day through sticky mud.

General Clowes moved his reserve troops in around the easternmost airstrip, No. 3, laid mines in the track coming from KB Mission along which the tanks would come and set up camouflaged anti-tank guns pointing in that direction. A company was moved forward to ambush the Japanese as they passed by, but it was poorly timed and the Japanese were able to respond and drive them into the high-country jungle. But not everything was going the invaders' way. Both tanks finally gave up their struggle with the deep mud and became irretrievably bogged near Rabi, four kilometres beyond KB Mission. The troops pressed on without tank cover. They made contact with the defenders forward of No. 3 Strip, meeting tougher resistance than they had faced all night. But there was little time to seriously test these defences or wonder where the increased strength had come from. The sun rose, the Kittyhawks appeared through the clouds and the Japanese melted into the surrounding greenery.

Little happened the next day. The only action—and the Japanese were unaware of it—was the movement of Kittyhawks from No. 1 Strip near Gili Gili to Port Moresby. It had been decided to relocate them lest they be captured. Any attack on the airfield was expected at night when the planes couldn't take off, so rudimentary was the bulldozed construction of the landing strip. On the other side, the assault force was resting up and taking stock under cover in the jungle. Soldiers examined the state of their feet after two days of crossing streams and marching through mud. Ankles and feet were inflamed and swollen, some so severely that boots wouldn't lace up fully and gaiters had to be wound around the ankles instead.[8]

The recurring problem of hunger was rearing its ugly head once again. Rations were reduced to dry biscuits, so there was monotony and poor nutrition as well as shortage. Help had been tantalisingly near the previous night but hadn't materialised. The destroyer *Hamakaze* had come into Milne Bay at midnight to land ammunition and rations for the assault force, but could not make contact in the rain. It had positioned itself off Rabi while the force was engaged in battle rather than further east, at Waga Waga, where support personnel were looking after the limited stores.

The next attempt to land men and materiel didn't make the same mistake. Apprised of the slow progress of the operation—its 'failure', according to Fleet command communications—Vice-Admiral Mikawa, commander of Eighth Fleet, decided to send urgent reinforcements. After the mishandling of the Coral Sea battle and the army's run of successes, the navy was in no mood to lose this one. Kure 3SNLP, with 560 men under Commander Minoru Yano and 200 men of Yokohama 5SNLP, left Rabaul on the afternoon of the 28th on three destroyers (*Arashi*, *Yayoi* and *Murakumo*) and three patrol boats, with destroyer escort. The convoy was attacked by Allied aircraft the next afternoon but took little damage. That night it was able to unload troops, ammunition and supplies (of tinned food and more *kammempo*) near KB Mission.[9]

Commander Hayashi had set up his command two kilometres east of Rabi. It had been a much-needed second quiet day when he met with Yano, moustache bristling and gung-ho for action. 'Let's go on the attack straight away.'

Hayashi, more the quiet achiever, replied, 'They're all exhausted. It would be unreasonable for them to attack the airfield straight away.'[10]

He was subdued and very tired himself, and worried that he had heard no word nor seen any sign of the Sasebo 5SNLP unit that had landed—he had no reason to think otherwise—on the ocean coast. It should have been making its way over the Stirling Range. Yano decided to move his fresh troops as near as possible to battle that night, then disperse them into the jungle to avoid enemy air attack. The following night they would mount a joint attack on the airfield with Hayashi's original landing force.

When night fell on 30 August, the fresh troops moved west and joined the original landing party. Action man Yano was now calling the shots. The combined force advanced towards No. 3 Strip and charged what was thought to be a significantly depleted enemy. There was no chanting this time, but still a great deal of yelling. The firefight was fierce, but the balance had shifted since the attack at KB Mission. The defenders had brought up American half-track armoured vehicles; their tracer fire lit up the battlefield, followed by machine-gun fire. Mortar fire was called on and lobbed well into Japanese positions. The assault force made three charges at the enemy front line. All were heavy, highly concentrated attacks—and all were driven back after taking dispiriting numbers of casualties. A flanking movement was tried, with a similar outcome. It was slowly dawning on the Japanese that they were seriously outnumbered.

Worse, the devastating Allied artillery was driving them backwards. Just before dawn, a bugle sounded and the ragged and much-reduced force withdrew into the jungle before the Kittyhawks arrived.

As the sun edged up on yet another dismal day, it cast its watery light over a macabre scene. The area east of No. 3 Strip had become a field of corpses, twisted, broken and mutilated by the impact of enemy artillery. Except for those unable to retreat, the Japanese were not in a position to see the extent of their losses. They'd been forced too far back. Australian and American defenders moved forward through the appalling carnage. Bodies were strewn higgledy-piggledy, sometimes across other bodies, with legs, arms and weapons pointing in all directions to some destination only their owners knew about. It was as if the gods in their annoyance had flung handfuls of men onto the ground. Some of the soldiers coming through vomited and went back.[11] No one made any effort to gather up the bodies. What was the point? Where would they take them?

Some Japanese had strapped themselves into the foliage of coconut trees and were sniping at enemy soldiers below. Others set up machine-guns to ambush troops moving down the track towards Rabi and KB Mission. Yet others lay still among their dead comrades, occasionally releasing a grenade or firing a rifle, their final gestures of the war. The Australians decided this was a planned tactical ploy and some went into a frenzy, bayoneting the bodies, a release of tension parading as an insurance policy.

The main assault force, or what was left of it, had either retreated to the jungle-clad slopes at the back of Rabi or fallen back towards KB Mission. They were in considerable disarray, shell-shocked by the unexpected fury and force of the ordnance storm they had been through. Had they had time to think about it they might have wondered what had become of the daily Kittyhawk patrol, but time was a luxury not available to them. Still, seven Zeros arrived in the morning and patrolled the skies over Rabi—and no Kittyhawks appeared.

One of the Zeros, on reconnaissance, reported sighting a Japanese flag and banner, indicating a no-drop zone, eight kilometres north-west of the airfield. It was assumed to be the Sasebo 5SNLP unit making its way from the coast. The spotter plane was unable to make any further identification or get any indication of the unit's condition, but it reported its findings to squadron command. An order was sent to Hayashi to make contact on the coming night with the unit supposedly now located, then attack and seize the airfield. It was an order to meet a unit that wasn't there—Sasebo 5SNLP was still marooned on Goodenough Island—and mount an assault for which it no longer had any capacity. Adding to the futility of the order, Commander Hayashi had been shot and killed in the afternoon's fighting.[12]

Retreating Japanese, now scattered in small groups, were repeatedly forced back during the day. By late afternoon, they had pulled back to KB Mission. The Kittyhawks finally appeared and strafed them in the coconut plantation, but air attack was now among the least of their concerns. In the constant rain the road had got heavier, churned into mud by troops and light tanks. Ensuring feet didn't remain ankle-deep in the boggy road was hard work. Troops were suffering from skin diseases, tinea and foot-rot. And still the rain fell. To make matters worse, Australians in pursuit had moved into the mission precinct and set up positions there. The retreating force tried to consolidate and mount a counter-attack that evening, but it came to nothing. It did, however, allow stragglers to slip by unmolested as they retreated east, and later enabled a larger force to get past after a costly ambush.

The previous night, Yano's fresh troops had tried unsuccessfully to outflank the Allies by circling to the north of the airfield. When the dawn bugle blew they had withdrawn into jungle; now, on the 31st, they made their way eastward past Rabi. Unaware that there had been an Australian offensive, they returned to the track at the Gama River expecting to be well clear of the enemy. They were about to cross the river when a militia platoon approached, coming back from overshooting its destination. The two groups started to exchange fire, but the surprises weren't yet over. A whole battalion was concealed in the coastal bush, waiting to ambush the Japanese stragglers they could hear coming back down to the track. In tight formation and at close range, they too opened up on the Japanese, who didn't have a chance. The survivors retreated into the jungle, circled and tried several times to breach the enemy's perimeter. It was a forlorn gesture. After a succession of costly failures they withdrew past KB Mission, taking their wounded with them, including a seriously injured Commander Yano.[13] When things start going wrong, they tend to keep going wrong until a circuit-breaker turns fortune around. There was no circuit-breaker this night. There wasn't going to be one at Milne Bay.

The naval landing force fell back through a series of holding positions on the morning of 1 September, under constant enemy pursuit. Their main aim was to delay the Australian advance to allow time for evacuation, should that become possible. The narrowness of the coastal corridor worked to the Japanese advantage—there was little room for flanking—but only because it slowed the Allies' forward thrust. Rabaul tried another way to regain the initiative. Zeros and bombers were sent to raid Rabi but heavy weather forced them back, while on the ground the landing force continued to be pushed inexorably towards the easternmost tip of New Guinea. Beyond that lay the Coral Sea.

On the morning of the 2nd, 130 men of Yokosuka 5SNLP left Rabaul. Travelling by patrol boat with the destroyer *Hamakaze* as escort, they were to reinforce the Rabi operation. At this time, Rabaul had little idea of developments in the campaign. As the reinforcement party was leaving, a message came from Yano that an enemy transport with cruiser escort had entered Milne Bay; there was no mention of Yano's condition. *Hamakaze* was ordered to cruise ahead at speed and intercept these ships while the transport held its position. Nine bombers and nine Zeros left Rabaul to assist, but the weather was so foul that three bombers were lost in it and this force also turned back. It didn't make much difference: there were no planes on the Milne Bay airstrips.

The destroyers *Hamakaze* and *Arashi* arrived at dusk to find that the Allied vessels had unloaded their cargoes and gone. They reported to Rabaul that there appeared to be heavy fighting near the original landing site at Waga Waga, but contact with land forces was hindered by heavy rain and poor visibility. These observations were not news to

Admiral Mikawa. The seriously wounded Yano had sent a sombre message to the Eighth Fleet commander that afternoon: 'We have reached the worst possible situation. We will together calmly defend our positions to the death. We pray for absolute victory for the empire and for long-lasting fortune in battle for you all.'[14]

Mikawa conferred with Seventeenth Army command and cancelled the reinforcement of RE Operation with the small landing force that was then on its way. Since the army's Aoba Force of 1000 men was due to arrive at Rabaul from Davao, in the Philippines, on 9 September, it was agreed to move them on to Milne Bay straight away and then launch a concerted attack on Rabi. Yano was told to hold his position until reinforcements could arrive on the 12th. Eighth Fleet Command was still unaware of Yano's injuries, or at least the extent of them.

Arashi and *Hamakaze* were ordered to contact the landing party during the day and enter the bay at night to evacuate the wounded. That was done successfully, the withdrawn wounded including Commander Yano. Mercifully, the evacuation site was far enough back from the Allied advance for the operation to take place without incident.

Next day the Australians tried to encircle the remaining positions, but found it next to impossible in the narrow strip along the coast. It was easy to get disoriented trying to find a way around the steep jungle slopes, and they were as likely as not to emerge and find themselves in the sights of well-concealed Japanese guns. Little headway was made in the face of intense fire from the assault force, now desperately defending. The one charge attempted by the Japanese was as unsuccessful as the Australians' had been, and for the most part they were satisfied just to hold their ground. The only result either side could measure was its heavy toll of casualties. At nightfall the Japanese and Australians both withdrew to secure their positions, each side unaware that the other was doing the same.

The destroyer *Yayoi* came into Milne Bay on the night of the 4th to evacuate more casualties. While the ship was there, it gathered more details of the condition of the landing force. All the company commanders had been killed, and only three or four platoon leaders were left. Fifty fully fit men remained in the force. The rest were incapacitated or could offer only token support. Many soldiers had foot sores so severe they couldn't walk and were fighting sitting down. The encircling enemy threatened annihilation, the ship's report concluded grimly. The following day Rear-Admiral Mitsuharu Matsuyama, commander of 18th Squadron coordinating RE Operation, conceded that the situation had become untenable even as a holding operation. He ordered the withdrawal of the Milne Bay landing force that night.[15]

By the 5th, the Japanese had withdrawn behind their supply base at Waga Waga. In the skirmishes that occurred from time to time as the Allies edged forward they were able to place a high cost on that advance, but they were suffering equal losses themselves. They no longer had even the minimum strength needed to sustain their position. They would fight off the Allied advance then pull back slightly, leaving behind their dead and near-dead. One Australian's description of Japanese bodies in an abandoned machine-gun nest captures the horror and the hopelessness: 'Their eyes shone in the jungle gloom with the glassy stare of death, but they were not all dead for I recall that one lifted his head at the sound of our approach.'[16] He doesn't say what was done with that soldier, but prisoners weren't taken.

In the final act of the Rabi operation, black barges from *Tenryu* appeared out of the night with a platoon of fresh troops to cover the evacuation. The wounded, then the walking wounded, then the few remaining fit soldiers boarded cutters towed behind the motorised barges. Once again Allied soldiers were not in evidence, so the operation went smoothly. The returning craft chugged slowly over the dark sea, but the relief was immense. No one noticed whether it was raining or not. At last, it no longer mattered. Of the 1940 troops landed during the operation 1320 had now been evacuated, including 310 wounded.[17] On board there was deathly silence, the men contemplating who knows what. They were alive, and that was what mattered most at this moment, but they had the air of a defeated force. And they were. RE Operation—or Milne Bay, as the Allies called it—was Japan's first defeat in a land operation in this war. After Midway and now Rabi, there was a

sense that fortune's wheel was turning. The spirited charge for empire
and emperor was grinding to a halt. For the Allies, Milne Bay broke the
myth of the invincibility of Japanese land forces that had lurked in the
shadows of their planning up till now. South Seas Force was on its own
now, its back-up buried in the Milne Bay mud.

◆　◆　◆

One chapter of the Milne Bay story remains to be told: the extraordinary saga of Tsukioka Unit. No one could account for the unit, which
was assumed to have landed on the north coast at Taupota and advanced
to the hills north of Rabi airfield. There had even been reported sight-
ings of the unit on its way across the Stirling Range, but they were false.
When the last soldier to be evacuated left Milne Bay, Tsukioka Unit was
still marooned on the south of Goodenough Island. It had arrived on
25 August to find there was no place suitable for concealing its barges.
The barges were spotted and destroyed by enemy aircraft along with the
unit's radio transmitter and all its provisions.

It wasn't until 2 September that the castaways managed to locate a
canoe and send three messengers paddling towards Buna. They reached
their destination a week later and collapsed, having eaten nothing but
coconut milk for eight days.[18] It was the first the navy knew of Tsukioka
Unit's fate. Two destroyers, *Yayoi* and *Isokaze*, were sent on a rescue mission, but were intercepted by B-17 Flying Fortresses and B-25 Mitchell
bombers. *Yayoi* suffered serious damage, became stranded and sank in
the late afternoon. *Isokaze* had evaded the bombers, returned to where
Yayoi had been and found only an oily residue. No *Yayoi*, no survivors.
Isokaze searched for both until well after nightfall, then returned to Rabaul.[19] Now there were two groups stranded in the Solomon Sea, one still
unlocated.

A message was air-dropped to the men on Goodenough Island on
the 10th, letting them know that rescue ships would arrive the next day.
Another message on the 12th, dropped with food supplies, advised that
the rescue had been postponed, but at least they knew the men had been
located.[20]

Rear-Admiral Matsuyama on *Tenryu* led *Hamakaze* next day on a search-and-rescue mission for both the *Yayoi* and the Tsukioka groups. These two ships could find no trace of *Yayoi* either, but they did find a number of Allied aircraft and returned to Rabaul, recognising there was no wisdom in conducting a search without air cover. *Isokaze* set out on the 22nd with *Mochizuki*, and they had better luck. Ten survivors were found south of New Britain in a launch from *Yayoi*. Learning that eighty-seven more survivors had drifted to the coast of Normanby Island, the two warships hastened there and searched into the night with searchlights and sirens. They could find no one.[21]

Further supplies were air-dropped on Goodenough Island on the 23rd. The same day, a passing Japanese plane spotted people on Normanby Island. They were assumed to be *Yayoi* survivors, and when they were evacuated on the 26th that was confirmed, but there were only ten of them. No further survivors from *Yayoi* were ever found. Rescue from Goodenough Island was a different matter, however. The Allies, by now aware of the presence of the stranded Japanese, made daily attacks on all rescue attempts. Worse, rations were getting threateningly low and the group was stricken with a serious outbreak of malaria.

The final scenes in the drama of rescuing Tsukioka's castaways were set on submarines. A sub arrived at the island on 3 October and landed rations, ammunition, a wireless radio and a barge. It was able, within its limited interior space, to evacuate about fifty sick men. Returning ten days later it landed medical supplies and more rations, but when a flare was dropped by an enemy plane the sub submerged and didn't reappear. A second landing craft was left behind. On the 15th, the stranded party got a message on their newly acquired wireless that the rescue was postponed for the time being and that they should conceal their barges.[22] Something was obviously brewing. Too much Allied interest was being shown in Goodenough Island.

Three hundred Australian troops landed on nearby Mud Bay on the night of 22 October and advanced in pouring rain towards the castaways' camp at Kilia Mission. The camp was no band of dispirited lost souls, however. The Japanese were now fed and well-positioned on a jungle-covered knoll, expecting Allied attention and ready to repel it. An Australian patrol came under heavy sniper fire and grenade attack as its men tried to climb up the bank of a nearby creek. A mortar crew was ambushed as it made its way to Kilia and abandoned most of its ammunition in the retreat. The attackers withdrew for the night and tried again the next day, but were stopped by accurate sniper fire. They tried approaching from other directions, but either found the jungle impenetrable or were driven back by Japanese fire. Air strafing of the Japanese positions was arranged for the next morning. It did not arrive until late in the afternoon. By the time the Australians, under air cover, moved in on Kilia Mission it had been evacuated.[23]

Tsukioka Unit had relocated to nearby Ferguson Island by barge during the night of the 24th. Two days later, they were rescued by the destroyer *Tenryu*.[24] It had been two months since they made the ill-fated overnight stop at Goodenough Island, and during that time the Japanese campaign in New Guinea and the Solomon Islands had deteriorated unimaginably.

As an ironic postscript to the Tsukioka Unit saga, an Allied officer expressed surprise at the end of the Milne Bay battle that the Japanese had not thought to mount an overland attack on the base's northern flank. To him, that seemed to be the weak point in Allied defences.[25] That thrust was exactly the role that RE Operation had mapped out for Tsukioka Unit after it landed at Taupota. But it was not to be. The initial air raid at Goodenough Island saw to that. Tsukioka Unit never made it to Taupota. On such slips can the fate of battles turn.

Chapter 9

To the end of the line

After the string of quick victories, Japan's war was starting to falter. Intelligence reports notified Seventeenth Army HQ in Rabaul that Allied troop numbers were building up in Port Moresby. This could make life difficult for South Seas Force, at that time tied down at Isurava and facing a looming supply crisis. On 28 August, General Hyakutake issued an order to General Horii to advance to the southern slopes of the Owen Stanley Range and hold that position until the second assault force was ready.[1] Soon after, the failure of RE Operation at Milne Bay ensured there would be no second force. If Horii was going to soldier on and attack Port Moresby, his force would be on its own and without air cover.

Stubbornness overcame the general. He pressed on despite his troop losses and increasing supply difficulties. The exhausted Australians had withdrawn to the next village, Eora Creek, their last counter-attack at Abuari having failed. Horii ordered 41st Regiment to chase after the enemy and held 144th Regiment in reserve. South Seas Force trudged on along the narrow, slippery track. The jungle got thicker, even at mid-day letting in only a dusky half-light. Fungus on tree trunks and on the ground had a phosphorescent glow. The humidity was unbearable, especially in the ravine-like valleys. Walled in by mountains, rising vapour hung heavily in the jungle. Rain fell almost every day and all night. Soldiers got wet through, shivering in the night and early-morning cold. The track was root-ridden and muddy, the ground elsewhere covered with decaying leaves and soft, velvety green moss; walking on it was 'like treading on some living animal'.[2]

Rather than retreat after Isurava, Brigadier Arnold Potts, the new Australian commander, chose to make a fighting withdrawal. Leapfrogging ambushes on the track, with fanning movements around the advancing Japanese, were followed each time by short pull-backs. A couple of strategic locations were chosen where the men could dig in for more substantial defence, while the wounded, sick and exhausted were moved out of harm's way.

The Australian wounded from Isurava had been brought back to a medical staging post at Eora Creek where medics, standing in mud, dressed wounds and carried out *ad hoc* surgery. Yellowish rain pelted down. When Japanese advance patrols moved up the mossy forested slopes above the medical post, it had to be evacuated. A unit was left behind to ambush and slow the advancing invaders. After exchanges of fire it withdrew and the Japanese moved on, having lost a few more men in the process.

Eora Creek village was perched on a side knoll, high above the white water cascading into the bottom of the ravine—a dreary, windswept and sunless place with high mountain walls on either side.[3] The Japanese found only abandoned huts, with corpses lying on stretchers outside. Some food was scattered about, but this time the storehouse had been emptied. They would encounter the same thing at the next storehouse, north of The Gap. The Australians had destroyed everything that couldn't be carried, slashing bags of rice and puncturing tins of bully beef.

Imanishi recalls, 'When the Australians retreated, they dumped all their rations on the ground. They made holes in biscuit tins and threw them into the valleys. Some valleys glinted with dumped biscuit tins. We ended up washing mud off Australian rice and eating it.'[4]

Provisions became damp and putrefied in the continual rain. Wet rice had to be put out in the sun to dry and eaten before other rations. With provisions getting desperately low, Horii ordered a reduction in the daily rice ration. Hunger was starting to grip. A dispiriting air hung over the men, try as they might to keep it at bay. Discipline was getting looser and having to be imposed more rigorously. In one action, officers had to wave their swords to get their troops moving. The men were urged on relentlessly, but casualties among platoon and company leaders were chipping away at South Seas Force's capacity for effective command in battle.

In the breaks between actions the men would sit around in a sort of trance, stripped of emotion, trying to reassemble their thoughts and motivate themselves to keep moving. Conversation was kept to a minimum. They went through all the checks they'd been trained to carry out, often like automatons. Their feet were puffy from constant soaking and white skin peeled off. Clothes stank; hair was matted with mud. But for all the difficulties, they didn't stop believing in their ability to carry out the mission. They were, after all, still moving forward, sometimes slowly, it was true, sometimes with more difficulty than they had expected, but always moving forward. They had suffered no reversals.

Koiwai Battalion, at the front of the advance, encountered another pocket of resistance at The Gap and was forced to press its attack all through the day. The Gap had been named by Allied HQ in Melbourne in the belief that it was a narrow pass like that at Thermopylae where a handful of Spartans held the entire Persian army at bay. The imagery was romantic and hopeful but wrong. A depression in the summit ridge, The 'Gap' is actually eleven kilometres wide.[5]

The simmering antagonism between Koiwai and his commanding officer flared up. Koiwai was cautiously preparing for an attack around a knob behind which he suspected enemy troops lay waiting. Colonel Yazawa became agitated. 'What are you waiting for?' he demanded. 'Attack now!'

Koiwai replied, 'I'm waiting for artillery support before giving the order to attack.'

'There won't be any artillery support,' Yazawa snorted.

Colonel Tanaka, General Horii's staff officer, said, 'This is my first opportunity to see an infantry attack for real. So please do it well.'

Koiwai was flabbergasted. This same Tanaka had written a training manual for the Infantry School![6]

Tanaka would have to wait longer to see his first infantry attack. A torrential downpour as night fell forced both sides to hold their positions in the biting cold while they waited for the rain to ease. However, the Australians withdrew during the night and Koiwai's men resumed their advance in the morning, crossing the saddle of the Owen Stanley Range. Japanese soldiers stood on the ridge, 2000 metres above sea level, among moss-covered trees on a cold and foggy day. They shouted '*Banzai*!' It was all downhill now, they congratulated themselves, all the way to Port Moresby. But this side of the Owen Stanleys would turn out not to be the reverse of the rapid rise from Kokoda that they expected.

The next objective was Myola, a flat alpine plain full of reeds and devoid of trees, often sodden underfoot from the chilly creeks that trickled across it. It had been used as an air-drop zone for Allied supplies earlier in the campaign. Allied Command signalled that Myola should be defended at all costs, even though Japan didn't have sufficient control of the air to make use of the place. As the advancing force began to work around the defenders' flank, Potts decided a wide, flat area was too easily circled and withdrew to a more defendable location at Efogi. In any case, the Japanese could come around an alternative loop of the track, through Kagi, and cut off any Australian retreat. Efogi was south of where the loop rejoined the track.

The Japanese entered Myola during a violent storm. Unhappy with the rate of progress of the 41st, Horii had returned the 144th to the front on crossing The Gap and again held the 41st in reserve. For the men from Kochi, it was like the train journey from their home town over the mountains to Marugame, every stop along the way a bustle of activity that only slowed the journey. Sometimes the soldiers, if they were at the front line, would be part of the bustle of circle, attack and crossfire, sometimes they came through the 'station' after that was over. At Myola, there was no bustle. Rather than risk encirclement, Potts's men had withdrawn after spoiling their remaining food. A delaying action was not feasible. The overland force moved in, soaked to the skin, and fell upon the remnants of Australian rations: corned beef, milk, jam. Whether the leftovers were deliberately contaminated or not, most of the troops were ill the next morning. Lieutenant Sakamoto notes in his diary: 'Many suffered diarrhoea by over-eating captured provisions.'[7]

◆　◆　◆

Dug in on new defensive positions across an unusually wide valley, Australian soldiers witnessed on the night of 6 September an extraordinary sight, spellbinding and threatening at the same time. About three kilometres away as the crow flew, a long line of small lights snaked slowly down the black slope opposite like an ancient religious procession, continuing all through the night, until dawn. Under any other circumstances it would have been a powerful and moving experience. Here it was disarming, giving an indication of the number of troops moving up to the front line. Each Japanese soldier in line carried a flaring length of rubber-coated signal wire left behind at Myola by the retreating troops. The glow guided their cautious movement down the slippery track. Pilgrims in the night, they made their way to Efogi River at the bottom of the valley that separated them from the waiting defenders. Occasionally a light jumped out of the line as a soldier slid and tumbled on the greasy, root-covered surface. Without their long-range Vickers machine-guns, the Australians could do no more than watch, mesmerised.

The village of Efogi sat where the Kokoda Track crossed the river before the path made its way up a long ridgeline between two smaller valleys. The exhausted Australian militiamen had been relieved of front-line duties and moved to the rear, out of the line of fire. Three AIF battalions had dug in around and above a small area of kunai grass high on the ridge, from which forested gullies fell steeply away on both sides. On the edge, a derelict Seventh Day Adventist hut gave the place its name, Mission Ridge. Potts's Brigade HQ was higher up, on a knoll where the ridgeline from Efogi joined the main east–west mountain line, running parallel with the Owen Stanley Range.

By morning, the front line of the Japanese attack force was occupying the deserted village of Efogi, with some troops gathering around the mission hut further up the track. The support was still making its way across the plateau at Efogi North, an open area covered with kunai grass and overlooking the valley. Eight B-26 Marauders and four Kittyhawks flew in, bombing and strafing these troops and inflicting significant casualties. The track was steep and movement down it slow, so the men bunched up. The Japanese called this Hell Valley. The planes tried for the same result down in the valley but were far less successful. Although the valley was wide enough, the canopy made pinpointing Japanese positions difficult. General Horii telegraphed Seventeenth Army HQ that enemy planes had caused heavy losses without Japanese fighter cover, but it was three days before this message got through to 25th Air Flotilla in Rabaul, too late for it to respond in any meaningful way even if it had the capacity.[8] The message had to be taken by runner back to Kokoda where the nearest radio transmitter was located, too heavy to carry further up the track.[9]

By mid-morning the Japanese started to probe enemy lines with machine-gun and mortar fire, looking for defenders' locations by noting points of retaliation. Horii and his senior commanders, including the now sick and stretcher-bound Colonel Kusunose, devised a plan of attack. Horie (2nd) Battalion would move up the western foot of the ridge, scale the sides and cut off the retreat line of their opponent's main defensive force, while Kuwada Unit (3rd Battalion) would conduct a conventional frontal assault. If successful, that would drive the withdrawing defenders into the line of fire of the flanking force.

Australian positions on Mission Ridge were subjected to artillery fire that evening. Taking advantage of the distraction and under cover of darkness, 2nd Battalion moved up the western flank along the foot of the ridge, Nishimura's company among them. In the dark and with a sloping slippery surface, it was 'like a balancing act in a circus'.[10] Crawling because of its steepness, they scaled the ridge's forested side well before dawn, reaching the track between Brigade HQ on the knoll and Mission Ridge forward of it. Lieutenant Sakamoto's company also clambered up the slope, dragging a Juki machine-gun. Defenders up on the knoll could hear the sounds of slashing vegetation and shovels digging somewhere in the dark, along with the sounds of a pre-dawn battle down on Mission Ridge, but couldn't work out what to make of it all.

Once on the knoll at its junction with the ridge the infiltrating troops dug foxholes along the sides of the track, each just big enough for one person, some hidden behind logs. Snipers took up positions in trees. Sakamoto's company set up its Juki to rake artillery fire over the rear of the three defender battalions. One company positioned itself behind where the Australian Brigade HQ had been, but Potts and his command group had already moved back even further. Nishimura's company dug in at the northernmost end of the Japanese wedge, nearest to the rear of the Australian forward defence.

'The Australians were very close to us,' he says, 'perhaps not more than twenty metres away, but we could not see them.'[11]

The infiltrated troops made no attempt to break the enemy perimeter below them, settling instead for woodpecker fire into those positions. The purpose was to isolate the Australian HQ and cut off their forward defenders. The Japanese did not want to reveal their positions, content to remain concealed until the withdrawing Australians were exposed to fire.

The frontal assault resumed in the cold pre-dawn mist, the strengthened Japanese attacking in several waves, each time forced back by machine-gun and rifle fire and grenades. But Horii's men had time on their side. As daylight came, the Australian defensive position was peppered with more gunfire and pounded with artillery. The Juki brought up onto the ridge cut across the command group behind the knoll. One of that group's soldiers was shot near the track high on the ridge while crossing to alert his comrades that the Japanese had infiltrated the higher ground—if they hadn't worked that out already.

The outflanking Japanese had cut the signal lines between the Australian forward defence and its HQ, so an unreliable wireless set was Potts's only means of contact with his front-line troops. With his three battalions sandwiched between two attacking battalions and with ammunition running dangerously low, he needed a tactic to extricate his men. In the mid-morning Potts brought them closer together, then ordered a charge from below in the afternoon to clear the track for withdrawal.[12] The alternative of bypassing the Japanese through precipitous bush on the eastern slope was considered, but it was decided against because of the need to get the wounded out on stretchers and get ammunition in.

Rain began to fall and intensified through the afternoon. In a straight line, with bayonets fixed, four Australian companies marched steadily through the downpour towards Japanese positions above the ridge. In the fierce firefight provoked by this desperate 'crash through or crash' tactic, most crashed. One company advancing on the eastern side got through to Brigade HQ, along with eight men from another company. Potts sent them back to attack the rear of the Japanese infiltrators, but in doing so they came under controlled fire from snipers and concealed positions. Few if any of this group survived that action.[13] By late afternoon those left at Brigade HQ started withdrawing to Menari, the next village on the track, taking the wounded with them. Papuan carriers had fled when the shooting started the day before.

The other companies in the clearing action, moving either along the track or to the right, remained pinned down under fire and were forced to withdraw with heavy casualties. Survivors fell back 100 metres to a track branching down the eastern slope, taking a wide path to Menari. Japanese pursuit was held off by two companies covering the side track's beginning while the remnants of all three Australian battalions made their way down this track, slashing through the undergrowth and carrying back their wounded in the drizzling rain. At dusk, the Japanese drew back in response to a short, unexpected counter-attack by the rearguard, as it covered its withdrawal into the overcast, black night.[14]

On several occasions, Kokichi Nishimura has told in extraordinary detail how his entire platoon—except himself—was annihilated during this day's fighting above Mission Ridge.[15] It is a story of four Allied charges during the day, of his taking shelter in a foxhole without a rifle and of a fight to the death with a young Australian, a fight in which Nishimura was wounded. The action at Mission Ridge 'was a key battle . . . in shaping the rest of Nishimura's life', as we will come to see.[16] The problem with his version of the events at Mission Ridge is that it is difficult to reconcile with the unit diaries of the three Australian battalions there or with the Japanese force's records—to the extent that they are available—although all four of those sources tell a consistent story. None talks of the wiping out of a Japanese platoon. Indeed, records on both sides refer only to heavy Australian losses on Mission Ridge. The nearest to Nishimura's description is a Japanese diary entry noting six of 5th Company (Nishimura's) killed in the action, but no mention of the annihilation of the smaller unit, a platoon of forty-two.[17]

A considerable part of Nishimura's day was spent in his foxhole without a rifle. Although a grenadier, he'd become the platoon commander's batman as well, handing Lieutenant Inoue his weapons as required. How much of the day was spent in that foxhole is not clear. There's no doubt Nishimura was wounded at Mission Ridge, but how that relates to the day's events, either Nishimura's telling of them or the armies' records, is equally unclear.

Nishimura had been shot in the shoulder by a machine-gun and was found the next morning by a machine-gunner from another company. He was taken by stretcher to a temporary field hospital, where a medic checked his wound but could find no bullet. The pain in his shoulder increased over the next few days, and Nishimura asked the man lying next to him to see what was wrong. A bullet was starting to poke out of the wound. The soldier took it out, but that was not the end of it. In a work-related X-ray forty years later, doctors discovered a second bullet deep in Nishimura's shoulder.[18]

◆ ◆ ◆

The day in which the Australians withdrew from the Efogi area was also the first day for some time that supplies got down the track to the front of the Japanese advance. They were distributed first to the front-line troops. The next day, Hirano's diary reports that he had a headache and upset stomach all day.[19] Sakamoto's diary notes that he ate rice that evening for the first time in three days.[20] The men had supplemented

their dwindling rations with raids on village gardens, the villagers having fled long before. This meant a diet of sweet potato and taro mostly,
but they often found they had been beaten to a garden by the retreating
soldiers. The Japanese supply line was collapsing because of air attacks
on the track as well as on ships coming from Rabaul, and from desertion
by native carriers. Hirano was pulled out of the front line and ordered to
take 100 men back down the track to get provisions.

Horii decided to press on south towards Port Moresby, despite
the state of his supply line and the Rabaul order to draw to a halt on
the southern slopes of the Owen Stanleys. He was a determined and
single-minded man, taking advantage of the imprecision of that order.
Mountain lines followed one after the other on this side of the range
in seemingly never-ending succession. At exactly which point in this
repetition was the halt to take place? Horii was driven by other demons
as well: vengeance for the high losses of his men to a stubborn enemy
at Isurava and Efogi; avoiding the disgrace of defeat; perhaps just sheer
bloody-mindedness. Port Moresby meant food, shelter and victory, and
an end to the supply dilemma that was plaguing his assault forces and
his battle plan.[21]

Okada, the newspaperman, walked through the Efogi valley next
morning and up Mission Ridge with Colonel Tanaka. A company commander from the previous night's fighting had told Okada there were
200 bodies, Japanese and Australian, scattered about the area. As they
walked along the red clay path through a dark cypress forest, he saw
corpses lying about in various contorted postures. 'One of them had a
twisted neck and broken legs, with his face smeared all over with mud
and blood,' he would later write. 'Another was in a crouching position,
his face resting at the foot of a tree. A third was lying on his back like a
fallen tree, and a fourth was shot through his forehead [while] in a prone
shooting position, his gun left on the ground in front of him. Another
again was hanging on a tree over the edge of a cliff; another lying with
his upper body in a ditch; and another leaning against a tree with his
body bent halfway forward—men in all postures and conditions showing how desperately they fought and fell.'[22]

The Japanese forward units were already moving on from Efogi by 9 September, the day after the Mission Ridge battle, hot on the tail of the withdrawing enemy gathering in Menari. By midday, the advance had reached an elevated position overlooking the village and opened up with mortar and machine-gun fire. The Australians immediately began withdrawing to Nauro, the next village on the track, and the advance troops occupied Menari by mid-afternoon. The three AIF battalions from Mission Ridge coming around a side track with their wounded on stretchers had to detour even further to get ahead of the advancing force.

◆ ◆ ◆

While the men of South Seas Force stalked the retreating Australians, they were themselves stalked. The black-cloaked spectre of sickness infiltrated the assault force the moment it arrived on the shores around Buna, ceaselessly swinging its scythe through the Japanese landing party. Pestilences of various sorts were taking a savage toll. More men had been taken out of the battlefield by disease than by enemy action, the most widespread afflictions being malaria and dysentery.

Physical exhaustion, poor nutrition and carelessness with preventative measures were all now making troops vulnerable to the ravages of malaria picked up in the swampy lowlands. Although the high country above Isurava was a little too cold for the mosquito that transmits the micro-organism, by the time the men reached there it was too late.[23] The disease takes a week or more to incubate, so it was often not until they were well down the track that soldiers would start to show symptoms of the malaria they had contracted in the lowlands or even earlier, in New Britain. Bouts of fever, shivering, chills and sweats were the usual first signs, along with muscle aches and tiredness. More serious forms of the disease led to kidney failure, mental confusion, coma and death.[24] Loss of life from malaria was high and rising among the men on the Kokoda Track, regardless of which side they were fighting on. Those who trudged on resolutely despite their fevers and chills found their ability to fight seriously hampered.

Japanese soldiers had been issued with a five-point instruction sheet, but it was largely ignored and cases of malaria started appearing after three days in Papua. Mosquito nets, veils and gloves were issued, but were not used and often discarded. They only added to the carrying load. Mosquito creams and smoke coils were used, but were in the same short supply as food. There were simply no protocols for malaria prevention in the harsh conditions of battle. Even basic sanitary measures were often abandoned. Soldiers with malaria were treated with quinine, Atebrin and plasmoquin, but supplies were irregular and sometimes treatment would not be available for days.[25] Only serious cases were evacuated. The rest travelled behind the advancing force and, if they recovered, were returned to their units.

The unsanitary conditions and hardship also ensured the spread of dysentery, with its symptoms of nausea, vomiting and diarrhoea. Both the amoebic and bacillary forms of the disease were prevalent. The usual method of containing the illness, by management of fluid intake, was not practical in the conditions of this campaign, so dysentery wasn't brought under control. It spread unchecked. The rugged terrain meant diarrhoea was not an easily disposable product, making the disease even more rampant. Streams flowed with faeces, especially after heavy rains. And the problem didn't dissipate with forward movement, because the Australian troops also suffered from dysentery. Advancing Japanese were moving from one infected area into another. Dealing with the continuing effects of dysentery was just a fact of life for most on the track, although soldiers with the disease would often die if they had malaria as well.

Two other diseases were part of the Kokoda campaign cocktail, less widespread than malaria or dysentery but even more devastating in their impact. The signs of dengue fever were sudden fever with severe headaches, muscle and joint pains (its nickname in English was 'bonecrusher disease') and bright red rashes on legs and chest. A viral disease spread by mosquitoes (a different species from the one spreading malaria), dengue is primarily treated by increasing fluid intake to combat dehydration, not at all easy in the contaminated mountains of wartime Papua.[26] Just as debilitating was scrub typhus, a bacterial disease spread by larval mites found in heavy scrub vegetation. The symptoms were often indistinguishable from those of the more common malaria and dysentery—fever, headache, muscle pain and gastroenteritis—making diagnosis difficult for inexperienced medicos. The more virulent form of scrub typhus would lead to haemorrhaging and blood clots.[27]

The extreme shortage of food, the exhausting march and the heat, humidity and cold of the mountains had a range of other impacts on the men's health. They suffered from pneumonia and other fevers, diet deficiency diseases, particularly beriberi and night blindness, and nervous breakdowns of one kind or another from their growing weariness and weakness and from the trauma of constant battle under such arduous conditions. Their physical strength was ebbing daily because of the scarcity of food. The prospect of food in Port Moresby drove them on.

By now Colonel Kusunose, commander of the 144th, was extremely ill with malaria but he continued to function, deploying his troops. He was carried forward by stretcher behind the main force each time it advanced. By the time South Seas Force was on the southern slopes of the Owen Stanleys, even serious cases were not being evacuated. Instead, they were carried forward behind the front lines by their units in the hope that they could be taken to the field hospital that would be set up as soon as the Japanese captured Port Moresby.[28]

◆　◆　◆

The 67th Line of Communication (LOC) Hospital had been set up as the base hospital for MO Operation at Giruwa, on the coast near Buna. It had been expanded with new buildings and tents to a maximum of 430 beds. The majority of patients concealed themselves in the nearby jungle to hide from Allied air attack. The hospital had to constantly improve and supplement its camouflage. Camps in the jungle at least had the advantage of natural camouflage. With peak staff of 400 and capacity to treat about 1000 patients, Giruwa was a staging point for seriously ill and wounded troops brought back from the field hospital at Kokoda and elsewhere for treatment before resumption of duties or for evacuation to

Rabaul. Ninety-eight were sent back to Rabaul on 17 September on the warship *Mochizuki*; 100 went on *Kazuura Maru* three days later.[29]

Maintaining a battlefield hospital in the tropics was testing. Sewage from patients with contagious disease had to be kept away from river water. It was dumped in deep holes filled with creosote liquid soap. When heavy rain in the mountains caused the Giruwa River to overflow, the medical supply depot was inundated. By September, the number of patients had outstripped capacity and the staff were depleted by illness.

The range of maladies was taking a toll on the establishment troops who had built up the base at Buna. Busily constructing defensive bunkers and trenches to guard against Allied attack on the northern beaches, these soldiers were more easily spotted from the air than those hidden under the forest canopy up in the Owen Stanleys. Enemy air attack was constant, often daily. The wounded from these raids added to the already untenable patient load at Giruwa.

Private Yokoyama, the medical corpsman in 41st Regiment, had operated from Kokoda while the front line advanced to Deniki, Isurava and beyond. Although there were hardships, the young medic also experienced uplifting moments. The grandeur of the countryside left a lasting impression: the magnificent, lonely vistas that changed every day; the view from Kokoda Plateau over the airfield and Mambare River. A hanging bridge at Kokoda would set him thinking wistfully of home— of the hanging bridges of Fukuyama.[30] He would recall the things that had been part of his past life, now so distant: young squeals reflected off the water of the Inland Sea in summer; snowballs thrown by naughty boys at school; the cool softness of falling snow; small black bears in the mountains with their white 'napkin' in front; all the things that were no longer part of his world, and perhaps never would be again.

Yokoyama's universe had become one of hunger and the constant threat of air attack. Few provisions got beyond the Kumusi, and a corpsman did not have a strong claim on those that did. Fear and hunger. Hunger and fear. In Kokoda, he was chased by planes prowling around looking for targets to pick off. One circled so low he could see the face of the young Australian pilot. It was hard to continue to think of him as an enemy then—easier when the Australians were faceless threats. As the pilot pulled out, having failed to line up the corpsman, he clipped the top of a palm tree and crashed just beyond the plantation.[31] It's a memory that haunts Yori-ichi Yokoyama to this day.

Eleventh Company of the 41st had been given garrison duties when Nankai Shitai moved on from Isurava. All, including the medical corpsman, were brought back to Giruwa to protect the base at Buna and the LOC Hospital and to work on extending the hospital. Given the options it wasn't a bad outcome for Yokoyama, although increased attention from Allied aircraft came with it. He and his comrades lived in a two-storey white house at the edge of a eucalyptus forest. Its previous occupant had left when the war came to Papua, as had most of the inhabitants of a nearby village. Yokoyama had little contact with the villagers.

The Japanese invaders had presented themselves as liberating Papuans from colonial rule. This had some appeal initially, as the Papuans north of the Owen Stanley were much less enamoured of Australians than their compatriots around Port Moresby. Although many of the local villagers had headed for the hills when the invasion force arrived, some of the district's Orokaivan tribesmen had joined the Japanese labour force, some press-ganged but many volunteering. They often scouted for the Japanese.

General Horii's instructions to his troops had been to deal fairly with the Papuans, but that didn't last. Papuans and New Guineans working for the invasion force carried supplies and evacuated casualties but they didn't get adequate rest, food or medical care, any more than those working for the Australians did. As rations were cut back, desertion severely punished and the promised rewards replaced with threats, Papuans became increasingly dubious about the notion of liberation. Many became too ill to work or disappeared, leaving volunteer Formosan and Korean labourers and Japanese troops to carry supplies to the front and wounded men back.

Villagers, other than the able-bodied men lured by promised rewards, had moved clear of the fighting. Their huts were often wrecked by army occupation by either side (or both), burnt by retreating troops or strafed by air attack. Japanese and Australian troops routinely plundered village gardens, sometimes out of hunger, sometimes just vandalism. Camping areas were often contaminated by the dysentery that afflicted the two forces.[32]

As the hardships that the Japanese had to endure increased, so did the brutality with which they dealt with incidents out of the ordinary. Training had ingrained in them decisive responses to a prescribed range of situations, but it left them poorly equipped to deal with anything not in the prescription. Several stories persist of atrocities against both combatants and civilians while the Buna region was serving as a base for MO Operation. Few of the reports are first-hand and many have no doubt been embellished, both by the people who provided them and in their subsequent use as propaganda or to motivate Allied soldiers against their enemy. Nonetheless, reports about each alleged atrocity are fairly consistent in essence and often supported by circumstantial evidence. In any case, it would be naïve to imagine that events of this nature would not happen in the course of a long and difficult military campaign.

The Special Naval Landing Parties, essentially navy marine units, had a particular reputation for harshness that could merge into brutality. Many infantry troops of the IJA had concerns (or say now that they did) about some of the behaviour they heard about. A unit often fingered for notoriety in this respect is Sasebo 5SNLP. Commander Tsukioka is generally said to have ordered several executions. As Tsukioka left Buna on 24 August for the Rabi operation and didn't return until two months later, either the atrocities attributed to him happened before that date or Tsukioka is a fall guy of sorts, automatically taking the blame for any unsavoury incidents on the northern beaches.

Another group that is frequently mentioned in relation to these activities is the *kempeitai*, the military police that accompanied the landing force. *Kempeitai* were volunteers who had already served elsewhere within the armed forces, a fairly hard-bitten lot often acting on their own judgment or whim and generally with considerable autonomy. Authorised to act as policemen to civilians, suppressing espionage and resistance activity, as well as to servicemen, they were feared by both.

When Yokoyama Advance Party landed in July, two women fled in the nick of time from their house among the sago palms, successfully eluding Lieutenant Ida's platoon. Young Anglican missionaries, May Hayman and Mavis Parkinson survived for several days in the jungle with an Anglican priest, Father James Benson, and a group of Australian soldiers and injured American airmen. The village councillor of Upper Dobodura, a Papuan named Embogi, advised the Japanese of their presence. The servicemen were killed, but Benson escaped and the two young women were taken prisoner. They were held in a coffee mill near Popondetta by the *kempeitai*, but refused to reveal any information during interrogation. It's not clear what useful information they might have provided: presumably, their refusal was an act of principled defiance. That doesn't go over very well with the Japanese military. The women were taken to a plantation near Buna on 13 August, made to stand over shallow graves and bayoneted to death.[33] Father Benson fared better. He was caught by soldiers and taken to Rabaul, where he was imprisoned until the end of the war. Embogi, on the other hand, was later captured by the Australian army and summarily executed by hanging.[34]

There is a history of Orokaivan antagonism towards the Australian administration. Some continued this by bringing Allied troops and occasional civilians to the Japanese. In one instance (according to notes from interrogation of a Japanese POW) they brought a party of seven Australians, including four women and a young boy. The group did not appear to have been brought in by force and probably had been deceived in some way by their captors, who left without reward. The prisoners were held in a building but were not bound or mistreated, according to the Japanese informant. He was retelling hearsay, not speaking as a witness to these events. The Australians were questioned by a civilian from Rabaul, Tashiro, who spoke both English and Pidgin. Eventually they were taken away from the camp and executed. They were made to kneel and were bayoneted one by one, except for the mother and her child, who were shot; the mother first, holding her son, then the boy. The POW believed the execution order came from Commander Tsukioka, although he didn't know why the captives were executed.

He said he thought their treatment unnecessarily cruel, but as he did so under interrogation his sincerity is open to question.[35]

The notebook of Toshio Sato, an interpreter working in Buna, tells another story of brutal killing of non-combatants, but again it is not first-hand. Sato was told of an incident involving Tsukioka's Sasebo 5SNLP, in which six or seven Australian men and women were beheaded. One, a sixteen-year-old girl, was so agitated, screaming and crying, that the sword stroke glanced or missed her head. She had to be held by force so the execution could be carried out, a messy and disturbing sight for those present. The tone of the diary note suggests the story is recounted out of horror, not glee.[36] The entry is dated 9 September, two weeks after Tsukioka Unit's departure for Milne Bay, so the story had been circulating for some time before it reached Sato.

Another item in Sato's notebook reports the discovery of a spy with a wireless set hidden in an extinct volcano in Rabaul. The Japanese were aware that there were Australian coastwatchers reporting by wireless on the movements of their troops, shipping and aircraft. Tsunoda, the Zero pilot, has commented that the Australians always seemed to be aware of a Japanese air raid before it got to its target. 'It seemed the Australians had an efficient intelligence network there,' he says. 'As soon as we got there, Port Moresby had detected our movements and attacked us.'[37]

The Japanese were clearly disinclined to give civilians much benefit of any doubt about their activities or potential activities.

Much was, and sometimes still is, made of the brutality of the Japanese use of bayonets in these summary executions. It is brutal in its physicality, but then Japanese soldiers, like their Australian counterparts, were trained to use bayonets and to see them as one of the tools to use in the 'kill or be killed' reality of battle. The environment created in warfare and the pressures that accompany it may well drive individuals to actions they would not normally contemplate and could be considered out of character. There is always a danger of this being used to reinforce stereotypes rather than to provide insight into human nature. Nonetheless, these incidents occurred, even if they don't get to be retold very accurately, and they should at least be used to give us some understanding of what human beings are capable of under the worst of circumstances and what some are capable of even under less severe circumstances.

❖ ❖ ❖

By early September, Allied air raids were taking place daily. Transport of munitions and supplies from Rabaul were suspended for the time being, as the Japanese navy's air units couldn't guarantee their protection. Rabaul had other worries as well. Now that the Japanese command knew there was a well-established base at Rabi on Milne Bay, concern arose that there might be an Allied landing in the Buna area, cutting off South Seas Force.

On 13 September, the commander of Buna airbase sent a telegram to Rabaul: 'According to army reports, an Allied force (strength unknown) has landed at Basabua. Great likelihood that paratroopers will land here and at Basabua from first light tomorrow. Request aerial patrols. Buna airfield not operational.'[38]

Twenty minutes later, a second telegram came: 'According to intelligence from the commander of the army's Tomita Unit, the enemy has undertaken a landing at Basabua. Strength unknown.'[39]

The two reports turned out to be furphies, but they put the wind up the Rabaul commanders. Two days later Yokosuka 5SNLP, the unit that was sent to Milne Bay but didn't land, landed instead at Buna to reinforce the garrison there.

General Horii had been told by Lieutenant Koya from the Kokoda Signals Base about the deteriorating situation in Guadalcanal. Horii's flippant response was that in all of the Solomon Islands and New Guinea area only South Seas Force was resisting the Allies. Rabaul wasn't so sanguine. A panic about the vulnerability of Horii's force crept into its thinking. General Hyakutake issued an order for a battalion from Nankai Shitai to be moved back to Buna to patrol that area. Then, on the 14th, he passed on Tokyo's decision to cancel the Moresby offensive and reassemble north of the Owen Stanley Range. The high command knew the prospects of rectifying the supply problem were not good, at least in the short term, and were still fearful of an Allied landing at

ler to Horii on 16 September, Hyakutake, in
cated. Horii was to secure the Ioribaiwa area
nsives. By implication, these were not yet to

◆ ◆ ◆

...anding and repelling an enemy ambush, the advancing troops of South Seas Force reached the highest point of the Maguli Range by daybreak on 12 September and for the first time saw the southern sea. Making their way along the ridge south from Nauro, and spurred on by the sight of the Gulf of Papua, they came down to Ofi Creek. Scattered in and around the creek were tins of Australian rations, bully beef and the like. The men couldn't believe their luck. They had had no further provisions from their own supply lines since Mission Ridge. A reduced rice ration had been supplemented by whatever they could pick up along the way, sometimes from village gardens (often after the retreating and hungry enemy had been through), sometimes just roots dug up in the mountain jungle or bark hacked from its trees. This was a gift from the gods.

The Japanese approached the creek cautiously, wading into the water. The rations were lying in an open area with bush around, but it all seemed quiet enough. The more adventurous—or the more starving— tore open the tins. Others, realising this was a limited bonanza, threw caution to the winds and moved down to the open area to join in the feast before it was all gone. They were reminiscent of seagulls with a fisherman's catch on the beaches near Kochi. Amid the pandemonium, a volley of rifle and machine-gun fire rang out from several directions high on the southern bank.[41] It was a cleverly laid trap, baited for soldiers the Australians expected to be as hungry as themselves, if not hungrier. Several of the diners were killed instantly, their hands still clutching at the precious rations. The rest retreated for cover and retaliatory fire but the Australians slipped away, their job done.

Apart from an occasional ambush, the advance to Port Moresby had progressed with no opposition since Mission Ridge. The Australians had withdrawn to Ioribaiwa Ridge, effectively the second-last razor-back ridgeline before the Papuan capital. The quagmire around Nauro Creek had not been a suitable place for them to dig in. The more north–south orientation of Maguli Range allowed Japanese flanking movement, which didn't make it a good position for holding up the advance either. The Australians dug in instead along the east–west ridge-line at Ioribaiwa, reinforced with three fresh battalions brought up from Port Moresby. Meanwhile, the Japanese set up a mountain gun high on the northern slope of the Ofi Creek valley. Engineers had to build steps into the steep incline further north so that the heavy parts of the gun could be manhandled up and over to its position. With a range of over eight kilometres, it was able to bombard enemy troops established along Ioribaiwa Ridge.

General Horii attacked Ioribaiwa with the 144th, holding the 41st back on the banks of the Nauro River. General Hyakutake had ordered from Rabaul that the 41st Regiment stay close to Kokoda because of the worsening situation in the Solomon Islands campaign. Nauro was Horii's version of 'close to Kokoda'. First Battalion of the 41st had remained in Rabaul when the regiment's other two battalions joined MO Operation. The intention was for it to be part of the Rabi operation, but in the end it didn't participate in that campaign. Instead, it was belatedly added to South Seas Force and joined the rest of 41st Regiment on 14 September.

Starting on 13 September, the 144th charged the defenders' positions on several fronts after a concentrated bombardment by mortars and Jukis, followed by a pounding with the mountain gun. Kuwada Unit moved in on the left, Horie Unit on the right. Grenades and gunfire from the higher ground enabled the defenders to keep the attack force at bay. Booby traps, grenades tied to trip wires, had been laid in the bush for patrols trying to infiltrate the defensive perimeter. On one occasion, the Japanese rushed up the ridge in a torrential downpour and the best part of a platoon was wiped out. It wasn't until late the following day that they managed to gain a foothold on the ridge, on its eastern flank, but they were unable to press the advantage any further.

The breakthrough the attackers were probing for came on the 15th. A militia unit in the ridgeline's mid-section defences had put its weapons to one side, ordered to dig its trenches deeper. Sentries had either not been posted or were distracted when a stalking Nishida Platoon rushed their position. With weapons out of reach, the Australians were defenceless. The section that was taken was a high point along the ridgeline. From it, the Japanese could fire down on defensive positions in both directions along the line.[42]

Counter-attacks failed to dislodge the Japanese from their new vantage point and the Australian command elected to withdraw further, to the next and last major ridgeline on the Kokoda Track. Imita Ridge, facing Ioribaiwa Ridge across the broad Ua-Ule Creek valley, was to be the Allied last stand. Behind it sat Port Moresby, and the Japanese knew it. 'Over there was Moresby,' wrote Lieutenant Nakahashi, 'the object of our invasion, which had become an obsession.'[43] The officers readied them for a final desperate charge to Moresby. Soldiers on both sides developed chronic coughs from the chilly nights. Sometimes the evening brought heavy, bitterly cold rain and gale-force winds shrieking and moaning through the trees. If it didn't rain, the still of night would be punctuated by coughing from the opposite lines while each army waited for the other to make a move. Nobody blinked.

The Japanese supply line had virtually ground to a halt, and the men were on the brink of starvation. The official ration had fallen to two *go* of rice (about three cups of cooked rice daily) for active soldiers and one-and-a-half *go* for others. The trickle of supply coming along the track was often being taken by men on the way, just as hungry as those at the front.[44] Lieutenant Hirano's men had carried their sick and wounded back to Isurava, but in drawing provisions there they found they would be returning almost empty-handed.

Exhausted and famished, the troops set about to install themselves securely enough on the ridge to resist any counter-attack. They dug their distinctive single-man foxholes with connecting trenches, and weapons pits for the Jukis and other artillery. The next morning, a platoon probed forward of the ridge down towards Ua-Ule Creek, in two lines led by

Soldiers of the 44th Infantry Regiment march through the streets of Kochi prior to deployment in China, November 1937.

Marching away from Asakura railway station to regimental headquarters, the 44th Regiment returns from China carrying the ashes of comrades who were killed.

Japanese troops follow the Australians who fled to the south after the capture of Rabaul.

A Japanese infantry regiment departs from Rabaul.

Troops of the Imperial Japanese Army (IJA) on board a landing barge heading for the Papuan shore.

A Special Naval Landing Party (SNLP) unit wades ashore.

The objective of MO Operation, Port Moresby in the 1940s.

A unit of South Seas Force sets out along the Kokoda Track.

Japanese soldiers haul their
mountain gun along the
Kokoda Track.

An officer marks a blaze on a tree indicating direction for troops following.

The view from Ioribaiwa Ridge of bombardment of Australian positions on Imita Ridge, September 1942.

The interior of a
Japanese defensive
bunker at Duropa
Plantation near Buna.

The exterior of a
Japanese dugout
at Buna.

A defensive
position dug under
exposed roots
on the northern
coastland.

Japanese soldiers washing in Papua.

Swamplands on the northern coastal plains.

American troops wading through a swamp near Buna.

General Stuart tanks put out of action at Duropa Plantation.

Emaciated Japanese captured at Buna

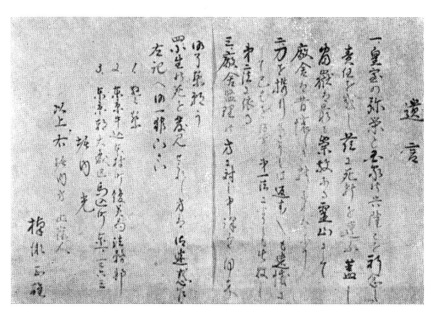

The letter left by Colonel Kusunose before committing suicide near Mt Fuji.

(Left) Major-General Tomitaro Horii, Commander of South Seas Force. (Right) Lieutenant-Colonel Masanobu Tsuji, who gave the unauthorised go ahead to MO Operation.

Colonel Masao Kusunose.

Colonel Kusunose, Major-General Horii and Lieutenant-Colonel Tanaka at Katsuharahama Beach, Kochi, before leaving for Bonin Islands, September 1941.

Papuan campaign survivors in Singapore, 1943: (left to right) unknown officer, Lieutenant Sakamoto, Colonel Tsukamoto, Captain Hamada, Lieutenant Yamasake and Lieutenant Nakahashi.

Colonel Shigemi Yamamoto, Commander of 144th Regiment.

Sergeant Kazuo Tsunoda, who operated for a short time out of Buna airfield.

Sadashige Imanishi.

Kokichi Nishimura.

Yukiharu Yamasaki.

Yuki Shimada.

No service photo of Yori–ichi
Yokoyama survives. They were all
in his home in Hiroshima when
the atomic bomb was dropped on
6 August 1945.

Yokoyama drops mini–sandals into the Kumusi River for the spirits of
soldiers killed in Papua.

a sword-wielding officer. Crossing a patch of kunai grass, they were cut down by enemy fire, a fusillade of about two deafening and deadly minutes followed by a quick withdrawal. After that timely lesson, patrols were much more cautious.

Horii set up his headquarters at Mawai, at the bottom of the valley behind Ioribaiwa Ridge. Colonel Kusunose was brought through on his stretcher, showing signs of recovery. On the 15th, Horii issued Operation Order A-115, announcing an advance to Port Moresby on the 20th. He assured his troops that the enemy was 'in a state of confusion'.[45] The next day he sent a message to the front: 'The regiment will secure the Ioribaiwa area and prepare for future offensives.'[46] Horii privately believed the attack would not start until supplies were replenished.[47] However, he needed to keep up the men's morale with the expectation of the final step in this long and tortuous journey. His plan was to scour the villages around Mawai for food and move support troops back to carry provisions. The 41st was to start withdrawing with its commander, Colonel Yazawa, while Koiwai Battalion would remain at Mawai under Horii's direct command. The troops on the ridge, meanwhile, dug their foxholes and trenches, their strength ebbing for lack of food, awaiting the order for the final assault that would secure fresh supplies.

By late September, South Seas Force was slowly starving. Rations were down to 1 *go* of race a day. Earlier in the month, Allied planes had destroyed supply barges at Buna and Sanananda and the airfield at Buna. They were constantly disabling the bridge at Wairopi as soon as engineers repaired it. At Ioribaiwa men searched the abandoned Australian dugouts, now filling with rain water, for scraps left behind. They foraged in nearby villages, eating tree roots, taro and sugar cane. Some became disorderly and argumentative. Military discipline got harder to maintain. Most of the men stoically kept up their spirit, a testimony to their training. Horii would appeal to their military pride with announcements from time to time. One 'Message of Instruction' said in part, 'Traversing mud more than knee-deep, clambering over steep precipices, bearing uncomplainingly the heavy weight of artillery ammunition, our men overcame the shortage of our supplies, and we succeeded in surmounting the Stanley Range. No pen or word can depict adequately the magnitude of the hardships suffered.'[48] He was playing to the gallery, but for how long would they be content with rhetoric?

The general was in a quandary. He was aware that intelligence estimated that 20,000 Allied troops were now garrisoned in Port Moresby. He realised the IJA's resources were being redirected towards the struggle for Guadalcanal. Rabaul and Tokyo were concerned about the possibility of an Allied landing near Buna, prompting Hyakutake's order for priority to be given to establishing a battalion at Buna. Five days later, another order had come for front-line troops to be pulled back to occupy a position north of Mawai. Either these orders failed to reach Horii or he ignored them.[49] He knew a command to withdraw was imminent but he didn't tell his troops, who were impatient to advance to finish the job and fill their crying bellies. Operation Order A-115, with its September 20 attack date, passed unactivated under an afternoon downpour. Two attempts to airlift food supplies from Rabaul were turned back by poor weather until supplies were successfully dropped over Kokoda on the 23rd. News of the drop came down the line, lifting spirits at Ioribaiwa, but news travels faster than food. The provisions only trickled down the track. And none reached the end of the line.

Chapter 10

'Change the marching direction'

At his makeshift base at Mawai General Horii received a telegram on 24 September from General Hitoshi Imamura, Commander of the Southern Area Army. Imamura had moved his headquarters to Rabaul. 'Stop attacking Port Moresby and wait for further instructions at present position,' the communiqué read. That night a second message came from General Hyakutake, Commander of Seventeenth Army and next in the hierarchy after Imamura: 'Withdraw from present position to some point in the Owen Stanley Range which you may consider best for strategic purposes.'[1] This was not an order that the obstinate Horii was likely to welcome.

The journalists Okada and Sato were with photographer Katayama in the rough thatched hut they had built adjacent to South Seas Force HQ at Mawai, finishing a paltry evening meal of sweet potato. Sensing something was afoot they hurried across to Horii's tent, which had been set up on a little cleared rise. Inside, the only light came from a single candle set on a ration-can lid. The general and his staff officer, Tanaka, were sitting cross-legged on a *tatami* in the throes of earnest discussion.

'I'm not going back, not a step,' exclaimed Horii. 'Are you prepared to go back, Tanaka? How can we abandon this course after all the blood the men have shed and the hardships they've suffered? I can't give an order like that.'

Horii grasped the sword that lay beside him and added with determination, 'I will not retreat an inch. I'd rather disguise myself as a native of these mountains and stay here.'

Tanaka, short, bespectacled and youthful-looking, was silent. Deep in thought, clearly uncomfortable, he avoided his grey-haired commander's gaze. A rustling sound and a cough outside indicated the arrival of the signal squad commander with a new wireless message, a more specific order from Hyakutake.

'The Commander of South Seas Force will assemble his main strength in the Isurava and Kokoda areas and secure these as a base for future offensives. In addition, the defences in the Buna area will be strengthened.'[2] Signals intelligence from New Caledonia the day before had suggested to Rabaul that an Allied landing was imminent in eastern New Guinea or the Solomon Islands. Rabaul was not prepared to take any chances.

Whatever reservations Horii might have had about complying with an order from his immediate superior, they were put to rest by the signal that followed directly after it. Sent from Imperial Headquarters in Tokyo, it confirmed the previous order to withdraw to Buna. The order now had the imprimatur of the Emperor. It had to be obeyed without question.

Horii was crushed. The order he'd been dreading had finally come. All the sacrifices and hardship of the last two months had now been rendered futile. He must have known this was inevitable, but hoped that some miracle might get them out of their predicament. No miracle had come.

The journalists withdrew discreetly, and Tanaka left to advise regimental commanders of the fresh orders and start planning for their implementation. Horii was left alone to brood about all that might have been and so very nearly was. In the end it had amounted to nothing. To failure.

Tanaka had his work cut out advising commanders of the latest orders and persuading the officers of their necessity. Having got this far they desperately wanted to stage a last-ditch charge at Port Moresby, but the imperturbable Tanaka reasoned calmly with them: 'It would be a suicidal action even if everything started well. Supply of food's in a hopeless state and our troops are too weakened for any sustained action. We don't know how large an enemy force we would face, but reports suggest they're well reinforced. It's more than likely we are greatly outnumbered. In that case, it would be pointless suicide.'[3]

Reluctantly, the officers agreed. No matter how much their hearts wanted to finish the job, their heads said it would be they and their men who'd be finished by such a reckless action.

The torpor that had overtaken the force in the last few days slowly turned to bustle. Headquarters began sending out messages to the front positions on Ioribaiwa Ridge, instructing them to make preparations for immediate withdrawal. Colonel Sasaki, the adjutant, dashed through the cold night drizzle, back and forth between headquarters and the signal unit. Tanaka too went over to the signalman's tent to reinforce the orders and clarify any necessary detail with front-line commanders. They were not happy with the turn of events, either.

'It's all very well for a staff officer to say that,' said one agitated voice on the telephone receiver, 'but how can we artillerymen leave our guns behind? We can't. They are a part of us.'

'I know. I know how you feel,' commiserated Tanaka, always the calmer of stormy emotions, 'but it can't be helped if you are short of hands. Guns are valuable, but soldiers are more valuable. If necessary, leave your guns and ammunition. We must take every living soldier with us. Every living soldier, sick or wounded.'[4] There were few carriers this far forward on the line.

The troops dug in along Ioribaiwa Ridge were told of the new orders the next morning. Their first reaction was disbelief. Then, as belief took hold, so did shock and, for some, bitterness. They couldn't accept that the mission was to be abandoned so close to their goal. Lieutenant Hirano noted in his diary that the order came 'like a bolt out of the blue', leaving him dazed and regretting a retreat from so near to

Moresby after so many sacrifices and casualties.[5] For these soldiers, the emotion of the moment 'could not be suppressed; it was compounded by feelings of anger, sorrow and frustration'.[6] Like their officers, the men were all for making the last push to Port Moresby even in their exhausted and emaciated state. The spirit that had driven them this far might have been waning, but it still had power in it. Gradually, however, sanity prevailed. The men bowed to the inevitable and started preparing to withdraw.

Sergeant Imanishi was among those at the front. He knew the next stage was not going to be easy. 'We never knew how to retreat because we had never done it before,' he recalls. 'The order was to "change the marching direction", but we knew what it really meant. I thought the enemy would launch a counter-offensive once we started retreating, therefore we must escape quickly. Otherwise we could not resist the enemy with our strength and number of troops. I thought it would be very difficult for the weakened soldiers around me.'[7]

Nankai Shitai had no protocol for retreat. General Horii and his senior officers had to devise an ad-hoc plan to meet the circumstances. They had already seen the value of a fighting withdrawal on this terrain and, consciously or subconsciously, the Japanese planned a similar strategy to that employed by the Australians in the previous two months.

A crucial cog had now fallen out of the machinery of South Seas Force. That cog was pride in the Japanese nation and its military, a pride sustained over the months by their victories and advances. Now they were preparing to 'advance to the rear' or 'change their marching direction'. They were no longer moving forward and, in their case at least, there would be no victory. They might not have been defeated by the enemy but they had been defeated by their circumstances, of which the enemy had been a part.

The men spent the day sifting numbly through equipment and personal belongings, trying to work out what to take with them and what to leave behind, as if they were refugee families about to abandon their homeland. The soldiers who carried the heaviest load were the grenadiers. Imanishi told the grenadiers in his platoon to throw away their launchers. They had no grenades to fire and they didn't have the strength to carry them all the way back. 'The men would not throw them away, no matter how much I told them to do so,' he recalls, 'so I removed the fuses, grabbed their launchers from their hands and threw them into the jungle.' He had to push his men onto the track back to Kokoda.

'The only thing I thought of was my men's lives. I couldn't let them die in vain, so I only thought how to make them survive. Sergeants and soldiers never think about the whole military operation.'[8]

The journalist group didn't hang around. As day dawned, they hurried past troops in the rear who were also making preparations to return down the track. The newspapermen were exhausted and hungry like everyone else and didn't want to be caught up in a moving body of dispirited men that could easily descend into disorder or worse as it tried to squeeze itself back along the narrow mountain path. In any case, their rice supply had run very low. They were worried they might starve before they got to the coast.[9]

Two units were also scheduled to be early starters in the withdrawal. Stanley Detachment had been formed from Horie Battalion of the 144th, with the addition of a mountain artillery company and an engineer company. Led by Major Horie, the detachment was to set up defensive positions leading up to the high ground overlooking Eora Creek. Their task was to delay any Australian pursuit of withdrawing troops. Koiwai Battalion of the 41st was to protect the rear. Kuwada Battalion of the 144th was also to start withdrawing its wounded and artillery that evening, to be followed by two of its companies and battalion HQ the following evening. The third company, with its machine-gun squad, would advance 500 metres as rearguard cover to disguise the withdrawal.[10]

The Australians were beginning to explore the strength of Japanese defences, unaware of the momentous changes afoot. They had spent seven days hauling an artillery cannon, a twenty-five-pounder, on wheels and ropes up the steep, muddy 'Golden Stairs' from Uberi, and set it up on Imita Ridge, where they had dug in. It was the first time the Australians had brought heavy artillery into this fray. As soon as the cannon started firing, it was clear it would be to no avail. Its shells fell short of Ioribaiwa Ridge on the other side of the wide Ua-Ule valley. Frustrated, the Australians returned to a familiar tactic. As soon as the Kuwada rearguard moved forward they subjected it to a frontal attack, but were driven back by artillery fire.[11]

Early on the morning of 26 September, the sick and wounded of South Seas Force were assembled at Mawai. In pouring rain, the remaining dead were buried and the living prayed to their gods. A few defiant rounds from the mountain gun were fired at the Australian lines before the gun was rolled down into the jungle out of sight. There it remains somewhere in the tangled undergrowth, to this day. 'This at least gave an uplift to our downcast spirits and to those of our dead comrades,' writes the artilleryman Nakahashi.[12]

The withdrawal of all remaining troops began at 10 p.m. and continued through the night under moonlight. There was minimal fuss or conversation. There wasn't much to talk about. Everyone knew the meaning of this occasion, and nothing anyone could say was capable of changing it or alleviating the intense feeling of disappointment. The rearguard 9th Company was the last to go. Its men looked back wistfully at the unoccupied ground they had so triumphantly taken ten days earlier before following their compatriots on the long path back to the northern coast.

Although there was no immediate Australian pursuit, the withdrawal was carried out under dreadful physical conditions, captured in the memoir of Major Koiwai: 'Our bodies were completely fatigued, so climbing even the smallest hill required a great effort. The majority of members of the unit were carrying wounded on stretchers. My battalion's 7th Company was meant to be protecting the rear, but they were carrying casualties from the field hospital, as were members of the force's wireless radio unit.'[13]

With food almost nonexistent, every step seemed to sap the last of each soldier's strength. The stream of bodies moved at a slow shuffle, trailing up and along the Maguli Range before reaching the horribly familiar series of ravines and razorbacks, 'counting each step, gasping for each breath'.

'Despite some encouragement to struggle through pain,' recalls Koiwai, 'many were stooped over, their eyes filled with tears and without even the strength to urge themselves on. My heart was filled with sorrow.'[14]

◆　◆　◆

On the day the Japanese abandoned Ioribaiwa the Allies moved three battalions into the field of battle, crossing the Ua–Ule Creek valley the following day. Unit diarists were puzzled by the apparent inactivity on the Japanese side, but no one drew the obvious conclusion. The 2/25th Battalion diary noted for 27 September: 'Quiet night. No activity on Bn [battalion] front. Patrol activity—report no enemy in area to W.P. Patrol from D Coy report enemy behind barricade on track.'[15] On 28 September, much the same: 'Quiet night. No activity on Bn front.'[16]

That night they shelled the unoccupied ridge and at dawn swept gunfire across it from right to left. Emboldened by the lack of response, two companies—about 200 men—scaled the ridge unopposed to find it empty apart from scattered dead and dying. Caught by surprise by this turn of events and alert to the possibility it was a trap, the Australians were wary of moving forward.

About two weeks before, as a sop to General MacArthur's criticisms of the Australian performance on the Kokoda Track, the Australian Commander-in-Chief, General Thomas Blamey, had relieved Brigadier Potts of command of Maroubra Force, the force fighting there. Next, he replaced his overall commander of New Guinea operations, Lieutenant-General Rowell, with Lieutenant-General Herring. Conscious of the tensions at the highest level of command, Brigadier Eather, the new Maroubra Force commander, gathered his troops at Ioribaiwa the following day. Patrols sent forward reported that the Japanese had withdrawn past Nauro. It was not until 2 October that a whole battalion began pursuing the retreating army. By then, South Seas Force had a start of six days.

Americans were now brought into land operations in the Kokoda campaign for the first time. General MacArthur sent 126th US Infantry Regiment along the Jaure Trail running to the north from Kapa Kapa, sixty-six kilometres east of Port Moresby. The object was to get to the Wairopi crossing of the Kumusi River first and cut off the retreating Japanese. However, the Japanese didn't repair the Wairopi bridge after it was bombed yet again on 4 October, so crossing the swollen river was going to be difficult with or without Australians to greet them. The Americans met no opposition along the little-used track but the going was tough for the inexperienced national servicemen, who in many places had to cut their way through matted jungle. The troops on the Jaure Trail called it 'one green hell'.[17]

Not all Japanese sick and wounded were capable of making the arduous journey back over the Owen Stanley Range. Those too ill or starving were left by the track for fate to take its course. As the forces withdrew, many of the immobile sick and wounded were given two grenades, one for the enemy and one for themselves.[18] It was assumed the Allies would not be taking prisoners, but in any case the soldiers had been taught that being taken prisoner was a shameful thing. Twelve men left at Nauro soon died of starvation or sickness or probably both.[19] Private Yamamoto, from a rifle unit of Kuwada Battalion, was lying down sick with diarrhoea when he was picked up by the advancing Australians near Ioribaiwa. He was taken prisoner.[20]

The walking wounded, afflicted with malaria, foot-rot or a fever of some sort, moved ahead a few steps at a time, leaning with both hands on long wooden sticks.[21] Some shook violently, others stopped from time to time to deal with the diarrhoea that ravaged them despite their lack of food. Private Nishimura was among these men, in pain even though his shoulder had been strapped and dressed. He made his way back to Kokoda unattached to any unit.[22]

The sick and wounded who were thought to have some chance of survival were carried out on stretchers. Few native or Formosan stretcher-bearers were this far down the track, so emaciated troops had no choice but to carry out their own wounded. The wounded were under great personal pressure, conscious that they were adding to the strain on their comrades, who were often barely able to get themselves through the series of deep ravines that took them up to the peak line of the Owen Stanleys. The stretcher cases would cry out from time to time, 'Please leave us here' and 'Let us die', but the bearers pressed on stoically, never letting on what the effort cost them. If nothing changed patients and carriers would die together, and some already had.

Some officers found the inner steel to do the only thing that could resolve this dilemma. Soldiers struggling under their load were ordered to put the stretchers down and go on. The hopelessly wounded were then shot where they lay, away from the direct gaze of their comrades. Those with a realistic chance of recovery continued on their journey, carried by anyone fit enough to support them.[23]

◆ ◆ ◆

Major Kobayashi of 41st Regiment's 3rd Battalion had been recalled from the Owen Stanleys while the front line was still at Ioribaiwa, and transferred to new duties in Japan. Grabbing the opportunity to impress on Rabaul the full extent of his plight, General Horii instructed Kobayashi to give Seventeenth Army command a clear picture of the conditions of battle in Papua.

'The supply situation for South Seas Force has already reached a crisis,' Kobayashi reported to Rabaul on 6 October. 'The number of troops who are collapsing continues to rise. Allied pressure mounts daily with no improvement in sight. An immediate transport of supplies by destroyer is needed to ease the situation.'[24]

Seventeenth Army was desperately trying to reverse Japan's fortunes in Guadalcanal, the first stage of operations having failed. The lack of supplies to Kokoda would have to be endured. General Hyakutake did, however, assign several staff officers to preparation of a revival of RE Operation, the sea invasion of Port Moresby.

Rabaul hadn't given up on MO Operation either. Hyakutake saw the withdrawal as only a temporary setback in the grand plan to secure Port Moresby against the Allied counter-offensive. As the counter-offensive had already commenced at Guadalcanal it's questionable whether this objective was still of great importance to the Japanese cause, but Hyaku-take was determined to achieve it nonetheless. On 30 September, he sent General Horii an updated set of orders. South Seas Force was to prepare an offensive base at Isurava and secure defensive positions in the Buna and Giruwa areas. The road from Giruwa to Kokoda was to be repaired, as was the horse trail from Kokoda to Isurava. With those measures accomplished, Horii's men were to secure a foothold once more on the southern side of the Owen Stanley Range. Clearly Hyakutake hadn't lost faith in Nankai Shitai; after all, they had achieved much so far in very difficult conditions. But the general was unable to see from his office in Rabaul how profoundly this battle-weary force had changed.

The 38th Division, under General Sano, was made up of three infantry regiments, mountain artillery, engineer and supply regiments, signals, munitions and medical units, all up a formidable force of about 20,000 troops. The division started arriving at Rabaul on 6 October with a view to re-launching the Rabi operation as a staging post for another attempt at a sea invasion of Port Moresby. General Horii telegraphed Sano to welcome the move. It meant the occupation of Moresby hadn't dropped off the Imperial HQ agenda and South Seas Force's sacrifices might not have been in vain.

Nothing would come of it. Horii's new hopes would soon be dashed in another false dawn. With the battle for Guadalcanal intensifying, 38th Division was deployed there instead and the Rabi operation was postponed once again.

The force on the Kokoda Track remained a solitary outpost of imperial ambition, battered by circumstance. At first stupefied by the abandonment of all they had striven for, the soldiers had finally understood that the unimaginable was happening: Japanese soldiers were turning their backs on the enemy, running away. And with that insight came a changed mentality that Okada detected and would later describe: 'They were seized with an instinctive desire to live. Neither history nor education had any meaning to them now. Discipline was completely forgotten. Each tried for his life to flee faster than his comrades, and the confusion was worse than it had been at the supply dump. During short respites on the way, we often repeated the popular Japanese saying, "Where there is life, there is hope."'[25]

The experience of returning along the track was different for different men. Once he had recovered from the shock of being ordered to withdraw, Hirano moved back with his unit in a fairly cohesive, mutually supportive fashion. Stragglers dropped behind, but the others would wait for them to catch up. The group eventually rejoined its battalion at Kagi to build defensive positions on top of a hill covered with bamboo thickets. The privation continued, however. One night was spent under pouring rain; on another, dinner was a handful of rice found by Hirano's corporal.[26]

On the other hand, Lieutenant Sakamoto, whose platoon had dragged their Juki to the top of Mission Ridge, witnessed a slow deterioration of everything that had sustained the men's spirits during the advance. They started out searching in the moonlight for food and smoking dried wild berry grass. Within a few days they had a handful of rice left and soon were spending the day gathering rice that had been spilt along the way over four weeks before. Finally, breakfast was 'only a sip of rice gruel'. Two-thirds of the men, including Sakamoto, came down with beriberi. Their eyesight was declining and so was their physical strength.

Sakamoto became increasingly despondent, complaining of the growing disrespect from lower ranks and that no one would help him make a fire when he woke in the middle of the night. He noted that discontented soldiers were grumbling about battalion administration, then joined them, complaining about the company commander staying back in Kokoda to ride a horse and Lieutenant Nagano taking himself off the battlefield. Sakamoto concluded philosophically that a man 'shows his true character when faced by hunger and hardship; he becomes rowdy and rude'.[27]

The Japanese spirit was weakening. Some of the soldiers had deserted. Rumours were rife. Men were saying that Lieutenant Ino had left Buna without permission and returned to Rabaul. Many of the troops were walking on automatic pilot, conversation between them virtually non-existent. They had no strength or interest in anything but walking. All they could think about was getting to the other end of the line. If they were wounded or fell ill there was no one to look after them, no room for altruism. Every man was doing his best to drag himself back to the coast. Each knew by now that he would lose his own life if he tried to save his fallen comrades. Anyone who had any strength left was already helping the wounded and sick.

Men lay motionless by the track, unable to walk from hunger and weariness. Some wandered around directionless, no longer knowing what their purpose was. All meaning had dissipated in sickness and exhaustion. Some Japanese were found by the advancing Australians sitting in a daze by the track. Corpses were examined by the medicos and found to be wasted, evidently starved. Some, in their desperate hunger, had eaten poisonous fruits and roots.

Very few prisoners were taken by the advancing force. Their own supply line was already too stretched; they had no desire to share their meagre provisions unnecessarily. Private Okino, the reluctant soldier posted to the packhorse unit, was one of the lucky ones. He had been told to make his own way back to Kokoda three days after arriving at Ioribaiwa. Exhausted and with very little food, he threw his rifle away and struggled back down the track. He wore the rubber-soled, 'camel-toed' canvas shoes called *tabi*, his army-issue boots having rotted off his feet.

Okino was sharing a native hut with a man called Tomiya he would tell his interrogators when they were found by a patrol from the Australian advance. The two men were tied to trees and told the main force would pick them up. Tomiya broke free and bolted but he did not untie Okino, who was too weak to free himself. He was brought in, shaking on a stretcher, half-starved and weakened by disease. Two weeks later he tried to wrestle with his prison guard, but had no recollection of it when interrogated the next day.[28]

On the Kokoda Track, the retreating troops were driven by the desire to escape starvation and the increasing air raids. Rumbling from enemy guns drew nearer. American air attacks grew more frequent. Nerves became strained every time the men crossed a patch of open ground without jungle cover, listening for the sound of approaching aircraft, for 'the roar of propellers that seemed to burst our eardrums and pierce our intestines, the ratatat of machine-guns, the sound of cannon fire that streamed forth'.[29]

The men of Headquarters Unit had been less involved in the fighting getting to Ioribaiwa. With their greater reserves of energy, they were constantly delayed picking up the sick and wounded on the way. At key points a platoon of the Yokoyama engineer unit would wait for the last man to pass through, then blow up the cliff side or cut off the log bridges to delay the Australians in pursuit. Those, like Okina, who hadn't kept up were left behind with the enemy. But still, every day the advancing force got a little closer and the air attacks became more vigorous.

◆ ◆ ◆

The press party and small independent units moved back quickly. They were among the first to retrace their steps down and through the Efogi ravine. Seizo Okada would later write about the experience, so extraordinarily surreal that he couldn't be sure he hadn't passed through some portal to the netherworld, a ghostly place suspended between life and afterlife. A dark path led through large cypress trees down to a valley buried below the forest canopy. A rumbling sound growled in the unseen depths. Rounding a rock, they saw 'a furious white serpent of water' plummeting from thirty metres above and roaring as it struck the giant boulders below. The humidity was high; mosses hung limp and dank in bunches on the trunks of trees like thick, shaggy uncombed hair. The branches overhead were so matted no sunlight was able to seep through. There was no day or night there, only a 'pale twilight and everything looked as wet as though it were deep under water'.

In the eternal dusk, bodies lay scattered about. These were men killed in the battles here less than four weeks before, and they had started to decompose. A suffocating stench, 'like that of burning old cloth', pervaded the place, the smell of rotting human beings. They were sprawled on the jungle floor in a range of postures, as if put there by a sculptor in the grip of some devastating insight into the depths of human despair. Some bodies were still standing, some were squatting. Some had fallen forward, others rolled on their sides, limbs sticking out in all directions like broken branches. What struck Okada was the presence on all their bellies of 'something like a heap of sand, black, glittering and wriggling all the time'.

He writes: 'I approached one of the bodies and found that it was a heap of maggots bred in the belly, where the rotting process seemed to set in before any other part of the body. They were little creatures about an inch long, with numerous slender legs like those of a centipede, and closely lined across their backs, which glittered like black lacquered armour. They crowded in a heap on the belly which had fallen in, pushing, fighting, dropping to the ground, scrambling up, eager to bite into the rotten bowels.'[30]

The trousers on these dead men were lying flat on the ground, as if waiting on an ironing board. The flesh that had once clung to their legs had melted away. On one body, hair and skin had gone from the skull; all that remained was the bone, exposed and white. On another the skin and flesh had parted from the chest, leaving ribs like chalk, bright in the forest's crepuscular light.

Okada turned a corner into an even gloomier part of the path. In front of him was a spectral figure moving noiselessly through the trees. It might have been the walking dead.

'Give me something to eat,' said a feeble, whispery voice in Japanese. 'Give me something to eat.'

His colourless face was bordered by black hair, and a piece of white cloth was draped over his emaciated, dark brown body. He must have been lying on the ground nearby, close to death, and struggled to his feet when he heard footsteps approaching. He staggered out onto the path. Okada recalled: '"Give me something to eat," he repeated over and over in his weak, husky voice, stretching out a thin hand which trembled like a piece of paper. I took a half-bitten rice-ball and a tiny taro out of my kit, put them in his outstretched hand and dashed away without ever turning my head.'[31]

Okada and his colleagues climbed up out of the ravine to Kagi, up the slope down which the all-night lantern procession had taken place, seemingly in another lifetime. Now they were with the vanguard of soldiers streaming back along the track. The journalists went on through Kokoda to Giruwa, on the coast.

The Australian advance reached Mission Ridge to be greeted by the stench of death and the same gruesome vision of scattered bodies, in treetops and in trenches, that Seizo Okada had seen a few days earlier. The entire retreating South Seas Force had passed along the ridge and across Efogi River since then. The Japanese were noted as having been buried under mounds, each marked with a single large pole with Japanese characters painted on it. A neat vine fence was staked around each mound. It appeared that the Japanese buried their own dead only. Australian soldiers remained where they fell, in the posture of their death. Some of the carriers from Rabaul had also died here, their corpses scattered about with the Australian ones. The Australian dead had not been interfered with. They still clutched their weapons and their haversacks were still on their backs, unopened.[32]

It is interesting to examine differences in the two eyewitness accounts of this macabre scene, both written some years later. Given the circumstances of the Japanese withdrawal, it is unlikely that any of their dead would have been buried with the attention to painted poles and vine fences reported by the Australian observer, William Crooks. Any burials must have taken place during the advance, before decomposition set in. Okada and Crooks would have described substantially the same scene with the same bodies. The Japanese writer doesn't ascribe nationality to the soldiers he saw. In fact, the degree of disintegration he notes suggests it could no longer be determined. Crooks describes the dead as Australians, and a few New Guineans.

Perhaps this indicates a need for caution with first-hand reports from the battlefield. They can be subjective and emotion-driven to the point of unreliability. Soldiers in the heat of battle, battered not only by enemy ordnance but by fear, privation and prejudice, don't always see things as they are but as they think they might or should be, under a weight of influences. Time and memory can also be factors. Even detailed descriptions may not hold up under analysis. They might tell of a torrential downpour on a day when it didn't rain. This doesn't mean people are lying, only that their testimony can be unreliable for quite understandable reasons. Sometimes an accurate version of an event can never be obtained, even when there were eyewitnesses to it. History can be fiction, a retelling of events as they felt, not as they were. Everyone relates his own truth but, when several people describe the same event, whose truth should prevail?

Chapter II

Buying time

The 144th Regiment and Koiwai Battalion from the 41st stopped withdrawing when they got to Kokoda and assembled around the village to restore their fighting strength. It was far from easy. The daily rice ration was increased to two *go* (360 millilitres) a day, but it was still insufficient. On the evening of 4 October, 10,000 forty-day portions of provisions were unloaded at Buna from the transport *Yamaura Maru*.[1] Without follow-up deliveries, that could be only a short-term solution to the supply crisis. Four days later, two months more of provisions could not be unloaded from the same ship because of air attacks. Supply remained in a critical state.

Colonel Kusunose had become increasingly ill on the trek back with a return of his malarial fever. The relapse was so severe he couldn't take effective command, even from a stretcher, and was evacuated to the rear. Colonel Tsukamoto took temporary command of the 144th, but the promotion did nothing to soften his relationship with his troops. Lieutenant Hirano's diary in early October alternates between accounts of digging for taro and of carping inspections by the new regimental commander. On the 3rd, as the platoon was preparing to depart, that 'thundering old man', Tsukamoto, 'passed by and started to bawl us out again'. On the 8th, he came for an unexpected inspection 'with his usual fault-finding attitude'. On the 11th he inspected again, and on the 13th he 'came again to nag'. Hirano, it appears, did not look forward to his commander's visits.[2]

At North Efogi, the Kokoda Track separated into two paths. The old prewar mail route went through Kagi. The other track diverted towards the treeless alpine plain of Myola, then traversed the upper reaches of the Efogi River and crossed over The Gap. The separate routes rejoined across Eora Creek at a junction the Australians called Templeton's Crossing. Stanley Detachment had departed early from Ioribaiwa in order to set up holding positions forward of and along Eora Creek. In readiness for the Australian forces, forward defenders occupied strategic sites on both branches of the track as they approached Templeton's Crossing. As with the Australian tactic nearly two months before, their objective was to buy time. This would allow fully fortified defences to be prepared on the northern coastal plains.

Stanley Detachment waited along sections of the track in dugout pits, well disguised and with covering fire from neighbouring positions. They occupied high vantage points, well placed to stall the approaching Australians. Details of the ensuing encounters are often difficult to ascertain from the various accounts. To soldiers of both sides, the Kokoda campaign was a story of trudging through a succession of mostly deserted Papuan villages in the most appalling of conditions. The names of these villages, if they ever heard them, would have been of no consequence. Survival was paramount in their minds.

It is only since the war that there have been attempts by veterans to reconstruct events from stored memories and situate them geographically. The Japanese and the Australians often had different names for the same place and sometimes gave the same name to different places. The place the Japanese knew as Gap, for instance, is about five kilometres from the place the Allies refer to as The Gap.[3] Names like Brigade Hill (above Mission Ridge) and Templeton's Crossing were given to those locations *ad hoc* by the Allies and were entirely unknown to the Japanese. As a result there are discrepancies and disjunctures in the various accounts, although they tell a consistent core story of the Eora Creek battle. It took until the end of October for the Australian attack to prevail over the entrenched Stanley Detachment in its well-placed defences, and with high casualties on both sides.

At the high point of the track's Kagi branch, Japanese forward defences were dug in along the narrow, densely covered ridge near Mount Bellamy. Foxholes were well-camouflaged, covered with logs and bushes. Japanese positions on spur tops enabled pre-emptive fire on any approaching enemy. The high ground provided both ample vision and concealment, but the extreme conditions on the highest parts of the Owen Stanleys made the wait torturous, damp and miserable. Downpours were heavier and more frequent. Trees covered with moss continued to drop water, even when the cloudburst stopped for a while. Under the canopy it was always raining. Fires could not be lit because of the continual dampness. Nights were cold and wet, with low cloud often shrouding the hills like fog. It was sometimes difficult to see a patrol approaching, but it was even harder for the patrol to see the concealed gun-pits. Thick undergrowth made movement difficult except along the narrow track, which fell away steeply on both sides. Patrols were forced to walk in single file, rendering the lead scout particularly vulnerable.

Two AIF battalions made their way up the track to its highest parts, still uncertain where the retreating invaders had got to. Patrols from one of the battalions—the 2/25th—moved up both paths from North Efogi, each straying into the line of fire of Japanese defenders on 8 October and again the next day, the first contact since Ioribaiwa. They withdrew both times with their casualties.[4]

On the Myola arm, units of Stanley Detachment had dug into positions forward of their main force. In a moss forest above the upper Efogi River they occupied another netherworld location, with lofty canopies of vegetation cutting out direct sunlight and with 'mud and soft, springy green mould' below.[5] The glow of phosphorescent moss and fireflies flitting about at night added a magical eeriness to the scene. With Japanese positions located by the 2/25th patrol, the 2/33rd AIF Battalion moved up from Myola on the 12th. Concealed in their muddy holes, the defenders

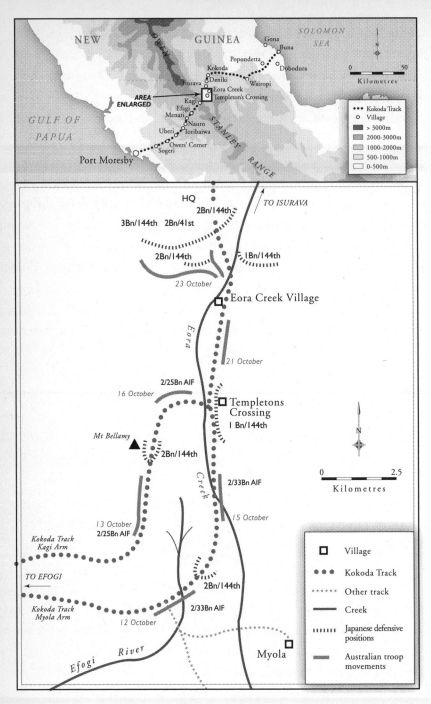

The Japanese defensive positions around Eora Creek and
Australian troop movements, October 1942

watched for the enemy's approach through gaps in the covering, adrenaline and determination temporarily sweeping aside the hunger, exhaustion and sickness that gripped them in calmer moments. The Australians had to find a path over fallen trees and up steep ridges, pushing their way as noiselessly as possible through thick curtains of undergrowth in search of machine-gun pits. About the only way a Juki could be silenced was with a grenade tossed into a firing slit. When the Australians were close the defenders fired a woodpecker or lighter machine-gun, cutting a swathe across the forest floor. The opening salvo would usually drive the patrol back but it would soon return, circling for a better point of approach, probing while trying to avoid fire from positions nearby.

On the first day of the moss forest engagement, a report filtered back that one of 2/33rd AIF's companies had taken the first ridge and driven the occupants back 300 metres. The battalion spent the rest of the day trying to gain the ridge that had reportedly been taken.[6] Reports moving around a battlefield are often little more than wishful thinking, but the attack pressed on regardless of this one and the defenders resisted. Forward dugouts were shelled the next morning by mortars brought in by the attacking force. Japanese mortars were fired in reply. An Australian company, which had set out the previous day to outflank the entrenched troops, launched a dawn attack but made no significant gains. The Japanese were effectively holding a line for over a kilometre up to Templeton's Crossing. Terrain on the south side of the ridge below the defenders was difficult to climb, a flanking company reported, making a surprise approach next to impossible.

On one occasion a group of Japanese were smoking near lean-tos in the main camp when an enemy patrol appeared over a ridge twenty metres away, taking both groups equally by surprise. Both tried to take the initiative, and both inflicted damage before the Australians withdrew to a ravine for the night. They ate cold rations in the chilly rain; the Japanese ate almost nothing.[7]

The Australians continued to be held at bay with mortar fire. A forward thrust was stopped in its tracks with grenades. By the third afternoon, heavy rain brought a lull in the action. It also caused an Allied air attack to be called off but the Japanese, unaware of this, began to withdraw. In the rain and under cover of the gathering darkness they pulled back towards Templeton's Crossing, where the Kagi track crossed the creek and rejoined the Myola one. The going was difficult in the dark, with that section of the track deep in mud. They blew up the first bridge over Eora Creek, enabling their rearguard to stage a nuisance ambush while the Australians picked their way across the swollen stream.

On the 15th, a militia battalion moved up to the front lines on the ridge and found the Japanese had gone after holding up the advancing troops for three days. In withdrawing, they had used the same delaying tactics that had served the Australians so well when the positions were reversed: resisting attacks stubbornly for a while then, when enough time had been bought, withdrawing to a new defensive position and starting the process all over again. There was nothing to be gained by fighting to the bitter end. The aim now was to hold up the Australians long enough for Japanese forces to consolidate their defences in the northern swamp-lands, where this time the Allied supply line would be stretched.

Meanwhile, on the equally damp and mossy Kagi track, where the other forward lines waited for an Australian advance, the AIF's 2/25th Battalion had hurried forward to cut off the Japanese at Templeton's Crossing. The 2/25th had received a report about the taking of the ridge that had not in fact been taken. The Japanese were supposedly withdraw-ing before the 2/33rd. In their haste to join the other battalion, forward scouts rushed into ambush positions and came under sustained fire from Japanese snipers near Mount Bellamy. Most of the advancing troops didn't see the hidden bunkers until they were on top of them and the defenders had opened fire with their jabbering Jukis. Retaliatory rifle fire under these circumstances was often ineffective. The Australians would have to circle the fortification and crawl close enough to lob in a grenade, no easy task in this terrain. The steepness of the ridges adjacent to the Japanese positions prevented outflanking. Fire lines were well placed and used relentlessly, so that little ground was gained. The Australians found themselves unable to make any further progress by the time night fell.

The defenders on the Kagi track continued to hold back Australian probing attacks over the next two days. Mortars were moved in but, with the Japanese bunkers so well concealed, their effect was fairly scattered. Several mortar rounds failed to explode as a result of being damaged when air-dropped in boxes to get them up the track quickly.[8] Mortars that managed to hit a defensive post and grenades lobbed in by men who managed to get to a post caused some casualties among the Japanese. On the other hand, forward scouts of Australian patrols were picked off from time to time. Casualties weren't heavy, but they were persistent on both sides. The Japanese had laid out a barricade of timber and wire in front of their positions. One attacking unit pushed through to the barricade but had to withdraw under sustained fire.

Wet days continued with no supplies getting through to the defenders. The nights were wet and bitterly cold, but quiet. The Japanese were not attacking, and the Australians were not interested in night attacks. On the third night, the Japanese quietly left their dugouts and withdrew behind the next line of defence, at Templeton's Crossing. An early morning patrol found the positions vacated, and the Australian battalion was at last able to press on.

Japanese positions at Templeton's Crossing overlooked the Eora Creek bridge. The advancing Australians didn't know it, but these were still forward defences. The main force was further back towards Isurava, sitting on a ridge overlooking Eora Creek village. With the time available—the best part of three weeks—and with the luxury of attached engineers, Stanley Detachment had built solid bunkers in a network of defences around the main camp. They were heavily fortified with logs, camouflaged and well positioned to cover approaches down the opposite slope to Eora Creek. Gun-pits were connected by fire trenches, allowing gunners to move rapidly between positions. In some places, tunnels connected bunkers. Jukis poked out from firing slits built into the foxhole's structure.

The defensive network had been reinforced. Tsukamoto Battalion, temporarily without its commander, who was still acting commander of the regiment, was ordered forward from Kokoda. Men led by Lieutenant Hirano and Sergeant Imanishi were in this group, joining Stanley

Detachment on the 16th. Hirano's platoon was sent further forward to Templeton's Crossing, while Imanishi's was sent to reinforce the area sloping down to Eora Creek, immediately in front of the main defensive perimeter up on the northern ridge.

While the Japanese main force waited above the Eora Creek valley, Australian patrols moving along the bank at Templeton's Crossing were subjected to mortar and machine-gun fire by their forward defence. A mountain gun targeted the area around the creek crossing where Australians were gathering. Patrols were sent out by Major Horie, more to keep pressure on the enemy than with any serious thought of counterattack, and they were soon pushed back. Hirano's platoon was among those covering this section of the track.

The Australian command had brought in three fresh battalions to relieve the men who had so far carried the burden of the forward thrust. The two days that followed saw a grim battle of attrition. The Japanese had occupied two spurs between Templeton's Crossing and Eora Creek village, sniping at forward scouts of a patrol forced by the terrain to move in single file. The Australians advanced on the defenders with grenades and machine-gun fire, using trees for cover. Jukis pinned them down, but their gun-pit fell to grenade attack by a group that had circled around it. A second Japanese machine-gun nest was captured. The defenders managed to get away, leaving equipment and rifles behind.

The Australians advanced 150 metres, but in doing so came under fire from the next defensive line. The advance unit was cut up in the fire-fight that followed and had to withdraw. A flanking movement ran into heavy Japanese fire. Another patrol coming around the left flank came under light-machine-gun attack but was unable to pinpoint the source of the fire. Even though the Australians knew they were only about fifty metres from Japanese gun nests, these were too well disguised to be easily seen. Both sides fired mortar rounds into the enemy, causing some casualties but mostly just adding to the confusion.

The intensity of Japanese fire caused several casualties but the attackers stuck grimly to their task and gradually pushed back the Japanese. The Australians moved forward to the new defensive line and, after a heavy fire-fight, the Japanese had to withdraw again, leaving behind two officers killed in the exchange. Maps and papers found by the Allies in the dead men's pockets were sent back for quick translation. The diary of Lieutenant Hirano was also found. The last entry, on 19 October, noted that an enemy attack under mortar cover had got close to his platoon's machine-gun position but had been repulsed.[9] The next day's attack was more successful: Lieutenant Hirano's diary, and his life, came to an abrupt close.

Another assault unit was brought in and it too was pinned down, but as darkness fell the Australians pulled back from contact. During the night, the Japanese withdrew again down the boggy, steep track. Next morning, the AIF moved cautiously forward and established that the enemy positions were now clear. In the afternoon they came under fire again from the remaining cluster of dug-outs forward of the main Japanese force. The attack swung units to the right and left of the track, but they made little headway. The jungle on the left was very thick, and it took till dusk to get to defender positions. With both rain and darkness falling, the attack was suspended until the morning. However, under cover of a very cold night, the Japanese pulled back yet again and melted into the main force on the other side of the Eora Creek ravine.

◆　◆　◆

The supply problem continued to plague them. Not so much with ammunition: this early in the first sustained confrontation with the Australians since the storming of Ioribaiwa Ridge a month before, and as Stanley Detachment built its positions around Eora Creek, munitions were brought up from a storage depot at Isurava. Food was a different story. The demand was continuous and stocks badly depleted. Coupled with the sheer shortage of food were the difficulties of maintaining even a trickle of rations to the front; village gardens on the way had already been plundered by both armies. Hunger was chronic. Examining the bodies of recently dead Japanese lying beside the track, Australian unit medicos saw the signs of death by starvation, in tandem with malaria or other diseases and exhaustion.

The resumption of engagement with the enemy at Templeton's

Crossing provided a gruesome solution to the hunger issue for some of the Japanese. On the verge of starvation, they dragged the bodies of Australians killed in recent skirmishes back to their dugouts like wild animals taking dead prey to their lairs. They tore off the corpses' clothing and cut strips of flesh from the thighs with knives or razor blades, then cooked it in their army-issue metal dixies.

In one account from the retreat, a soldier with severe diarrhoea and malarial fever was barely able to walk. A comrade said, 'You'll die without taking food. Eat this. There's too much for me.' The soldier knew without being told what the cooked meat offered was. It had a pleasant aroma and he ate it without hesitation. He had no second thoughts then, such was his desperate hunger, or for some time after his return from the war. Eventually, though, as he immersed himself back in everyday life, what he'd done began to nag at him. He developed an unexplained deep pain like that from his old war injuries, and he imagined voices saying, 'You have done what must not be done.'[10]

Interestingly, the reports by Australians who went through the area later mention only Australian bodies being found mutilated. Mutilated Japanese may have been regarded as unremarkable or as diminishing the reports' propaganda value; more likely, the Japanese were reluctant to eat the flesh of their dead comrades when there was an alternative. Cannibalism continues to provoke revulsion in people who have never faced starvation, which is most of us who aren't Uruguayan rugby footballers.[11] It has been suggested (by Australian researchers) that on at least one occasion Australians might also have resorted to eating the flesh of their dead comrades rather than die of starvation while lost in the Owen Stanley jungle.[12] No evidence of this has been found of Australians on the Kokoda Track, although they too had supply-line difficulties. They, however, were only very hungry. The Japanese, at times, were starving. Soldiers on the brink of death, already in mental and physical no man's land, might well suppress any moral objections to the thought that one more meal could get them to another day.[13]

◆　◆　◆

General Horii had chosen to position his main defences at this stage on the northern ridge overlooking Eora Creek valley and its village. To stall the enemy advance, he had spread his men along the ridge in their network of machine-gun posts and fire trenches, with Kuwada's unit occupying the right flank. The Kokoda Track arrived at a bare ridge opposite them before descending into the ravine to the village and creek. The Japanese watched and waited. With such a clear view of arrivals on that southern ridge, there would be no surprises. They would know the Australians had arrived well before the Australians knew they were there, waiting.

The first Australians got to the southern ridge by the morning of 22 October. The defenders watched them from the northern ridge but held their fire. A platoon advanced down the steep, slippery side of the valley to where Eora Creek village sat on a flat area projecting out from the scarp. Exposed among the remnants of native huts, they came under mortar and machine-gun fire from Japanese positioned low in the valley side opposite. Those who weren't wounded or killed took cover and tried to pinpoint their ambushers.

The advance force continued coming up to the open high ground overlooking the ravine, gathering there or waiting down on the track until the pocket of defence in the valley could be dealt with. They had no idea they were being observed by a much larger force hidden high on the ridge opposite. A company was sent along the southern ridge to attack the ambushers from above. Another was sent to skirt widely around Eora Creek village to Alola further north, but they took insufficient rations and returned four days later. Advancing troops had concentrated on the southern ridge by the afternoon, when they were unexpectedly pounded with mortars and shells from a mountain gun set among the main defence positions. Losses were high as startled Australians tried to withdraw back up the slope, grabbing desperately at tree trunks and roots to stop themselves sliding to the bottom.

Down in the valley, the company pinned in the village sent out patrols to find a way across the creek. No path forward could be found, and machine-gun fire made reconnaissance difficult. The creek banks were found to be impenetrable from the village. The two bridges over Eora Creek were held by the Japanese, who had cover from the slope behind and above them. The Australians couldn't go back up the slope on their side, and supplies couldn't be brought down to them. They had no alternative but to weather the mortar and mountain-gun storm until dark.

The Japanese had retired for the night to positions behind the second bridge, intending to return just before dawn. Australians had so far shown little inclination for night attacks and, in any case, with rain continuously falling there was no moonlight to assist movement down the steep, greasy path that zigzagged to the bottom.

At 2 a.m., the rain eased and the moon came out. Two Australian officers crept down to the creek and crossed the first bridge without attracting Japanese fire, much to their surprise. At 4 a.m., with the moon still out, they signalled their company to follow, guided by pieces of paper on sticks the officers had earlier stuck in the ground. The company crossed the first bridge and half the men were over the second bridge before the Japanese became aware of what was happening. Machine-gun fire caused a few casualties, but the rest of the Australians eventually got across both bridges, dodging bullets as they went. Then the moon went down and the valley was plunged into darkness again until the 6.30 a.m. dawn.[14]

With the moonlight switched off, the Japanese in their defensive pits couldn't see enemy movements in front of them. Some of the platoons moving forward in the dark stumbled across Japanese positions, causing considerable surprise and a number killed and wounded. They were moving blind. By dawn, the Australians found themselves wedged in a cul-de-sac between the torrent of Eora Creek and a sheer rock face.

A second company attempted to follow the night-time advance, but machine-gun fire stopped it before it even got to a bridge. These men moved around on the left and tried to get up the main track, but Japanese guns pinned them down. Another company moved up on the right until their way was blocked by a waterfall and matted vines. In turning back, they encountered stiff opposition. They inflicted casualties but couldn't drive the Japanese out of their positions. Instead, a Japanese unit worked around the slope above them, causing heavy Australian losses. Another Australian platoon went further up the ridge on the right and put a machine-gun nest out of action before it too was driven back.

Imanishi was among the defenders below the ridge. 'That one was terrible,' he says of the battle. All day the Australians, down in the valley and up on the southern ridge, were hammered with mountain-gun, Juki and mortar. It was a day when the two opposing forces in the valley took turns to overrun each other's positions. Losses were considerable for both sides. At sunset the Japanese withdrew from the basin and around the bridges, pulling back to the next spur.

The attackers had now infiltrated up the side of the valley and were precariously dug in fifty metres below Japanese mortars. Engineers built a new fortification for the mountain gun to be repositioned. The Australians in their holes could hear the chopping of wood on the ridge above them. They were hemmed in, but one of the other battalions had moved up on the Japanese far right flank and was making inroads there. During yet another bitterly cold night and in a continuous downpour, the Australians built a pit for a Vickers gun on the southern ridge, apparently still unaware of how clear a view the Japanese had of that ridge. In the morning, the gun and its crew were blown out of the pit.

That morning also, two Allied aircraft strafed the Japanese positions, but they hit behind the defenders and caused little damage. For much of that day and the next, the opposing forces exchanged mortar fire and sent out patrols that either ambushed the enemy or were ambushed by them. As casualties mounted in a battle of attrition, no one moved decisively forward and no one moved back. This was stalemate.

General Horii walked up from his command headquarters at Kokoda and toasted the front-line officers with *sake*. Ill and hungry, South Seas Force had held its ground against a larger, fitter army, although the Australians too were starting to feel the effects of fighting in appalling conditions at the end of a badly stretched supply line. They had ongoing problems with defective mortars, and they had been subjected to trenchant criticism by a senior command with no comprehension of the agonies they had to endure. Though it poured every night, not even drinking water was readily available. The Japanese had built their defences around the only clean water on the ridge. The Australians had to catch rain water in their gas capes or from the thick vine of the 'water tree' that, when cut, 'dripped fresh drinking water for hours'.[15]

Horii recognised that the stand at Eora Creek had served its purpose, but his men could not hold out for much longer. With his two battalions down to half strength, the risk was growing that the enemy could infiltrate through gaps in his defensive line. He had insisted over the protestations of Colonel Yazawa that the men were too stricken with malaria and beriberi to resume battle, that Koiwai Battalion from the depleted 41st Regiment recuperating in Kokoda must be brought forward to reinforce Stanley Detachment. Koiwai unit arrived at Eora Creek on the 26th, four days after the battle there had started. Horii was now able to put into place his end-game strategy for this phase of the tactical withdrawal. Stanley Detachment would continue to repel frontal attacks and pull back on the evening of 28 October, with Koiwai Battalion acting as rearguard.

Imanishi remembers those terrible last days at Eora Creek. 'We were under a barrage and it was like "bullet rain". But we were not allowed to withdraw and were told to hold our position until the designated date. Because it was an order, I thought we would have to hold the position until we all died.'[16]

An Australian attack along the track was held up by Juki fire, but out on the extremities a patrol got through and cut Japanese telephone cables before being driven back. Elsewhere the Australians were getting more mobile in their flanking attacks, and their mortar barrages were having a telling effect. Many of the defenders felt trapped even though they were still holding the enemy at bay.

'We detected the Australian infantry coming round,' recalls Imanishi, 'so we climbed up the hill and waited for the enemy to approach, but the Australian mortar attacks were so strong there.' Instead of coming up the hill the Australians skirted up a ridge to one side, so the unit's move had been to no avail.[17]

At the bottom of the valley, the heavy rain had caused the creek to rise several feet and wash away part of one of the bridges. The break-away section got jammed between rocks downstream, with the walkway below the water line. The Australians were trying to get supplies through and the wounded back from their forward positions, something that could be done only under cover of darkness. Getting across the partly submerged bridge and bringing casualties back was extremely hazard-ous. It needed a line of men at night bracing themselves in the icy water against the sunken bridge and passing each stretcher above water. These desperate actions took place under constant mortar fire.

On the night of the 26th, the Japanese moved back 500 metres to stronger positions on a steeper part of the slope. This was to be the last defence before full withdrawal. The attack troops moved forward and dug into shallow trenches, sheltering under the concave lip of the ridge, sometimes only twenty metres below the Japanese. These new positions had the Australians even more restricted than before. The defenders had so many rifles and machine-guns trained on them that they couldn't move without attracting fire, except at night. Grenades were bounced down the slope at them. The Japanese also rolled boulders onto the Aus-tralian positions.

Up on the far right flank, however, the Japanese perimeter was becom-ing vulnerable. The defenders were fighting hard to resist an Australian unit that was now firmly entrenched there. Another patrol penetrated to the track on which Japanese supplies were run to their men on the outer edge. In this area there were constant clashes between opposing patrols without any decisive result. Patrols moving about were never quite sure who was where in a game of blind man's buff. They could never see more than ten metres in front of them in the dense undergrowth.

The Australians brought a 3-inch mortar into the attack, but a round that had been brought up to the mountains in air-dropped supplies blew up in the gun, killing its crew of three. On the right flank they fared bet-ter. In the afternoon on the final day, two platoons probed the perimeter and were followed by a larger force which drove the Japanese back. In the face of severe machine-gun fire, the Australians rushed in with gren-ades. Both sides suffered heavy losses.

The Japanese had only just managed to hold their strategic position above Eora Creek until the date Horii had earmarked for the withdrawal. During the morning of the 28th, they had to withstand attacks on both flanks. Scouts from Koiwai Unit found signal wires, indicating that a sustained Allied attack on the main camp was in preparation. Kuwada Battalion bore the brunt of that attack, on the high ground of the right flank that afternoon, until mist rolled in, masking the defenders' movements. Major Koiwai had met with Colonel Kuwada in the early afternoon to coordinate their defence and withdrawal, the latter to start after dark. Tsukamoto Unit, including Imanishi's platoon, would be holding the road behind.

Kuwada's men arrived after 8 p.m., the prearranged time for their major's meeting with Koiwai. The attack force had penetrated their positions and had engaged them in close fighting. They hadn't been able to withdraw until they could push the enemy back, although that would have been no more than a temporary respite had they remained in position. Only the HQ and machine-gun companies came out with Kuwada. They waited for the rest of the battalion until the moon came out at 10 p.m., making it riskier to linger. Kuwada said, 'We cannot wait any longer for the unit. We have to leave. The company commanders may somehow be able to withdraw.'

'No,' Koiwai replied. 'Our unit is to defend the withdrawal. We must leave friendly forces to the rear of the unit. Let's wait for another hour.'

'But perhaps a company will come out further down the track. If we wait here it will be a waste of time.'

They could hear coughing from the Australian positions. Taking special care to conceal the sound of footsteps, they reached the main track safely by midnight.

The Kuwada troops who had engaged the Australians on that final day and hadn't retreated with the rest of the battalion lost their way in the dark jungle when they were finally able to withdraw. Carrying their wounded with them, they managed to find a circuitous route across the mountains and rejoined their battalion below Isurava two days later.[18]

As the 29th dawned, Australian forward patrols reported that the

Japanese had withdrawn. An advance unit moved up over the ridge and down the track towards Alola. They scooped up anything of use that the Japanese left behind: machine-guns, mortars, a wireless set and papers.

South Seas Force, dug in around Eora Creek, had resisted the enemy advance for over two valuable weeks. Horii had less than a thousand men still fit to fight. Of the original 500 in Koiwai Battalion, only sixteen were still battle-capable.[19] The story was similar across the battalions: 170 of the original 744 in Kuwada Battalion remained able to fight, and 180 of the 797-strong Horie Battalion.[20]

The remnants of Stanley Detachment and its reinforcements moved back past Kokoda. The village was no longer part of Horii's battle plan. It was a reasonable location for defending against an attack from Mambere valley to the north, but no place to stop a push from behind. The Japanese had already abandoned Kokoda. The field hospital had been evacuated to Giruwa when troops started withdrawing from Ioribaiwa over a month before. Kokoda didn't have the iconic significance for the Japanese that it had for Australians. The Kokoda campaign of the Australians was MO Operation to the Japanese, who hadn't even been able to put its airstrip to any good use. The retreating Japanese headed instead to the high ground around Oivi, near the Kumusi River.

On 2 November, the Australian advance force entered the abandoned village of Kokoda. Next day, amid much fanfare both there and back home, they hoisted the Australian flag. Little mention was made of the fact that the Japanese were no longer there.

Chapter 12

General Horii's last stand

Day and night throughout October 1942, men of the Imperial Japanese Army streamed along the Kokoda Track towards the coast, their hair and beards shaggy, their uniforms ragged and soiled with blood, mud and sweat. Some had no uniforms at all: instead they wore blankets and straw rice bags. Many walked barefoot, their boots and *tabi* having rotted in the constant mud underfoot. They carried the remnants of whatever rice or taro they had in dirty kits. Some wrapped meagre food scraps in corners of blankets or tied them up with cloth onto belts or hung over shoulders.

By the end of the month this stream was joined by troops withdrawing from the Eora Creek defence, a few still fighting fit, many of them showing unmistakable signs of exhaustion, sickness and the other effects of a long, hellish campaign. Some were 'skin and bone, plodding along with the help of a stick'.[1] Those fit enough to support a stretcher staggered in groups of four with the sick or wounded on their shoulders; others carried them on their backs or, out of desperation, dragged them on the ground through the mud. They helped each other to the extent they were able and by so doing stayed ahead of the enemy they'd held up at Templeton's Crossing and Eora Creek. Soldiers fell exhausted on the side of the track, lay for a while, then struggled to their feet—or never got up. Sometimes sturdier, younger men passed by briskly and left their slower comrades behind.[2]

Sergeant Imanishi was among the withdrawing troops. When he got to Deniki, he saw a group of planes flying over Kokoda up ahead of him. Parachutes opened ominously behind the planes. Imanishi thought they must be the enemy's airborne troops. Then, to his relief, he saw the rising sun on the fuselage. When he got to Kokoda he was told, 'The navy bombers just dropped food here. You can go and grab some.'[3]

Sergeant Tsunoda was one of the navy pilots who made the drop. They had been told South Seas Force was starving, that their food was being carried by the army's Korean civilians who couldn't help eating it before they got on the Kokoda Track. The pilots decided to air-drop rice packs to their fellow soldiers.

From the sky, Tsunoda couldn't even see the Kokoda Track. It was hidden beneath the jungle, but he saw some soldiers marching on top of a rocky hill shortly before he dropped the supplies. They waved Japanese flags as he flew over them.[4]

When the drop was completed and the planes had flown away, the men on the ground went into the bush and came back with rice. They were far enough in front of the enemy to make a fire and cook it. Feeling full for the first time in weeks, the men sprawled on their backs and said to each other, 'Now we are off duty for a while.'

They weren't off duty for long. Within a couple of days, Kokoda was evacuated. Ridges and plateaus might be good places to stop a force coming up the track, as the Japanese had found in their advance three months before, but not against a force coming from behind, as the approaching Australians would soon be doing. General Horii wanted to set his defences in a position of advantage.

Battle-fit soldiers were assembled in a clearing in the jungle at Ilimo, near the Kumusi River, and addressed by the general. They were to recover their strength and health and prepare for a fresh offensive. Engineers had meanwhile constructed defensive bunkers on the high ground near the village of Oivi, back up the main track a few kilometres. The 41st Regiment was the primary unit to be deployed around Oivi. The 144th Regiment would remain in reserve, occupying the area around Gorari, five kilometres further back. This regiment's Stanley Detachment, having borne the brunt of the action at Eora Creek, had earned a stint out of the immediate line of fire. South Seas Force's headquarters, with Horii presiding, was to be established south of Gorari, near Waju, with Kuwada (3rd) Battalion of the 144th providing a defensive perimeter. A decisive phase of the Kokoda campaign was rapidly approaching.

Morale in the force went up and down. The air-drop of rice near Kokoda had symbolic value and had boosted the men's spirits. It was not enough to end their hunger, however: for that a bulk landing of supplies was needed. Two army transport ships, *Choryo Maru* and *Kiyokawa Maru*, landed ammunition and provisions at Buna on 2 November. Bags of rice and wheat were taken to Waju and stored, along with barrels of pickled plums. For the first time since Ioribaiwa, the men of South Seas Force were fighting only disease, exhaustion and Australians. Starvation had been beaten for the time being.

On the other side of the morale ledger, one incident in particular fuelled the growing discontent of the troops with some of their leadership. It is described in the memoir of Lieutenant Kanemoto, who was in charge of trucks carrying the wounded to the hospital at Giruwa—the same Kanemoto who had made the ill-judged reconnaissance flight for Yokoyama Advance Party before the Kokoda campaign began.

Kanemoto was accosted by a major he didn't recognise, accompanied by his batman. 'Hey, Transportation Unit,' said the officer. 'I'm Major Horie, going back to Japan by order of Imperial HQ. Let me on your truck.'

The transport officer sat him next to the driver. He thought, 'He's supposed to be commanding Stanley Detachment in a bitter fight to hold off the enemy. Why is he going back to Japan?'

During the journey, Allied fighters flew overhead. Jumping out of the truck and sprawling on the ground away from it, Kanemoto found himself next to Horie's batman. He asked him why the major was going back to Japan.

'I heard the major will have to take an exam at the Army College, sir.'

Kanemoto was incensed. He couldn't understand how an exam could be more important to an officer than staying with his men, then still in the Owen Stanley Range and no doubt believing it their duty to follow the major's orders at any cost. Major Horie, he decided, 'must have told his men, "It is extremely hard to leave you all," or something like that and I can accept that he really believed such words in his own heart. However, at the same time I believe he felt relieved and thought, "Thank God!" No matter what he might say, he gave up his men for his career.'

Colonel Tsukamoto was livid when he heard this report. He said to his men, 'What the hell! So the guy wants to enter the Army College that much and wouldn't hesitate to leave his men behind. Very well, let him go home and disappear from here. I don't want to see his face again.' Tsukamoto might have been difficult to get on with, but he was a dedicated soldier.[5]

Imanishi too was disillusioned with what amounted to a desertion of his men by one of their appointed leaders. 'The quality of the commanders,' he says, 'got worse and worse.'[6]

The rumoured instigator of this extraordinary move was none other than Colonel Tsuji, the man who had jumped the gun with MO Operation, now recovered from his wounds and transferred from Tokyo back to Rabaul in a liaison role.[7] Horie was later replaced in the field by Major Kokichi Kato as commander of 2nd Battalion.

◆　◆　◆

By the time the advancing Australian force reached the vicinity of Oivi and Gorari, the Japanese were waiting in foxholes reinforced with palm logs and well camouflaged under vegetation. Ragged, unkempt and looking like scruffy street urchins, they still knew how to go about the business for which they had been so intensively trained. Once again, they had stationed themselves to provide covering fire for adjacent bunkers. Snipers had taken up positions in the surrounding rubber trees and palms. The main force of the 41st Regiment occupied two areas of

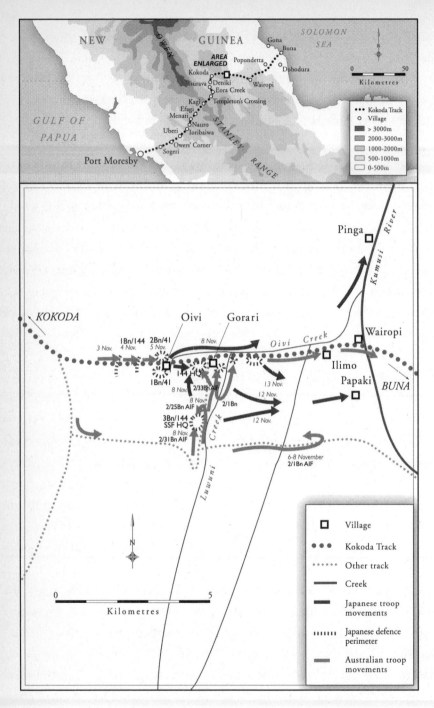

Troop movements during the battle at Oivi and Gorari,
November 1942

high ground that straddled the main track adjacent to the small village at Oivi, Koiwai (2nd) Battalion to the north of the track, Miyamoto (1st) Battalion to the south. A more mobile defensive line had been set up forward of those positions with elements of 144th Regiment's 1st (Tsukamoto) Battalion, including Sergeant Imanishi.

The Australians first appeared on the afternoon of 3 November and were immediately pinned down with the rifles and machine-guns of the forwardmost defenders. Two Australian platoons had to skirt around each side of the track and create distractions so the front group could extricate itself and move back. The Japanese lookout withdrew at the same time. This was a tactical manoeuvre, not a 'do-or-die' operation. An Australian patrol then crossed a small creek and was immediately stopped by a volley of woodpecker fire. It had made no further progress by dusk, when it withdrew. During the night the front defensive line of the 144th disengaged, having done its job of making a nuisance of itself. Its men moved back with their weapons to join the main group a couple of kilometres behind.

The next day the Australians crossed the creek again and attacked on both flanks, only to find the Japanese no longer there. Moving down the main track, a forward patrol came under fire from another Japanese lookout unit, which then withdrew. Behind them, 3rd Company of 55th Mountain Artillery Regiment under Lieutenant Yoshifumi Takagi had set up a mountain gun. By early afternoon, the Australians found themselves under attack from it and a number of Juki emplacements. The advancing force tried to circle under severe shelling without much success. In the late afternoon, the remainder of Tsukamoto Unit moved back behind the entrenched positions of the 41st on the Oivi rises. The 55th pulled its mountain gun on its wheels four kilometres back to a new position on the western side of Gorari village.

These were just preliminary skirmishes in the battle to prevail at Oivi–Gorari, and the Australian field command knew it. The Allies had intercepted Japanese army signals for the first time on 28 October.[8] These indicated that fresh troops were joining the battle and that the Japanese had abandoned Kokoda, withdrawing to the Kumusi River. The part about the fresh troops may have been out of date. Although troops of the 41st were brought across from Buna, the signal may also have referred to the decision of General Miyazaki, Chief of Staff in Rabaul, that 1st Battalion of 229th Regiment, then due to arrive in Rabaul, was to reinforce South Seas Force. This order raised for Horii the possibility of a renewed thrust to Port Moresby, but it was short-lived. The situation in Guadalcanal had deteriorated to such an extent that the order was cancelled and the battalion diverted to that island instead.[9] The Australians may have known of the Japanese decision but not of its reversal.

Thinking they had a fair idea of the defending troop strength, the advancing troops moved into the line of sight of 41st Regiment, firmly dug in on the Oivi rises. It was the morning of 5 November, already the third day of this action. The Japanese were on a long high ground with spurs running off it, each covered with machine-gun lines protected by snipers and supported by mortars. They had heard the earlier skirmishes with Tsukamoto's men and the thud of the mountain gun. The Australians were approaching, and the defenders in their damp gun-pits were ready.

The first patrols, coming under heavy mortar fire from Major Miyamoto's men on the southern of the two defensive rises, were unable to make much progress. A second battalion was brought in, but it too was unable to penetrate the Japanese defences. At the end of a day during which the attackers had suffered considerable losses, they dug in fifty metres from the Japanese positions. It would be a night of little sleep for either side.

Next day, the Australians probed the defences with flanking patrols and direct attacks, but made little headway and took severe casualties. A machine-gun post fell, but a counter-attack forced the assault unit back fifty metres. The attackers eventually pulled back to their previous positions. In the late afternoon, a Japanese counter-attack with machine-guns, accompanied by yelling, was also forced back. A stalemate had developed.

The Australian General Arthur 'Tubby' Allen had been sacked on the eve of the move beyond Eora Creek and replaced with General George

Vasey by an impatient Commander-in-Chief Sir Thomas Blamey. Unable to make progress on the western flank of Oivi, Vasey ordered a second line of attack. Another track ran parallel with and south of the main track through Oivi and Gorari. Vasey moved two battalions along it to the area below Gorari, where air reconnaissance had indicated troops dug in, to get behind the Japanese front line. A third battalion was to continue down this same track to Ilimo to cut off any retreat by the Japanese, but it ran out of rations and returned to join the other two battalions at the junction of the path up to Gorari. Vasey had seven battalions at his disposal, giving him strength of numbers if not of position. Aware of the capriciousness of his senior commanders, he wanted to leave as little to chance as possible.

The Japanese knew the terrain they were defending much better than their enemy, whose geographical neighbourhood this nominally was. The Australians had only just arrived and these troops had not been in the area before, while the Japanese had been operating from the northern coastland for over three months. Yet Horii appears not to have put guards on the southern track, leaving this flank of his defences exposed. Perhaps the disappointments and distress of the arduous campaign were catching up with him. On the other hand, Australian troops found Japanese cigarette cases and the remains of cooking fires along the southern track, suggesting it had been occupied before the battle.[10] It is possible that the general placed a guard on the southern track which then relocated for some reason. Horii had in mind a circling movement for when the enemy had closed in on his front-line defence,[11] more plausible with troops tucked around the corner on the southern track. In the end, however, it was the Japanese who got caught in an enemy pincer, with devastating results.

◆ ◆ ◆

Luwuni Creek, east of Gorari, ran along the eastern side of the plantation track the attack force would most likely use to get from the southern track to the village. At this time of the year the creek was fast-flowing and difficult to cross except by the suspension bridge on the main track to Buna. First Battalion of 144th Regiment was dug in on both sides of the creek, with the regimental headquarters, still temporarily under Colonel Tsukamoto, on the western bank. Crucially, the Japanese field command had placed snipers and a unit with mortars on a three-metre-high rocky outcrop overlooking the bridge from the far bank. Anyone attempting to get onto the bridge would move into their line of fire.

On the afternoon of the 8th, Australian soldiers made their first push up the plantation track to the forward line protecting the southern rim of South Seas Force HQ. These men, of the AIF's 2/31st Battalion, were drawn into an exchange of mortar fire. A second Australian battalion (the 2/25th) swung wide to their right and came behind the troops already dealing with the opening thrust. Although there was little penetration of the perimeter on this afternoon, the Japanese defenders sensed they were in trouble here. They were right, and it would get worse. The next three days would see confused and bitter fighting at close quarters, costly for the Australians, catastrophic for the Japanese.

Horii began evacuating his headquarters staff that first afternoon from positions that were rapidly becoming the front line. The beginnings of panic were seeping into the force as control of the strategic agenda—so evident at Eora Creek even in the context of withdrawal—slipped from their grasp. To make matters worse, torrential rain started falling in the afternoon and continued through the night. Those withdrawing had to do it in the most difficult of conditions as they made their way in the dusk and then the dark up the plantation track to Gorari and the banks of Oivi Creek. The number of troops that subsequently crossed the Kumusi suggests a significant proportion of the men stationed around Gorari were evacuated at this stage. Reduced numbers of defenders stayed to hold off the Australian pursuit.

Private Nishimura was there. Having recovered sufficiently from his wounds, he had been returned to the battlefield. He was allocated to a new platoon, either because his previous platoon no longer existed or perhaps because he was unwanted there.

The sun rose on a flooded countryside, with foxholes full of water.

Men were drenched to the skin, their gear wringing wet. Two more Australian battalions joined the fighting around Gorari, moving even wider to the right around the previous day's attack units and the defensive positions they had surrounded. They pushed all the way up to the main Buna track, one (the 2/33rd) veering left to engage the defences at Gorari village, the other (the 2/1st) moving to the right, where positions had been established around the 144th supply depot. The Japanese were now simultaneously fending off attacks in three separate battles: around Gorari, north of Waju and still on the high ground near Oivi.[12]

Colonel Yazawa's men of the 41st continued to hold off attempts to penetrate the front at Oivi. In doing so, they had to withstand Allied bombing and strafing runs over two mornings. However, Japanese positions were hard to pinpoint from the air, and fighting on the ground was at such close quarters that the pilots feared they would hit Allied soldiers. The Australians returned to mortar attacks to try to dislodge the defenders from their height advantage. The Japanese replied with mortars and mountain guns. At the same time, the defences were being gradually thinned in a piecemeal withdrawal. The two Australian battalions at Oivi noted in their unit diaries at the time that the Japanese response seemed to be getting lighter, but they were still unable to make any significant headway.[13]

Five kilometres away, the infantrymen of the 144th were trying desperately to choke off enemy attacks on two fronts: around Gorari and down the plantation track towards Waju. Kuwada Unit's front-line troops, on the occupied area to the south, halted any progress with sustained mortar attack. They tried to change the battle's momentum the next afternoon with a charge on the stalled Australians, but it was thwarted with Tommy guns and bayonets. Having seized the initiative, the Australians advanced on Japanese positions and, although casualties were heavy on both sides, succeeded in pushing the defenders back from their forward arc of bunkers. Headquarters personnel who hadn't already withdrawn were caught up in the close-quarters exchange of bayonet thrusts and machine-gun sweeps as the AIF pressed home its advantage.

The area behind them now occupied, Kuwada's guard and the remaining headquarters men had nowhere to retreat to. Their line of withdrawal towards Gorari had been cut off. However, advancing troops had to cross open ground under heavy machine-gun fire from camouflaged positions. An afternoon attack penetrated some of the defensive line, but could not hold the ground gained. Under constant machine-gun fire, the Australians withdrew. They had sustained heavy losses, but they still held the tactical advantage. Although they had been unable to move forward, the Japanese were unable to move back. Pushed up against a stone wall, they found themselves squeezed into a diminishing space. Something had to give.

Meanwhile, north of this action and blocking the avenue of escape from both Waju and Oivi, more Japanese positions were under sustained attack. The defences established in and around Gorari brought the advancing troops under heavy fire as they crossed an open area strewn with boulders. The men of the 144th attacked the pinned-down Australians, driving them back a short distance. As night fell they could hear sounds of battle 1500 metres to the south and 500 metres to the east. The latter was the engagement of Japanese defences by the AIF's 2/21st Battalion further along the main track, where it crosses Luwuni Creek rushing towards Oivi Creek. These defensive positions, protecting a medical post and the supply stores of 144th Regiment's headquarters, were overrun in the late afternoon, scattering defenders in all directions. It would prove to be the most decisive of the Australian attacks at this time, with profound implications for the Japanese withdrawal. The approach to the bridge, the easiest means of crossing the swift, deep-cut Luwuni Creek, was now under heavy Australian guard.

General Horii's defensive strategy was starting to unravel disastrously. He was no longer in a position to carry out his planned circle-and-destroy movement. Troops of 41st Regiment withdrawing from Oivi found themselves confronted by enemy forces. The Australians had pushed past the 144th, which had been assigned to protect the rear. For many years after the war, this would be a bone of contention between the two Japanese regiments.

A decision was made for the general withdrawal of South Seas Force from the Gorari area, but the Australians had so deeply infiltrated their lines that this could only be done piecemeal, as opportunity arose. Horii regarded a withdrawal to the Kumusi as a last resort, but last resorts were becoming his reality. The first withdrawals from Force HQ, which included the general and his staff, retreated over Oivi Creek before Australian units got around to their rear. From there they made their way along the north bank towards the Kumusi River.

The first troops to withdraw from Oivi had made their way directly to the creek's north bank. When the 144th became caught up in battle, however, the 41st went back along the track to assist their fellow defenders, only to find that the downpour of the 8th had made Oivi Creek treacherous for exhausted soldiers to cross. Retreat via its north bank was now difficult. An alternative was to push through the Australian positions and try to get across the suspension bridge over Luwuni Creek and back along the track to Buna, but this had become a no man's land. Australian troops, unable to cross a bridge covered by fire from the rocky outcrop opposite, had laid booby traps of trip wires and hand grenades around the approach to the bridge so the retreating Japanese wouldn't be able to cross it either. The potential lines of retreat were becoming fewer and more dangerous.

Japanese numbers at Gorari had been expanded by the 41st's withdrawal from Oivi. The last of them abandoned their high-ground advantage on the night of the 10th, using vines tied to trees along the track and a series of shielded candles as a guide.[14] They carried with them all their equipment, arms and wounded, having buried their dead. Nothing was left behind but empty, muddy weapons pits.

By then the 144th had been pushed backwards out of Gorari village, in the reverse direction of their intended retreat. They desperately needed to turn the tide, even if only temporarily, to give themselves space to retreat along with troops from Oivi, who now shared their predicament. A dawn clash between patrols resulted in both Japanese and Australian losses. Yelling theatrically, the Japanese then rushed enemy positions with rifle and machine-gun fire. They knew they were hemmed in, and this was the only possible way out. It was all or nothing now. Lieutenant Takagi's artillery company dragged its mountain gun up from west of the village and fired high-explosive shells at point-blank range. The air over Gorari village rained shrapnel during two hours of shelling. Some of the Australians started running back in the confusion and had to be pulled forward again.[15]

Even with the mountain-gun barrage, the Japanese were unable to force their way back into the village. At noon the following day, they ran out of shells and the bombardment stopped. The desperation had been there, but the outcome had eluded them. For two days, groups of soldiers had probed around the Australian positions to find a route— any route—through to the Kumusi River. Those who got around came across further enemy positions blocking the bridge and turned back instead towards Gorari and the Australian positions in and around the village. Small groups of the 144th ran back and forth, often with little thought beyond escape, bumped like balls in a pinball machine between the enemy-occupied areas at Gorari and Waju and on the approach to the bridge. It was happening by day and by night and there was confusion on both sides, even though the Australians held the upper hand. Groups from both armies would stumble across each other in the dark and the pouring rain, exchange gunfire, maybe take a poke at each other with bayonets, and slip away as quickly as they could.

Further south, the 144th was crushed in its defensive positions. Kuwada's men tried before first light on the 11th to break through the surrounding AIF. It was to no avail, and twelve were killed in the attempt. That morning, the surrounding Australian forces launched a major attack from both flanks with grenades, rifles and bayonets. The defenders were driven into the Australian flanking advance with heavy losses. It was all over by morning's end. Those who were not killed in the onslaught slipped away, trying to make for Papaki, on the Kumusi River. Machine-guns, ammunition and documents were left to be gathered up by the Australians.

The defenders of Gorari village had been driven back, not surrounded and overrun like their comrades to the south. They could either withdraw across Oivi Creek, which had eased a little in the last couple of days but was still turbulent, or they could cross the smaller but still swollen Luwuni and head for Papaki. Those near Oivi Creek took the first option, following the path already being taken by Horii's group. Those further from Oivi Creek, often with Australian troops both in front of them and behind, headed for the Luwuni even though that route required finding a way through enemy lines.

The men were to leave behind their large weapons so they could carry out the wounded. Lieutenant Takagi was ordered to bury his company's mountain gun and instruct his men to help carry the wounded from other units. Takagi, a young graduate of an elite officers' academy, was unable to bring himself to bury the artillery piece.

He went to the commander and begged, 'If we can carry out the wounded, then please let us carry the gun as well.'

The request was refused. Takagi returned to his unit to gather his troops. The breech was broken up and the gun buried. After the artillery company had given a final parting salute to the buried gun the soldiers dispersed, leaving their leader at the burial mound. Lieutenant Takagi took his pistol, raised it to his head and shot himself.[16]

Sergeant Imanishi was nearby at the time. 'I can never forget the sound,' he says. 'Only one shot, like "Pom!" The battlefield was so quiet, and many of us could hear the sound.'[17]

Takagi's men screamed, 'Lieutenant Takagi's killed himself' and went running back to him. He took some time to die, but his action made a strong impression on those around. Imanishi says, 'I was so impressed by his officer spirit.'[18]

'The news of First Lieutenant Takagi's final gesture . . . did much to lift the flagging morale of the Japanese troops,' writes Lieutenant Nakahashi.[19]

Major Koiwai comments in his memoir: 'Artillery officers fresh from officers' college hold equal sentiment for their guns and military orders. Older army commanders hold human life as the fundamental principle . . . The military spirit which compelled the lieutenant to act will live forever. At the same time, even the decision of the commander to bury the gun was principled when seen from a wider perspective, owing to his desire to save the young troops in his charge.'[20] Koiwai had a capacity to sympathise with both sides of an issue. To some this confirmed him as a soldier-philosopher; to others it meant he was indecisive.

The Luwuni bridge remained no man's land even as the surviving Japanese around Gorari were slipping away. Japanese riflemen overlooking the bridge from the rocky outcrop continued to prevent the Australians from taking it and moving along the track to the coast. Australian army engineers followed Luwuni Creek upstream out of the firing line to build a temporary bridge. With three logs laid across a narrow point of the swift-flowing creek a platoon was able to cross and move up the opposite bank, looking to charge the rock from behind. The rest of that battalion, left to maintain its bridgehead, was attacked in the night's downpour in close combat. At the cost of a handful more lives on both sides, the bridgehead held fast and the Japanese fell back.

The next day, a whole Australian company crossed the improvised bridge upstream. Attacked from the rear, the Japanese were swept from their position of advantage on the rock. The Australians were now able to cross the creek by the main bridge. Their forces converged on that point and advanced on a 200-strong Japanese rearguard dug in down the track to Ilimo and the Kumusi River. It was an area that had been used for corralling mules and packhorses. The rearguard was surrounded, with devastating results. Some Japanese broke through, but many were killed in the attempt. Only the tethered horses and mules stayed behind. The rest of the battered survivors of the battle at Oivi–Gorari were up ahead, retreating towards Papaki.

The remnants of the 144th had slipped through gaps in the Australian lines. In the extreme dark of the night-time jungle they, like the Australians, had followed Luwuni Creek upstream; crossing it, they headed for Papaki. An advance group ran into Australian troops, and grenade explosions lit up the jungle. The rest moved undetected along a ravine, reaching a creek at Ilimo, where they waited for others to join them. With night and the Australians closing around them, they forded the creek chest-deep in the moonlight.[21]

Now, the retreating forces walked through boggy, trackless jungle, some along the northern side of Oivi Creek, some on the other side off the main track but in the same general direction. They didn't know how far back the pursuing Australians were. Although rations had been available when they were dug in at Oivi and Gorari, they were once again without food and their physical strength was fading as a result. Boots had been wearing down and rotting away for some time. Many soldiers were now walking barefoot. Many had swollen feet, making walking more painful. Heavy firearms were discarded, along with their ammunition. Eventually, even rifles were tossed away, though many were reluctant to break this connection with their military training. Discarding weapons without permission would ordinarily bring heavy punishment.

Major Koiwai, retreating with some of his men of the 41st, came across a group of stragglers. Some lay on the ground; others tottered on, their rifles still by their sides, dragging their legs as if in a slow-motion film.

'Throw away your weapons!' Koiwai yelled at the exhausted men. 'You'll travel lighter without them.'

Some looked bewildered and showed no inclination to lose their rifles.

'I am Major Koiwai of the 41st. I'll look after the rifles for you.' He took the weapons. 'If the company commander asks you where they are, tell them Major Koiwai has taken charge of them.'

He discarded the rifles after he had moved out of their sight.[22]

In the 'every man for himself' principle, Private Nishimura wandered alone and lost in the jungle. After a week of pushing in what he thought was the direction of the coast while avoiding Australian soldiers, he stumbled into a village. Relations between the Japanese and Papuans had become strained by this time, but that mood wasn't apparent in this village. The people fed Nishimura and pointed him towards the coast. He arrived at Giruwa a couple of days later.[23]

The troops of 144th Regiment had retreated along the main track from Kokoda, crossing the Kumusi River near an old ford at Papaki on 14 November, ahead of pursuing Australians. They were in various stages of emaciation, many with blood-soaked rag bandages around heads or arms. To get the wounded across the river, the men made rafts by tying together logs that were lying around. Some of the New Guineans who had been brought from Rabaul went back to get more food. They returned quickly with agitated reports that Australian troops were arriving. The moment that news landed, panic erupted. Some of Koiwai Battalion, there with the 144th, drowned when their hastily built rafts sank.[24]

Among the last to cross were the men of Sergeant Imanishi's platoon. A company commander, Lieutenant Hamada, told Imanishi the men would have to make their way to Giruwa individually. They could no longer be expected to move as a unit. Imanishi asked Hamada if he could swim and he said, 'I'm not good at swimming.' Together with a private and two Rabaul locals, the lieutenant got onto an improvised log boat and pushed out into the river. On the way across, it snagged on a tree and overturned, drowning the four men.

The horses and mules that had been used for transporting supplies in the area were milling around, many of them as malnourished as their human companions. Since they could potentially be used by the advancing enemy, some were shot. Imanishi was followed by one of the horses to the river's edge. It looked lost in the morning mist. 'I couldn't even think about killing it and just wished it would go away,' he recalls. 'I felt so sorry for the horse, but I still went across the [Kumusi] river and climbed up the hill.'

This was the same river Imanishi had waded across, bicycle held above his head, when he and his comrades had landed in Papua in July in the dry. It was a different proposition now, over a hundred metres wide in places and flowing strongly and swiftly, in flood from the constant downpours of recent weeks. Still, Imanishi was confident he could swim across. He had spent much of his childhood swimming in the Yoshino River near his home at Motoyama. 'I thought, "OK, I can deal with this river." I carefully checked the speed of the stream and the width of the river. Then I jumped in.'

He had an Australian tent that he'd picked up somewhere during the campaign and had put his remaining belongings into it: pistol, shoes, clothes and a sword. The package was bound to a cane which he held in his teeth as he swam, first dog-paddle and then, as he felt his scant strength draining, on his back. Eventually he stretched his leg down and could feel the sand at the bottom of the river. Near exhaustion by this stage, he almost wept with relief. He had made it to the other side.[25]

◆　　◆　　◆

The headquarters cohort of South Seas Force, also undetected by the Allies, grouped further north on the Kumusi on 18 November. They had made their tortuous way along the northern side of Oivi Creek with some of the 41st and down the bank of the Kumusi, away from Wairopi, where the Australians were headed. Halfway to the sea, they camped on flat ground at Pinga. Heavy rain fell during the night, and the river overflow flooded the camp site. The men, officers and soldiers alike, had to stand upright until dawn 'like horses, shivering from the intense cold'.[26]

By then, the Australians controlled the river around Wairopi. Crossing there, they too moved towards the coast. At Pinga, General Horii could hear the sounds of artillery fire from the direction of Giruwa on the coast and guessed that the base was already under Allied attack. Anxious to get to Giruwa as quickly as possible, he decided to go down the remainder of the Kumusi by raft with several of his staff officers. He left South Seas Force in charge of Colonel Yazawa of 41st Regiment, with orders to cross the river there and advance towards Gona. Horii, his staff officers and adjutant and a small number of troops boarded a large palm-log raft and headed down the Kumusi. 'I'll go on ahead,' was his parting remark.

With the senior officers at Pinga trying to decide how best to cross the swollen Kumusi, one of the Takasago Volunteers proposed a method he had seen used in Formosa. Four or five saplings were lashed together to form a raft, not for soldiers but for their clothing and weapons. They could reach the other side if they pushed the raft as far as possible into the middle, where the river curved, then cling to it as it was carried around the bend. The method worked, although not without hitches.

Some of the soldiers were so exhausted that they lost their hold and drowned. Sometimes the raft was upended, with equipment and clothing disappearing into the surging Kumusi.[27]

The raft that General Horii and his group set out on down the Kumusi became stuck on a submerged tree two kilometres downstream. Despite frantic efforts to release it, it remained caught. It was abandoned and all aboard clambered to shore. Making their way along the bank, the ragged men found a small canoe tied up at the river's edge. Horii commandeered the canoe for himself and his chief of staff, Colonel Tanaka. Horii's orderly, Private Shigeji Fukuoka, happened to be a fisherman in civilian life, so he was ordered to paddle the canoe to the mouth of the Kumusi River.

The gunfire from the direction of Giruwa continued, the booms growing louder and more frequent. Horii was anxious to get there as fast as possible so he could lead the battle. When they reached the mouth of the river he decided, despite the risk, to try to reach Giruwa by sea. To stay out of range of enemy artillery, they took a course some distance out from shore. Fukuoka was a strong paddler, but unfortunately for the trio the weather turned bad. A fierce tropical thunderstorm struck, whipping up the sea. The canoe capsized and sank instantly.

It turned out that Tanaka could not swim. Implacably loyal to his commander, he had kept that to himself when the general decided to take the sea route to Giruwa. Tanaka's bespectacled head bobbed above the turbulent surface a few times, then disappeared. He was never seen again.

Horii and Fukuoka began swimming towards the shore. After a while the general began to tire badly. Debilitation and prolonged hunger made the effort of staying afloat in surging water too much for a man in his fifties.

He said to Fukuoka, 'I haven't the strength to swim any further. Tell the troops that Horii died here.' He then lifted both arms above the water, cried '*Tenno Heika banzai*' (Long live the Emperor) with his remaining strength and sank beneath the waves.

Fukuoka, the young fisherman, swam the remaining distance to shore and joined his comrades, grimly defending their bases on the north Papuan coast. He told them the story of the drowning of General Tomi-taro Horii.[28]

Here was a man characterised by determination, often to the point of stubbornness. His desire to lead his force from the front—he always set up his headquarters just behind his front line—was eventually to be his undoing in this heroically futile final gesture.

Chapter 13

Dug in on swampland

While South Seas Force stalled the Australian pursuit along the Kokoda Track through October and well into November, Japanese engineers and labourers built a network of defences on the northern coastal strip their troops had occupied since July. Beachheads were established at Buna, Gona and Sanananda; defensive positions were also set up along the road to Sanananda, which ran over swamp country. Over four months, the engineers constructed hundreds of bunkers using coconut-palm logs and compacted earth. The walls were reinforced with forty-four-gallon drums filled with earth. Some were strengthened further with concrete and steel. Bunker roofs were covered with earth and rocks and then camouflaged naturally under fast-growing vegetation. When the Australians eventually arrived they would find the bunkers hard to spot and resistant to bullets.

This was a landscape of fetid swamplands, scraggy jungle, palm groves and kunai grass. There were small scattered patches of relatively firm ground, and it was on these that the Japanese built their bunkers. Approaching troops would have to wade through swamps or cross open grassland to get to them. Crawl trenches joining the bunkers allowed defending troops to move around the network and served also as lateral lines of covering fire. As an extra precaution, heavily camouflaged snipers would be placed in treetops when the enemy reached the coastal plain.

Behind the defensive network, grey sand beaches fringed with romantically swaying coconut palms marked the edge of the Solomon Sea, by which the Japanese had come to this mosquito-infested coast of pouring rain and suffocating humidity. Malaria was rampant on the northern beaches, and the grassland was home to the mites that carry scrub typhus.

Soldiers and non-combatants who weren't part of Stanley Detachment or the subsequent defence of Oivi and Gorari were arriving at the coast now in twos and threes. Most wore tattered rags; some were stark naked. Some had only a kitbag slung over their shoulders; others wore no more than a dirty cap.

Among the first to return to the coastal plain were the three Japanese newspapermen, Okada, Sato and Katayama. Okada notes that even without having been in the fighting the trio looked like the walking dead, with shaggy beards, deep sunken eyes and rough skin 'like wet yellow earth'. Filthy with mud and sweat, their clothes were torn to shreds.

Making their way over the flat coastland the trio came to Soputa, where their radio operator had set up in a coffee plantation in a hut 'as charming and light as a painter's studio'. There, Okada fell on a pile of grass heaped on the floor, covered himself with two blankets and stretched his limbs. Weariness seeped away. He fell into a deep, sweet sleep, his Kokoda assignment completed.[1]

The sick and the wounded were arriving at the field hospitals at Gona and Giruwa every day. When the Japanese evacuated Kokoda field hospital there were no carriers available, so those unable to walk or commit suicide were shot. The walking wounded made their way to the 500-bed Line of Communication Hospital at Giruwa. By November, the hospital held 2000 patients. As huts could not be built fast enough to keep pace with their arrival, they lay on straw mats by the road or in the jungle. There were so many of them that there was hardly room to stand. Many had been lying there since the retreat began, keeping alive with whatever food the medics could scrape up.

Private Yokoyama was one of the medical corpsmen attached to the hospital. He had remained in Giruwa with the rest of 11th Company of the 41st. Diarrhoea and malaria were rife among the workers down on the plain, Yokoyama included. Although they weren't faced with the close-quarters fighting of the Kokoda Track they were subjected to daily Allied air raids, living in dread of the sound of approaching aircraft. It got to the point where they could work only at night. Casualties from these attacks added to pressure on the hospital at Giruwa.

A report by medical officer Lieutenant Fukunobo Okubo gives some idea of the state of the facilities there by the end of October. Food was running short, he noted, along with basic medical supplies like painkillers. There was no morphine left at the hospital. Medical panniers were corroded, and surgical instruments were rusting in the humidity. Tents were rotting, and merely touching their canvas would make a hole in it, but the hospital was so overcrowded that a temporary annexe was built with these same tents.[2]

There was little medicine other than tincture of iodine ('red tincture'), which was applied to serious wounds. Stomachs had been damaged from eating tree shoots, grass roots and caked earth. These people were no longer able to digest food, even when there was any; they vomited blood and died. Everywhere, men were breathing faintly and dying silently.[3]

Ashes of those who died on the Kokoda Track were sent back to Japan. If it was not possible for the whole body to be cremated, a limb would be severed for the purpose. The dead man's ashes would be placed in his mess tin and wrapped in paper. If the body was not able to be recovered or cremation wasn't possible, the mess tin would be sent home with a seal or identity disc, capturing the dead man's spirit.

By late November, the ashes of the dead were no longer being sent to Japan. At Buna, bodies were left lying on sand or in grass or leaning against trees, gradually rotting away until they were no more than white bones. The living had no strength to bury the dead, and made no attempt at cremation.[4] They were facing the looming shadows of starvation and death themselves.

◆　◆　◆

The movement of the battlefield to the area around Buna brought a new focus to the Kokoda campaign. The Allied strategy was driven by American inter-service rivalry. The US Army's General MacArthur wanted a quick victory before the navy won at Guadalcanal so he could take the front seat in the drive towards Tokyo.[5] MacArthur was also aware that although it was dangerous at that time for the Japanese to land reinforcements with so few aircraft in New Guinea, they could deploy 80,000 troops to the South Pacific if they regained air superiority. This posed a threat to the recently secured Allied airbases at nearby Kokoda and Dobodura. MacArthur was determined to pursue the total annihilation of the remaining Japanese force in Papua rather than settle for the less costly (in lives) strategy of starving them out.[6]

On 14 November, MacArthur ordered the Allies to finish off the Japanese as expediently as circumstances would allow. They advanced on four fronts. Australian and American infantrymen were already coming along the Kokoda and Jaure tracks. Unknown to the Japanese, Allied troops had been airlifted through October from Port Moresby and Milne Bay to Wanigela and had marched up the coast to Pongani. More Australian reinforcements would come in December by sea from Milne Bay to Oro Bay, south of Buna. There followed three months of intensive, vicious fighting, hampered by heavy rain, sweltering heat and swampy ground. A starving, sick, exhausted Japanese army, relying on a fragile supply line, reduced a far larger Allied force to a state of 'baffled impotence' for much of that time.[7]

Japan's strategy in the south Pacific was to thwart MacArthur's ambitions. On 16 November, Imperial Headquarters issued an order to General Hyakutake in Rabaul insisting that Buna be held 'at all costs' and that the enemy airbase at Dobodura, south of Buna, be destroyed. A loss of Buna would put future operations in the area, and the Japanese position in Rabaul, in serious jeopardy. On the other hand, removal of the airbase would frustrate the Allies' attempts to bring in reinforcements and weaken their capacity for air attack. Tokyo resolved to land extra troops to strengthen the defence of the north Papuan coast. Army command, concerned about abandoning soldiers in Guadalcanal to starvation, asked whether boosting the numbers in New Guinea would make it harder to supply Guadalcanal. The navy countered that capture of the Dobodura airfield would remove a major impediment to supply. To the end, however, the base would remain in Allied hands.

The areas around Buna and Gona were defended by mostly non-combat troops. Apart from Private Yokoyama's 11th Company, all the infantry units of South Seas Force—144th and 41st Regiments—had been fighting on the Kokoda Track. Only 3rd Battalion of the 41st, under Major Gohei Murase after Major Kobayashi's recall to Tokyo, had come back to Giruwa and stayed there. Miyamoto (1st) Battalion had come back, but was returned to the defence of Oivi. Koiwai (2nd) Battalion had been part of the defence of both Eora Creek and Oivi, and was only then making its way to the coast along with other survivors from Oivi and Gorari.

Colonel Yokoyama, commander of 15th Independent Engineers and leader of the original advance party in July, was in charge of the defence of Giruwa and Gona. Three anti-aircraft guns of Colonel Sadahide Fuchiyama's 47th Field Anti-aircraft Artillery Battalion dealt with the regular morning attacks by Allied bombers and fighters. Most of Yokoyama's men were either enfeebled by disease or were engineers or supply troops, not combat soldiers. The log of the 47th throughout October reported daily attacks by enemy planes, some brought down with anti-aircraft fire, some driven off, but some finding their targets which included the anti-aircraft gunners on the ground. Over the month the 115-man unit was reduced to four able soldiers, although most of that attrition was caused by malaria.[8]

Until South Seas Force drifted back, in whatever state of battle-readiness it was in, or reinforcements were landed, Yokoyama's defensive options were extremely limited. Down the coast, the defence of Buna was in the hands of Captain Yoshitatsu Yasuda and his Yokosuka 5th Special Naval Landing Party, with 900 engineers and two anti-aircraft guns. Combat troops at Buna were the survivors of Tsukioka Unit's three-month ordeal on Goodenough Island in their thwarted journey to Milne Bay, and those naval troops of Sasebo 5SNLP who had not been sent to the Rabi operation.

At Gona, Major Tsuneichi Yamamoto was in charge of an 800-strong road construction unit, mostly Formosans of Takasago *Giyutai* (Volunteers). In the absence of General Horii, whose fate was then unknown, command of the South Seas Force was temporarily in the hands of Colonel Yokoyama. Until reinforcements arrived, there was little in the way of trained combat troops to take on the Allied forces being deployed in their vicinity.

Yokoyama knew this was going to be a desperate defensive operation, with nowhere to withdraw to. An edict was issued to the men of the 41st under his temporary command: 'It is not permissible to retreat even a step from each unit's original defensive position. I demand that each man fight until the last.'[9] This time all units in the occupied area, including non-combatants and army employees, would be expected to join the fighting. Yokoyama's order added: 'Those without firearms or sabres must be prepared to fight with sharp weapons such as knives or bayonets tied to sticks, or with clubs.'[10]

The Takasago Volunteers had been working as carriers and labourers up to that point. They had the strength and natural agility in mountain and jungle that came from living all their lives in such terrain. Formosans have almost legendary status among Japanese veterans, who compare them favourably with the other colonial group, the Koreans. The story is frequently told that on the track Koreans would eat the rice they were delivering, whereas Formosans had been found lying dead from starvation alongside unopened bags of rice.[11] Formosans were 'excellent workers', according to Lieutenant Riichi Inagaki, the paymaster. The Korean volunteers were 'attracted by the high rates of pay', but they were a 'lazy, shiftless and thieving lot'.[12] The Takasago Volunteers were paid less at the request of the Formosan colonial administration to avoid 'spoiling them for the future'. Both Koreans and Formosans mostly sent their pay back to their families.

Takasago had been a generic Japanese expression for indigenous Formosans since their country became a Japanese colony fifty years before. Not a disparaging term, it was comparable to Australians' use of 'Kiwis' for New Zealanders. Colonial education had sought to make loyal

Japanese citizens of the Formosans, with broad success. They had been encouraged to enlist in the Japanese army as war approached, but only as citizen volunteers.[13]

With their sharp hearing, Formosans were often the first to pick up sounds of the approaching enemy. At the same time, they could move noiselessly through the jungle and had an uncanny ability to enter the enemy's camp and pilfer food from inside tents. Masami Suzuki, a military doctor, writes about the beautiful singing voices of the Takasago. When he heard a young Formosan singing in the shade of a coconut palm, he writes, 'I was so moved that I wanted to embrace him lovingly.'[14]

Hidden behind the beauty of their singing was a romantic culture of the warrior. They carried the curved-bladed hunting knives their headhunter ancestors had used,[15] and some were said to have applied as volunteers by writing in their own blood.

'The Formosan Volunteers kept asking us, "Sir, please let me use your gun,"' Imanishi remembers. 'They were given guns and fought alongside us, keeping a lookout for the enemy.'[16] They were eager and courageous. Whether they were effective is not so clear.

◆   ◆   ◆

On 16 November, three luggers and a Japanese barge captured at Milne Bay were spotted by a Japanese lookout fifteen kilometres south of Buna, unloading their cargo of supplies onto a lighter in Oro Bay. One of the boats had General Edwin Harding, commander of the Buna assault, on board. They were protected only by deck-mounted machine-guns, their air cover having left to get back to Port Moresby before dark. Eighteen Zeros swooped on them and all four craft were soon ablaze, the ammunition in their cargo exploding. Harding and many others swam ashore, but twenty-four men were killed in the attack.[17]

Both sides were intent on bringing in fresh troops. The following night, a first echelon of Japanese reinforcements arrived further up the Papuan coast in five destroyers—1000 troops together with Colonel Shigemi Yamamoto, who was to take command of 144th Regiment. The malaria-stricken Colonel Kusunose had been repatriated to Japan a few days before. Colonel Tsukamoto, somewhere between Gorari and the coast, was relieved of his temporary command of the regiment and continued as leader of 1st Battalion.

A second echelon of 500 men was landed at Buna the next night from three more destroyers. The two nights' arrivals made up a battalion of 229th Regiment, veterans of fighting in China under Major Heishichi Kenmotsu; an artillery company; and 700 replacements for the 144th. With Japanese and Allied troops converging on the region—some fresh, some battle-weary—the stage was set for a fight to the finish at the Japanese defences across Buna, Gona and Sanananda. It would turn out to be a devastatingly drawn-out affair.

The Australians, weary and depleted from crossing the Owen Stanley Range, were ordered to attack and capture Gona and Sanananda, supported by US troops who had tramped up the Jaure Trail parallel to and south-east of the Kokoda Track. They too were worn down by the long, slippery march over jungle-clad mountains, although they had yet to experience fighting in New Guinea. In addition, two American regiments that had advanced unopposed along the coast were to attack Buna.

Gona was an Anglican mission—a church, a school, a hospital, a mission house and a few Papuan huts. The adjacent beach was lined with more huts. The village of Kikori sat on the other side of Gona Creek's estuary; the village of Gona five kilometres further west. Unobstructed by hidden reefs, the bay in front of Gona Mission served as a useful anchorage for Japanese ships ferrying supplies and personnel into the area. The mission itself, used as a base by Major Yamamoto's road construction unit, had been damaged by his troops' occupation and Allied bombing.

The mission area had natural defences: a narrow beach, perhaps ten metres wide, and a thick canopy of coconut palms and banyan trees, which could absorb much of the impact of any mortar attack. Small Creek made attack on the eastern end difficult, and the wide, deep estuary of Gona Creek made it impossible from the west. Stretched to the south in front of the Japanese positions were swamps and kunai fields, some of which had been burnt out by the Japanese to open them up. Colonel Tomita, based near Giruwa, had positioned the Gona defences so arcs of fire would cross and placed snipers in coconut trees. Lines of machine-gun posts connected by zigzagging fire trenches circled the mission area. Another line, with a post every five metres, ran along the fringe of the beach.

The pattern was similar in Buna. Its garrison, the 1000 experienced infantrymen recently landed with Colonel Yamamoto, took up positions within Duropa Plantation, a prewar commercial copra operation at Cape Endaiadere (the Outer Camp), and at key points outside two airstrips to the south of the plantation (the Eastern Sector). The Old Strip had been built by Australian forces and completed before the Japanese invasion. It had been used by Japanese naval aircraft in August, but had been heavily bombed and proved difficult to keep in operation. Several disabled Zeros and transports stood abandoned by the runway including the Zero Sergeant Tsunoda had left behind. The New Strip had been constructed east of the old one as a dummy airfield to confuse attacking airmen. A line of defence ran through the plantation to the airstrips and across the bridge between them. Outposts covered approaches to this line. A log barricade was built across the coastal road to the cape; it could be protected by covering fire. The track between the landing strips ran onto a wooden causeway, forty metres long, crossing the Simemi Creek as it cut a deep trench through the swamp. Covering fire would make it difficult to use this track to cross to the north of the airstrips.

Colonel Yamamoto's new command, 144th Regiment, was still working its way back from Gorari. Meanwhile, with an Allied assault on Buna imminent, he took charge of the reinforcements on the eastern flank of the Buna defences.

The marine units, Yokosuka 5SNLP and Sasebo 5SNLP, were deployed around Buna village and the government station nearby (the Western Sector). Captain Yasuda had a honeycomb of bunkers on the main approach between swamps, and in the coconut grove and gardens behind. They were sufficiently close to each other that troops could move quickly between areas under attack. Yasuda had established headquarters on a large grassy strip south of these defences, presumably in the belief that the Allied attack was likely to come from the sea. The two main buildings were canvas and frame constructions with *tatami* mats on wooden floors. There was also an infirmary there, and huts for storing weapons, ammunition, food and medicine. Heavy barbed-wire entanglements laid across the track on the southern approaches would make an attack more difficult if it should come from that direction—which in fact it did.

◆　◆　◆

The Allies began their offensive at Buna on the morning of 19 November in torrential rain that continued all day. Troops were drenched and air support grounded. An assault force of 700 from the Americans' Warren Force advanced along the coast through swamp and jungle towards Cape Endaiadere. It was the first time American infantrymen had confronted Japanese ground forces in New Guinea. Told they were up against tired, disease-ridden survivors of the fighting in the Owen Stanleys, they found they were actually taking on fresh Japanese troops, well fed and well armed. It was the beginning of a two-week-long attack that was unconvincing at best, and sometimes a fiasco.

The Americans, mostly national servicemen, were ill prepared. Heavy foliage made mortars ineffective. The forward troops particularly were mown down by machine-gun fire from posts so well camouflaged they were all but invisible. The source of the gunfire couldn't be identified because Japanese machine-guns and Arisaka rifles emitted no flash and the sound reverberated in the jungle. The Japanese rotated weapons around several positions, creating the impression that they had the attacking force surrounded with superior numbers. Defensive fire seemed to be coming from all directions.

Major Porter, a US engineer observing, recalls: 'Our troops were pinned down everywhere by extremely effective fire. It was dangerous to show even a finger from behind one's cover, as it would immediately draw a burst of fire.'[18]

Advancing troops were allowed to pass by. Then the defenders opened fire, on the rear elements from the sides and on the front elements from behind. The forward troops took heavy casualties. The rest pulled back.

Another US unit attempted to move down Simemi track between the airstrips, but came under such intense fire on the wooden causeway that it was forced to a halt. Pushing waist- and chest-deep through oozing swamps alongside Simemi Creek, the Americans could carry only light weapons. The defenders in the concealed bunkers of the Eastern Sector watched them coming and cut them down with machine-gun fire. For the first time, the Americans experienced the insistent rat-tat-tat of woodpecker Jukis. Grenades got wet and became ineffective. Some Americans trailed a Japanese group, but not one of the seven grenades they hurled at them exploded. Japanese return fire brought down a third of the patrol.

Troops of the 229th, new to fighting in tropical swampland, were also trying to settle into the surrounds. Lance-Corporal Seiichi Uchiyama was among those deployed to the Eastern Sector. As soon as he arrived he found himself in a 'fierce hand-grenade battle with the enemy twenty metres away in the jungle'.[19] His unit retreated firing, suffering several casualties in the process. They constructed trenches overnight for protection from the concentrated fire. Uchiyama had no sleep for two nights, so often did they change positions.

The next day, a frustrated MacArthur ordered the storming of Buna's defences: 'All columns will be driven through to objectives regardless of losses.' After artillery and air bombardment in support, an Allied push along the coastal road in the morning came under Japanese air attack as well as fire from snipers and concealed bunkers and was driven back. MacArthur was apoplectic and issued the same order again on the 21st to General Harding. 'Take Buna today at all costs. MacArthur.'[20] It was to no avail.

The assault was becoming an embarrassment. A morning attack by Allied bombers was to be followed by a ground attack, but front-line commanders had not been notified. One of the planes dropped bombs on Allied forward troops between airstrips, killing four. There was no ground attack. Harding arranged a second air attack at midday, but that did not eventuate. An afternoon attack did, but most planes couldn't find the target area. A-20s dropped their bombs on the sea, and a B-25 bombed the US front-line forces on the coast, killing six.

The American troops were unnerved by this turn of events. Some had to be ordered back to the line. The force advanced with light weapons, ineffective mortar shells and a handset radio that didn't work in the jungle, against Japanese untouched by the earlier Allied bombardment. A few machine-gun outposts fell, but at a high cost in American casualties. An Australian company, ordered to take the first of the airstrips with US support, got to within sixty metres of it, but the Americans refused to advance and the Australians were eventually forced back.[21]

On the same day, Yasuda's naval troops near the Buna government station in the Japanese Western Sector faced an advance by a second US force under Harding. The Americans of Urbana Force found the track largely mud, the swamp water knee-deep and Entrance Creek along that perimeter unfordable, except at points well covered by machine-gun. Urbana Force got bogged in the swamps. Mortar shells got wet and failed; machine-guns and other weapons became clogged with swamp muck and jammed. One company's leader decided to press on towards dry land as darkness fell, but the swamp kept getting deeper. The disoriented Americans had to stop and spend a long, miserable night standing in watery ooze, waiting for first light so they could move again.

The assault force was plagued with glitches in its communications with battalion headquarters, a result of misunderstandings ('neck-deep' was heard as 'knee-deep') and confusion between Urbana Force's two commanders, Colonel Herbert A. Smith and Major Herbert M. Smith.[22]

By the fourth day, Urbana Force had made no progress. The daily Allied air attack accidentally strafed Colonel Smith's command post, and accurate Japanese machine-gun fire countered the Allied advance. The Americans dug into foxholes, which proceeded to fill with water. Intense covering fire by the Japanese prevented the enemy from getting past the barbed wire on the frontal approaches. Members of a Japanese unit relocating an anti-aircraft position were surprised by advancing Allied soldiers opening fire on them, but with the advantage of numbers they were able to drive their attackers back into the swamp.

The Japanese defence had been effective but Yasuda, recognising that he had set up his headquarters in a vulnerable position, ordered his men onto the attack and had his staff start destroying key documents. Yelling, the Japanese advanced on Americans gathered on a flat area of kunai at dusk. With many of their weapons jamming, the Americans were no match for them; they pulled back to the swamp, leaving the useless guns behind. Following a further series of miscommunications and malfunctions, all of Urbana Force started withdrawing on the morning of the 25th despite an order to remain on the kunai flat.[23]

Warren Force, meanwhile, had reorganised its communications and observation points for artillery fire. Harding had decided tanks were necessary for this phase and requested that three General Stuart tanks be brought up from Milne Bay. However, the only available transports there were Japanese barges abandoned in the Rabi operation, and the first tank was found, too late, to be overweight. The barge slowly capsized, and the tank sank into Milne Bay.

An advance on 26 November without tank support was pinned down then strafed by Japanese fighters from Lae despite Allied attempts to intercept them in the air. Finally, on the 30th, attacks were ordered from both Urbana and Warren forces. Urbana Force advanced in the pre-dawn to the front line of machine-gun posts. In the ensuing pandemonium of rifle and machine-gun fire, shouts and screams, a few outer posts were overrun. A unit advancing on Buna village lost its bearings and ended in a swamp. It moved back to the village at dawn, but was unable to penetrate further. The Americans arrived at Yasuda's headquarters to find him and his staff gone and documents, diaries and a large radio set strewn across the floor.

Warren Force moved towards the posts in Duropa Plantation, but even with mountain gun and mortar support it made no progress. It could not get past the log barricade, which couldn't be dislodged even with heavy artillery. The only ground lost by the Japanese was a crossing over Siwori Creek, to the west of Buna village. Land communication between Buna and Giruwa was cut as a result.

The daily pattern at Buna into December had been largely one of the Japanese holding their positions and the Allied force making incremental or no advances. By the end of November the defensive line at Buna was undented. But the Japanese had nowhere to go anyway. All they could do was defend and defend. There was no plan to advance from the coastal defences and nowhere to withdraw to—except across the sea, and that wasn't a decision for Colonel Yamamoto. Although the Japanese held fast, inflicting serious casualties, they suffered slow attrition at the same time.

A diary found at Buna reports a reconnaissance patrol on which a Private Kimura was shot and killed. Under enemy fire, his comrades had no choice but to hide the body and withdraw. When Americans appeared twenty-five metres in front of them, the Japanese fired on them; the Americans withdrew, leaving one dead soldier behind. The patrol returned in the evening and collected Kimura's body.[24]

The defences were subjected to constant artillery fire, limited by the small number of guns the Allies had there. The daily pattern seemed to be mountain howitzer and air attack followed by a ground advance, with further bombardment only if something went wrong for the Allies in the morning, which it often did. The regularity of the attack schedule allowed the defenders to stay in their bunkers during strafing and bombing runs, then emerge unharmed to take up concealed firing positions. The level of air attack from both sides increased significantly, as did the attrition rate. Japanese planes had recovered some of the initiative in the air, reflected in increased strike success: on the 22nd, two dozen of their fighters and bombers engaged fourteen Allied fighters over Buna and strafed an enemy-occupied village; two days later, bombers raided Dobodura airfield; on the 26th, planes sank an Allied transport ship and hit an armoured vessel; on the 28th, another transport ship was left in flames.[25]

The American ground troops found fighting in the unsanitary, swampy conditions exhausting. After wading, sometimes chest-deep, through foul-smelling swamps, they were expected to climb out and charge camouflaged bunkers with wet, clogged rifles. They had little artillery cover and often even less air cover. Food and ammunition were running low as air attacks frayed the supply line. By the end of November 492 Americans had been killed or wounded, and more had been taken out of action by malaria, dysentery and scrub typhus. The GIs had had enough.

Chapter 14

Madness and desperation

The first two weeks of the Allied thrust on Buna saw mostly green American reservists pitted against fresh, fit Japanese troops. Militarily, these were probably the best equipped of the defending soldiers. Elsewhere, the defenders were non-combatants or troops who had returned from the Kokoda Track. Those who took part in the Oivi–Gorari defence were still trickling back to the northern beachheads when the Allied assaults got under way. A large proportion of the Japanese who had crossed the Owen Stanleys were in little condition to fight, but along with their more fit confreres they were organised, where possible, into the defensive positions. Some of the men, however, had broken down completely and were mental shipwrecks.

Journalist Okada wrote about a chance encounter with such a man. Suffering himself after his Kokoda experience, Okada would go down to the shore at Giruwa most days to see if a ship had come in that might return him to Rabaul. For days there was none. All he saw was a 'straight, monotonous coastline of burning sand'.[1] Papua was taking its toll on his mind; he was becoming unhinged.

On the beach one day, he met a young officer from Osaka. At first the soldier talked sentimentally about his family. Then he asked Okada if he had any sushi to spare, and launched into a disjointed rant about gold bars hidden along the New Guinea coast and about how much he had enjoyed Charlie Chaplin in *The Gold Rush*. His eyes focused over Okada's shoulders, scanning the distant horizon, he gabbled on and on, about a major at hospital, about what was funny, about rice balls and when his ship might come in. This last subject was a key element of his manic monologue.

Okada turned away, but the officer went on ranting into empty space until a hospital orderly arrived. The orderly explained that the man was Captain Hanai, a medical officer who had suffered a violent fit in the mountains from malaria. He had been carried back to a field hospital, where he lay delirious, tossing and groaning, for several days. One morning, his fever lifted and he disappeared, but he came back to the hospital in the evening. He did that every day, going to the beach, talking to anyone he saw about his ship coming, or else sitting silently till sunset, when he would return to the hospital. It was time for him to return to his refuge once more. 'Looking after the emaciated mad man,' wrote Okada, 'I was suddenly seized with fear that my ship would never come.'[2]

As it happened, ships came that evening. The transports left at midnight, loaded with the sick and wounded—and Okada, who was neither sick nor wounded, just a journalist for whom war was no longer new or appealing. On the way his ship was sunk by Allied planes, and passengers had to be picked up by another transport. Eventually, however, he reached Rabaul.

There he attended a press briefing by Colonel Tsuji, the Tokyo emissary who had set MO Operation in train. Asked about the New Guinea campaign, Tsuji was scathing.

'A blunder,' he replied, as he thrust maps and papers into his leather bag. 'Cross the mountains and you'll get the worst of it. Don't you see that?'

He stood up, again spat out, 'A blunder,' and left.[3]

Those not evacuated from New Guinea were ordered to hold the beachhead for a renewed assault on Port Moresby if Japan should prevail in Guadalcanal. The Buna action might have been a battle between well-trained Japanese and inexperienced Americans, but at Gona the balance shifted. Gona was defended by a unit called Basabua Garrison, under the command of Major Tsuneichi Yamamoto. It was largely composed of non-combatants and camp followers: a 700-strong road construction unit, mostly made up of Formosan labourers of Takasago Volunteers, a hygiene unit and infirmary troops. The hygiene unit, more formally 55th Division Disease Prevention and Water Supply Unit, was under the command of a Captain Yamamoto, no relation to the garrison commander. Not only was this garrison not really a garrison, it was not actually stationed in Basabua. The Japanese command often confused the adjacent localities of Gona and Basabua. The Japanese never occupied Basabua village.

There was also, however, one infantry unit left in defence of Gona. Early in the campaign 11th Company of 41st Regiment had been redeployed to the northern region to assist with construction of bases there. By the time of the Allied advance it had become part of the garrison at Gona, sixty-eight men led by Lieutenant Jiro Soda. He was also Private Yokoyama's company commander, but the medical orderly had remained in Giruwa under Lieutenant Takenaka. Soda was a popular and respected junior officer who had risen through the ranks from private. He was constantly saying to his men in the frequent times of food shortage, 'If I die, eat my body and keep fighting.' The irony, says Yokoyama, is that he was always too skinny to eat.[4]

On paper, the Australians assigned to capture Gona were a vastly superior force. Trained infantry, they had Middle East combat experience—though how useful that would be in the humid, mosquito-infested swampland of the Papuan coast was open to question—but, unlike the men of Basabua Garrison, they had just come through the gruelling ordeal across the Owen Stanleys. They were tired and their supply line was stretched.

The Japanese road labourers-cum-soldiers at Gona fought with a single-minded ferocity born of desperation. They had sufficient time to set their defensive lines to maximum advantage so that anyone approaching their positions would pass through intersecting fields of fire from mutu-ally supporting posts. The Allied command has been criticised for not reconnoitring Japanese positions or getting aerial photos of them. There is evidence that they did get aerial photos, but the bunkers may have been too well camouflaged for the photos to provide useful intelligence.[5] As a result, the Australians didn't know where the defence posts were and Japanese gunmen were able to pick them off wading through swamps or advancing through fields of kunai grass. The Australian troops were also hampered by poor tactical decisions made during the advance.

◆　◆　◆

A group of Japanese were eating near a lone tree when the first advance patrol appeared on 19 November. They raced off as the Australians fired at them, but the arrivals then walked into a curtain of heavy rifle and machine-gun fire and dropped into a culvert by the track. Moving to either side of the track, they were pinned down in kunai fields. Jap-anese defenders in their concealed gun nests watched the enemy bring in more troops for a flanking movement, then brought it to a halt with sweeps of gunfire. Over the afternoon, a short advance was achieved at great cost. The Australians could see Japanese activity on the water-front—trucks, crates and a motor boat—but it was beyond their reach. That night they withdrew three kilometres, having lost thirty-two lives in the day's fighting.[6]

Australian rations were running low. They waited two days in pour-ing rain for fresh supplies, then renewed the attack at dawn. Coming again from the south, they were again pinned down in the cut-back kunai grass. Some managed to get to front-line Japanese pits and push grenades through the firing slits, but the attack was too weak to con-tinue. The attackers withdrew under fire, carrying their wounded back through the swamp on stretchers. An advance was also attempted from the east through the strip of coconut palms fringing the beach. This was an area infested with Japanese snipers. Progress was insignificant, but casualties weren't.

The next day, the Australians applied the same tactic with the same

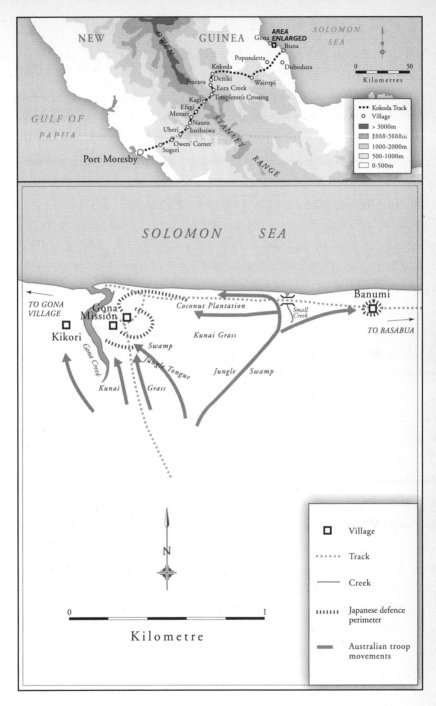

Japanese defensive positions and Australian troop movements,
Gona, November/December 1942

result. Troops moving across kunai patches and swamps were mown down by crisscrossing lines of machine-gun fire; those pushing through the coconut grove to the east were easy prey for snipers. Casualties were once again high for very little gain. By the end of the 23rd over 200 Australians had been lost at Gona, killed or wounded, and an even greater number put out of action by sickness. A worried General Vasey wired his immediate commander, General Edmund Herring, 'The Jap won't go till he is killed and in the process he is inflicting many casualties on us. I am beginning to wonder who will reach zero first.'[7]

Watching an advance coming through the scrub and kunai, Japanese riflemen picked out the choicest targets. Officers were recognisable from their gestures while moving forward: killing them weakened the attack. A Bren gunner put out of action forced the Australians to spend time organising a replacement crew. The Japanese had set up traps, cutting down palm trees and leaving them in the line of fire so they could pick off attackers tempted to use them as cover.

To the hard-pressed Australians the Japanese seemed to be sitting pretty, almost invulnerable in their cleverly laid out defences, but as at Buna they had nowhere to go. Their defeat was inevitable, even if they didn't yet realise it. They could hold out for now, but once the Allies figured out how to crack the nut their fate would be sealed.

In pursuit of that kernel, the assault force tried to bring more pressure and vary the attack with air strafing and bombing. In the morning Wirraways raided the Japanese defences, both guiding artillery and strafing, but to little effect, since the post positions were not well known and hard to spot. Midday air bombing seemed not to hit many targets either, but one Japanese diary notes for that day, 'Bombarded by enemy with considerable casualties.'[8] There was no infantry follow-up.

That day also, eighty Japanese reinforcements were landed at Gona among the waterfront traffic. The infantry unit, under Lieutenant Yamazaki, included two Jukis and was deployed at the south end of the mission, where the Australian mortar attack was strongest.[9] The newcomers were in the thick of it from the moment they arrived.

For the Australians, things weren't improving. Day after day, artillery and mortar bombardment would be followed by a ground attack making little gain. Some artillery fire from behind fell on the Australian lines, wounding two. A Japanese patrol advanced with bayonets fixed and backed by machine-gun and mortar fire, but it was held at bay by the Australian defence. All the time, barges were coming and going on the Gona beachfront. The assault force needed to occupy the beach if it was to stem the flow of supplies.

On the 28th an Australian battalion moved further east from Small Creek, already 750 metres east of the mission, to the village of Banumi, known to the Japanese as Pago and to the Australians as Cemetery Village. It's not clear which unit of Basabua Garrison was responsible for holding the eastern perimeter, but it was more likely to have been made up of non-combatants than infantry given its peripheral placement and the relative speed with which it would soon be overrun. The village had become a satellite citadel, with well-positioned and well-defended firing posts. The advance patrol took heavy casualties from the 'hornet's nest of concealed positions'.[10]

The whole battalion moved into the village the following morning after peppering it with mortars. Rifle fire was met with rifle fire, and initially the Japanese were able to resist the attack. An Australian Bren gunner fired from an open area and was killed by crossfire. An attempted bayonet charge by the attackers was cut down. The front line withdrew to allow a second mortar barrage, with devastating results. A machine-gun post was hit and the occupants shot as they ran for shelter. With the defenders reeling there was another Australian advance under cover of smoke, but the Japanese recovered sufficiently to pin it down. There was no further advance before night fell.

The defenders were losing heart. In the pre-dawn, ten Japanese tried to escape along the beach; five were killed. During the day, some defenders were picked off by an attack happy to play the waiting game and hold its position while preventing infiltration back to Gona. A Japanese unit isolated in Banumi village posed little threat to the assault on the Gona fortifications. The defenders sent out a patrol in the afternoon to probe the Australian line, but it was ambushed and put out of action. Soon after, the Australians' end-game began. An advance followed another artillery and mortar barrage, but for the few remaining Japanese the hopelessness of their predicament was clear. They broke and ran, some swimming out to sea, some heading into the scrub. There was nowhere specific to swim to, though, and many of the swimmers were shot as they floundered desperately. Those who ran into the jungle fared better, and some got away. An Australian patrol moved into the village and confirmed that 'Cemetery Village' was clear. The cemetery after which it was nicknamed could expect some new occupants.

While the Japanese eastern flank was being cleared, the main body of defenders at Gona held fast. They watched unseen as Australians crossed a kunai patch earlier reported free of Japanese. Wading through a swamp at dusk, the advance came under enfiladed fire from bunkers they could not locate in the dark. The Australian dead and wounded lay in the line of fire. Fit troops and the walking wounded had no choice but to withdraw through swamps and scrub, leaving them behind.

Next day the Allies replied with heavy aerial bombardment from fighters, A-20 Boston bombers and US B-17 Flying Fortresses. Three-hundred and 500-pound bombs and parachute bombs were dropped on the Japanese positions; among the casualties was the newly arrived unit commander, Yamazaki. But the Australians were slow to advance after the raids, and by the time they did the defenders were ready for them. Pushing down the beach and through the coconut palms, the attack made some progress before machine-gun fire from concealed bunkers and sniper fire brought them to a halt. The Australians had taken a foothold at several places along the beach, but Gona Mission was still firmly under Japanese control.

Although on the surface the Japanese held the upper hand they were worn out, with only a few hundred fit men left. Diarrhoea was rampant, but the men could seldom go far from their bunkers to defecate. Green flies were everywhere, with a bite that itched for days. The fighting was so intense that there was no time to bury the dead. Instead corpses remained where they fell and were used as sandbags, to stand on when shooting or to bolster bunker walls. The living slept side by side with the dead in posts constantly filling with rainwater. The stench of bloated, rotting bodies had become so bad that soldiers were putting on gas masks despite the humid heat. 'Everywhere, pervading everything, was the stench of putrescent flesh.' One Japanese soldier, unable to stand the strain, pointed his rifle at his own head, put his big toe on the trigger and blew the top of his head off.[11]

These defenders were isolated. The wire connection to South Seas Force HQ at Giruwa had been severed. In order to deliver messages, dispatch troops swam out to sea to get around the Australian perimeter. Among the messages was a plea for reinforcements, but evacuation was becoming more and more likely. Major Koiwai was instructed to stage a rescue by sea of the Gona troops. Two companies of his 2nd Battalion, about 120 men, left Sanananda in three barges on the night of 30 November, reaching the beach along from Gona Mission after midnight. Unable to identify the landing point in the dark, they lit signal flares—and drew fierce machine-gun fire from the shore. They returned to Sanananda, having accomplished nothing.

Koiwai's abortive rescue wasn't the only Japanese attempt to land at Gona. Barges moved up and down the coast transferring supplies and personnel. It appears there was little coordinated strategy driving the defensive effort along the coastline. Rather, disparate garrisons were making up tactics as they went. Although Koiwai's rescue failed to make contact, a similar but seemingly unrelated incident was observed from a distance a few days later by an Australian unit holding its position overnight near the beach. About midnight, two Japanese landing barges were spotted pulled up on the sand. A voice called out in the night, 'Give us a light, George.'[12] It was a ruse the Japanese often employed, calling out in English, and a line that had been used frequently.

The barges on the Gona beach appeared to hold no troops, just a couple of crewmen, who pushed the barges back into the water and glided into the darkness. Seen beaching again further up, they eventually left. It wasn't clear what their mission was, and the presence of concealed gun nests discouraged investigation. It was assumed they were evacuating some of the wounded.

Barges were also sent from Gona to rescue troops returning from

Oivi and Gorari as they reached the Kumusi mouth after crossing the river at Pinga. Colonel Yokoyama had ordered all available barges to be sent on this mission, but there wasn't enough space for all the troops gathered there. Most of 1st (Miyamoto) Battalion of the 41st was left behind. Those who were on the barges were attacked by Allied planes on the way and only about 500 men reached Giruwa the next day.[13] Some barges beached along the way to shelter from the attack. Miyamoto's bedraggled remnant drifted down the coast on foot towards the western side of Gona Creek.

A small Australian force had been dispatched west of the creek to block any support moving in from that side. Several Japanese attempts to land were reported, but they were always driven off with mortar fire. These were probably the returning soldiers. Some barges landed out of sight of the Australians, in addition to those landing further west and moving towards Gona. A Japanese tent on the beach was subjected to mortar fire. The occupants were mostly barefoot and dressed in tatters. Some were unarmed. They were clearly part of the retreat from Gorari, but they would soon be joined by much fresher troops.

◆ ◆ ◆

In Rabaul, steps were being taken to fill the senior leadership vacuum in New Guinea. General Hyakutake of Seventeenth Army had been ordered by Imperial HQ to concentrate on the war in the Solomons, with particular emphasis on the arm-wrestle in Guadalcanal. Responsibility for New Guinea was transferred to the newly formed Eighteenth Army and its commander, Lieutenant-General Hatazo Adachi. Major-General Tsuyuo Yamagata was commander of 21st Independent Mixed Brigade, formerly an Indochina garrison but without combat experience. Adachi put him in charge of all units in the Buna region that were not under South Seas Force command.[14] His command was designated Buna Detachment.

Yamagata's orders were to repel the Australian attacks, then secure a line from Gona through south of Giruwa to the navy airfield at Buna. Adachi felt the commander needed to be on the spot to determine how best this could be achieved. On 28 November, after waiting for the full moon to wane, Yamagata left Rabaul without air cover on a convoy of four destroyers. With him were two of his staff officers and the first echelon of a planned major reinforcement of the Papuan coastal defences. It was apparently thought that darkness and the speed of the destroyers would be enough protection for the convoy. The belief proved to be misjudged. The convoy was attacked in Vitiaz Strait, between New Britain and New Guinea, by three waves of twelve Flying Fortresses. One of the destroyers was substantially damaged and returned to Rabaul. Another burst into flames and followed soon after. The remaining two destroyers anchored in poor visibility but were driven off by another air attack without disembarking.

A second echelon—made up of 3rd Battalion of 170th Regiment (1st Battalion had been in the first echelon) and a signals unit—was on board and standing by to follow the first. Yamagata and his HQ staff attached to that convoy. This time it went down the other side of New Britain, supported by Zeros. An attack by B-17s was successfully intercepted by the Zeros, and the convoy reached Basabua anchorage before daybreak on 2 December, the night after Koiwai's failed rescue attempt. There the convoy came under such intense air attack that boarding barges wasn't feasible. Relocating to the mouth of the Kumusi, it landed troops and supplies there with great difficulty. Helped by orange flares that lit up the pre-dawn sky, Allied planes dive-bombed and strafed ships and landing craft. Five hundred troops and a large part of the supplies were brought ashore, but there was no opportunity for an ordered landing according to military procedure.[15] The barges headed to different parts of the shoreline, leaving the troops dispersed along the beach with instructions to make their own way down the coast. Yamagata, the new force leader, had only a company and a signals unit for protection. It was an operation fraught with risk.

The landed troops pushed down the shoreline, reaching Gona village on the evening of 6 December. There they joined up with the residue of Miyamoto's battalion. Troops who landed further down the coast moved east much faster. Crossing the Amboga River, halfway to Gona

Mission, they met forward units of the Australian force patrolling the area. The Japanese attacked but were driven back. The Australians noted, and duly recorded in their unit diary, that these troops had new clothes and equipment.[16] This was clearly a different opposition from the one they had been dealing with until then.

◆   ◆   ◆

At the mission precinct, the Australians continued to press for some sort of advantage with the same tactics that had so far yielded so little. After a pre-dawn artillery and mortar barrage, they advanced on the mission under smoke cover with bayonets fixed. Once again fierce machine-gun and sniper fire from the Japanese inflicted heavy casualties. Some of the attack force was pinned down in kunai, others took some Japanese bunkers by the beach, and another group dashed towards the huts yelling through a shower of Japanese fire.

In the afternoon, artillery shells rained down on the mission area and the Australians had to withdraw to shelter. An exchange of fire followed, but the Australians had lost the initiative. A militia unit in the attacking force missed the rendezvous point and failed to link up with the other units advancing through the coconut-palm belt. The Japanese successfully counter-attacked the occupied gun nests. The Australians fell back from their gains and had to withdraw with their casualties across Gona Creek. It had been a frustrating day, 'stinking hot', and the enemy remained maddeningly well concealed. An Australian sergeant has recalled, 'Through three attacks at Gona, I didn't even see a bloody Jap.'[17]

The next few days saw a slow turning of the tide in the battle of attrition at Gona Mission. The mornings would begin with artillery and mortar shelling of Japanese positions. The Japanese, with no artillery units at Gona, couldn't respond. They sat out the barrage amid the stench of the decomposing dead and the hygiene imposed by circumstance, each man hoping his post would not be hit. Then would come an assault on more Japanese beach positions. Much of the time these attacks were driven off with machine-gun fire, but occasionally a post would be overrun. Sometimes a counter-attack would recover a lost position, but as the days went by the Japanese defensive line along the water's edge was gradually whittled away until the Australians controlled the entire beachline running east from Gona Mission.

The story was similar with the defensive lines around the mission itself. Australians were still advancing across the kunai with significant losses. A smoke screen would be used as cover, although this often made the concealed Japanese positions even harder to see. Once they got close enough, the advancing troops could be seen through the smoke. Nonetheless, the outer defences were eliminated step by step. The Japanese were being squeezed into a small area, about 300 metres by 400 metres. Australian patrols often moved among the mission huts at night but they usually had to withdraw, having failed to take control.

An Australian militia unit was added to the assault force on 2 December. The 39th Battalion had initially held up the Japanese advance an eternity earlier at Isurava. Now its men were back to book-end the Kokoda story—and immediately had a taste of the chaos that ruled. Strafed by mistake by an RAAF Beaufighter, the 39th lost five men wounded before it got into battle.[18] On the 6th, they moved in under a smokescreen after a pre-dawn mortar barrage of the Japanese positions. Once again, the smoke made it difficult to locate hidden machine-gun posts and the crossing lines of fire ensured no significant penetration. For a gain of fifty metres, twelve men were killed. On the right flank, a platoon was caught by Japanese fire while it was shoulder-deep in sago swamp slime.

Heavy rain overnight filled the trenches and dugouts. Australian night patrols entered the mission precinct and flung a few random grenades with no discernible result. About midday eight Wirraways dive-bombed the area, but their targeting was inaccurate and had little effect on the Japanese. The ground attack was postponed.

The Japanese sensed that a major attack was imminent. They knew the end of their brave stand was near, inevitable and irresistible. Now reduced to perhaps a couple of hundred men who existed in utter squalor, soggy and stinking, they had held off a larger enemy force for nearly three weeks. It was a challenge for which most of them, as non-combatants, had not been trained. Now they waited and watched. An abandoned car on the edge of the mission was used as an observation post to track the comings and goings of the Australians.

A soldier's diary picked up later contained, for 7 December, these poignant words: 'At daybreak, enemy attacked us fiercely. Most of the frontline guards are injured. If we are defeated now, the wounded will be annihilated. We stir our injured bodies and defend our protective line.' It was the journal's last entry.

The Australians of the 39th brought a new tactic that hastened the inevitable. The Japanese endured the expected artillery and mortar barrage in the late morning of 8 December. As usual, they kept their heads down until it finished, after which they expected to set up in their posts with Jukis and light machine-guns to repel the usual advance. On that day, the pattern changed. Australian infantrymen moved up two minutes before the scheduled end of shelling. Their artillerymen lengthened the shells' trajectory to reduce the risk of friendly fire casualties. One attack came in not through the open kunai but from the south-east, using a jungle tongue as cover. Another came from the beach behind.

The attackers were up at the Japanese line before the shelling stopped, rushing machine-gun posts while the occupants were still setting up. Defenders were subjected to grenade and Bren-gun fire while they were sheltering from the bombardment.[19] The beach-side attack was held off at first but, with surprise on the side of the Australians, several posts on the opposite perimeter fell immediately. The breach provided an opening for more Australian troops to push in towards the centre. The attackers kept up the momentum all day, and now defences facing the beach began to crumble as well. By night, the Japanese had lost control of half their perimeter and the centre of their defences. Their cause at Gona Mission was clearly lost.

That night, garrison commander Yamamoto and 100 of the defenders tried to steal through the Australian lines and escape to the east towards Sanananda. Bren-gun fire cut them down in the darkness as they moved through kunai grass below the coconut-palm belt or waded out to sea. Less than half of them were later found not to have been armed with anything other than grenades. With the odds so stacked against them, a handful still managed to break through and join the defensive positions at Giruwa. Major Yamamoto was among those killed. He had entrusted his papers to one of the Takasago Volunteers. With characteristic resourcefulness born of life in the Formosan jungle, the runner found a path through the Australian positions and made his way to Giruwa.

At first light another forty defenders tried to rush past the beach strongholds, but it was a futile move made out of desperation and doomed to failure. The Australians spent the day snuffing out pockets of resistance within the mission grounds. One group of Japanese was encountered in a bunker, nine of them on stretchers. They had no intention of surrendering. Instead, they opened fire with grenades and rifles until they were either killed or too badly wounded to go on.

As the Australian troops moved through the precinct, they found ammunition, medical stores and rice green with mould. In a dugout, sacks of rice had been piled on the dead and more Japanese had fallen on the rice, their ammunition still stacked alongside them.[20] The surrounding area was testimony to the dreadful conditions in which Japanese had been living during the Allied assault. Gona beach was a filthy mess. Rotting corpses from both sides were floating in the lagoons and swamps, the mouths, eyes and nostrils filled with maggots. For the Australians, the long, costly mission was completed. By mid-afternoon on the 9th the 39th Battalion commander, Colonel Ralph Honner, was able to wire to his Brigade HQ, 'Gona's gone.'[21]

◆　◆　◆

While the Japanese forces were being swept out of Gona Mission, the troops that landed with General Yamagata on 2 December had crossed the Amboga River and were moving towards Gona village, five kilometres west of the mission. The unit of 280 men under Yamagata's direct command dug gun posts in and around the village. Australian patrols on that side of Gona Creek tried to deal with the advancing troops as they encountered them, but soon realised they were no longer the remnants of the Owen Stanleys campaign. Considerably outnumbered, the Australians pulled back. Following a fierce electrical storm overnight, a patrol was sent out to test Japanese strength. It came under intense machine-gun fire and withdrew.

The next day, the 11th, an afternoon patrol was pushed back across the creek by Japanese fire, but the Australian attack was reinforced with another battalion and the balance of strength at Gona village shifted. Scouts killed three Japanese officers near the village. The newly arrived force made its way by accident to the far side of the Japanese line and mounted a surprise attack across a swamp. In the firefight that followed the Australians' charge was eventually halted, but by then they had taken several posts and inflicted many casualties.

A Japanese counter-attack in overnight rain recovered some of the posts, but only some. Supported by relentless air bombing, the Australians advanced steadily over the next two days towards the village against a determined defence that would not pull back. Yamagata and his immediate staff, however, did withdraw to Napapo, three kilometres up the coast from Gona. The first echelon of reinforcements from 21st Brigade was still waiting to be successfully landed. Yamagata resolved to 'secure our current position in the Gona area, wait for the arrival of the second echelon of reinforcements, and plan subsequent strategies'.[22]

By then, the defenders around Gona village were reduced to 100 men. They fought on to the bitter end as the Australians chipped away at their line. By the 16th, the Japanese were encircled. The next day a No. 68 AT Grenade launcher[23] was brought into the attack and immediately destroyed a bunker containing a Juki and two lighter machine-guns. The 68 grenades were the last straw for the defenders. When the Australians swarmed through the village on 18 December to take out the remaining pockets of resistance, there was little opposition. Only a few Japanese remained, in hiding. It had been a more orderly defence than at Gona Mission. The wounded had been evacuated over sandbars or by barge at night. The dead had been buried outside the village.

The original echelon, another battalion of 170th Regiment with artillery and field machine-cannon companies, had left Rabaul on 8

December, but nine Flying Fortresses attacked in waves as it approached the Papuan coast the following afternoon. Three of the destroyers were set on fire and the convoy turned back.

It was another week before the next attempt was made to land reinforcements, and this time it went remarkably smoothly. On board with the 800 troops were the newly appointed commander of South Seas Force, Major-General Kensaku Oda, replacing the ill-fated General Horii, and a staff officer for the Buna Detachment under Yamagata, Colonel Kikutaro Aotsu. The weather turned bad, the poor visibility protecting the convoy so that it arrived undetected in the 14 December pre-dawn at the mouth of the Mambare River, fifty kilometres up the coast from the Kumusi's mouth. The ships had come equipped for rapid, efficient disembarkation. Decks were loaded with waterproofed cases of supplies lashed to empty drums, which were pushed overboard into the sea to be washed ashore by the tide. The ships also brought their own landing craft so troops were able to get to the beach soon after anchoring without needing to make contact with the shore. Allied planes arrived eventually, too late to cause any significant damage or loss. The landed troops were still sixty kilometres north of their army's beachheads, but they had barges.[24]

The Japanese got their supplies safely under cover of the shoreline vegetation. Unknown to them, they were observed by an Australian coastwatcher on a ridge overlooking the Mambare's mouth. Coast-watchers were military officers who operated behind enemy lines, often alone, gathering intelligence and reporting their observations by radio. Alerted by the Mambare coastwatcher, Allied aircraft bombed the supply dumps the next morning, destroying several barges at the same time. The Japanese would move the positions of their tents and supply dumps, still under the hidden eye of the coastwatcher, only to suffer repeatedly from bombing runs on new positions.[25]

General Oda was delayed several days at the mouth of the Mambare. He could only move a portion of his troops by night to the mouth of the Amboga River to join the Japanese forces already operating there. Oda and Aotsu joined Yamagata at Danawatu, where he had moved back to from Napapo, and were ordered by the senior officer to take direct charge of the fighting along the track to Sanananda. The troops from both reinforcement echelons—those who had survived the fighting around Gona village—were transferred to Giruwa by barge on 26 December. General Yamagata followed three days later.

Oda had previously been in charge of Toyohashi Reserve Officers' College, so he had come to New Guinea from administrative duties, not active service.[26] He and General Yamagata, who also had not come from combat duty, were of the same rank and had been in the same graduation year at military college. There appears to have been some tension between the two officers, but whether that predated their time in New Guinea is unclear. Yamagata seemed reluctant to move close to the fighting, something rectified eventually by General Adachi. However, Yamagata, senior to Oda in the Buna hierarchy, readily sent Oda up to the front line.

Chapter 15

On the track to Sanananda

Behind the thin strip of coarse sand that was the beach at Sanananda ran a low bank covered with tropical growth, mostly coconut palms and banyan trees, that rapidly gave way to extensive swampland. The swamps rose and fell with the tide, but after a torrential downpour they only rose, flooding the patches of kunai grass.

Across this sodden landscape and sitting slightly above it ran a track from Sanananda village south-west to Soputa, ten kilometres inland. Built up with earth, the road was laid with 'corduroy', logs placed side by side across its surface. This gave some firmness to the track, enough to carry vehicles in the dry season, but any movement off it was made precarious by the swampy ground. The heavy rains of October and November meant that treading on the earth at the edge of the track turned it to mud.

The Japanese had concentrated their defences on this part of their northern beachhead along the track to Sanananda, setting up posts from their bases around Giruwa on the shore for five kilometres up to the junction of a side track that led to Cape Killerton. This effectively cut off any land approach to Giruwa from the south or west. Any approach from Basabua, further west, had to contend with impenetrable jungle and swamp, as the Australians had discovered when moving eastward from Gona Mission.

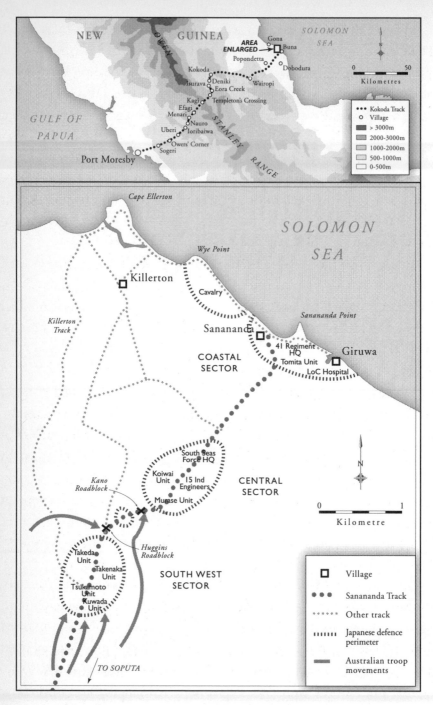

The Japanese defensive positions around Giruwa and along the
Sanananda track, November/December 1942

Japanese defensive positions were deployed in three separate sectors. The Central Sector, south of Giruwa, contained South Seas Force Headquarters. From the drowning of General Horii and Colonel Tanaka in late November until the arrival of General Oda a month later, HQ had no commander or staff officer. Also in this sector were mountain gun and anti-aircraft artillery battalions and 300 troops of the Independent Engineers. Koiwai Unit would be deployed in this sector when it returned to the coast. At the front was Murase Unit, with some of the residue of 3rd Battalion of the 41st, along with 800 reinforcements under Lieutenant Ogi, who arrived in late November. Major Murase himself did not join his unit until 18 November.

Spread along the coast from Wye Point to beyond Giruwa, the Coastal Sector held logistic units under Colonel Tomita, the headquarters of 41st Regiment under Colonel Yazawa, and a cavalry unit, as well as medical units and patients (about 2500 all together) associated with the hospital east of Giruwa. Buna Detachment headquarters would be set up in this sector when General Yamagata arrived at Giruwa.

At the front, on the Killerton track junction, was the strong point of the Giruwa defences, the South-West Sector, under the command of the grizzly Colonel Tsukamoto. This sector included much of the remains of 144th Regiment at its front end, although Sergeant Imanishi's platoon had been assigned up on the coast for guard duty at the barge landing site. In the South-West Sector there was also a unit under Lieutenant Hideta Takenaka, made up from the 41st, and Takeda Unit of field hospital patients. The medical corpsman Private Yokoyama was now with Takenaka Unit.

As at Buna and Gona the defences were solidly constructed bunkers, reinforced with earth-filled steel drums and palm logs. As the water table was about half a metre below the surface in many places the bunkers were built half into the ground, half above, as large, long, low-ceilinged rooms. The part sitting above ground was well camouflaged with awnings of vegetation that had to be replaced daily. A network of linking trenches, easily dug into the black soil and sandy loam, provided mobility for firing positions. They also were under camouflage. A layer of water from rain or seepage through the walls generally sat on the muddy bottom of the dugouts. Narrow wooden benches were built to give some respite from it. Although occupying most of the small elevated areas reduced seepage into the dugouts, they were never completely dry. The bunkers were prisons for their occupants. Except when they moved down the fire trenches or ventured out on occasional patrols the men stayed in them, waiting, eating, sleeping, toileting, firing at the enemy—but mostly waiting. Many of them would eventually die in their dugout or its attached trenches.

This was a landscape swarming with mosquitoes. Surrounded by swampland, so densely covered with mangroves and sago palms that troops moving through it became disoriented, the ribbon of the track to Sanananda was eminently defendable. The Allies would confirm this to their cost.

The Australians who had crossed the Kumusi at Wairopi began arriving at Soputa, at the inland end of the Sanananda track, early on 19 November. A party of Japanese at a supply dump was surprised by the arrivals and pulled back down the track, leaving behind several trucks. A bigger group that had remained in Soputa engaged the Allied advance patrols then withdrew to Tsukamoto's defences.

Lieutenant Kokichi Nakahashi was ordered to direct mountain-gun fire on the patrols that had moved into Soputa village. The Allied advance was temporarily stopped, but as darkness fell shadowy figures were seen moving around the Japanese artillery positions. A runner sent back to Tsukamoto's perimeter was intercepted, and Nakahashi realised they were in danger of encirclement. After dismantling and burying their gun, his crew avoided the enemy by crawling through the jungle for two hours to reach Japanese lines.

Australians moving down the track to the coast struck the front end of Japanese defences before the Killerton junction. In the afternoon of the 19th the advance clashed with Kuwada Battalion, initially making significant ground with a charge on battalion headquarters. Seventy of the defenders were killed, including Colonel Kuwada.

The regimental colours of the 144th had been kept in a hut in 3rd

Battalion HQ. By dusk the hut was occupied only by dead or dying men, but fighting had eased and the Australians had fallen back. With a burst of gunfire that torched the hut, Australians moved up again in the flickering gloom shouting 'Fire!', unaware of the significance of the burning hut's contents. Regimental colours are of such totemic importance that the last standing member of the colour guard was ordered to prevent them falling into enemy hands. He ran through the flames, wrapped his arms around the huge banner and its wooden rod as best he could and leapt into a trench, escaping up its length. Warrant Officer Shimada was given the responsibility of keeping the scorched colours of the 144th in safe hands.

The day after the colours were rescued defenders counter-attacked, recovering the ground they had given up and inflicting damaging losses on the Australians. The early story on the Sanananda track was much the same as in the first engagements at Buna and Gona. Defenders in their concealed dugouts were able to subject approaching troops to deadly enfilading crossfire, causing considerable losses with each approach. In two weeks of daily attack at different points of the South-West Sector perimeter, the Australians suffered many casualties with very little progress. What small gains were made were subsequently recovered by Japanese counter-attack. The Australians, having come off tough fighting on the Kokoda Track, were a near-spent force, down to about 15 per cent of their original strength.[1]

Although the Japanese had been through the same debilitating experience, they managed to defend effectively from their well-placed bunkers. But at Giruwa a different mindset was needed. Imanishi says he found the defensive operation on the Sanananda track much more stressful than advancing in attack over the precipitous pathway towards Port Moresby.

'When you fight offensively, you have more fighting spirit,' he says, 'but for defence everything is different. When we arrived at Giruwa, we had no food. Giruwa is flat and swampy, and we had to hold our positions under the enemy's heavy artillery fire and air bombing. You never knew where the enemy's infantry would come from, either.'[2] The passive nature of dug-in defence was unnerving. At least in attack there was movement and an element of skill. This wasn't even a fighting withdrawal now; it was just backs to the wall.

Like other refugees from the Kokoda Track fighting Imanishi had got to Giruwa by a circuitous route, driven by an instinct for survival. After crossing the Kumusi, his group inferred the direction of Giruwa from the sound of anti-aircraft gunfire during the day. Unoccupied Allied tents along the way were raided for food. Without officers in command, they found a way through enemy lines by wading through swamps. Arriving at Gona Mission during its siege, they were ordered to transfer to Giruwa by barge. In the evening, while they waited on the beach near the mission, they saw in the distance a group of Japanese soldiers chased by Australians and trying to swim to safety. Bullets raised a spray of water around them. Imanishi's group felt like observers from another dimension. They left by barge soon afterwards.

American troops from 126th Regiment joined their Australian allies in late November. At first they were welcomed, despite their tendency to brag. One Australian unit diary noted that the Americans were 'keen to get to grips with the Japs',[3] another that they told the Australians they 'could go home now as they [the Americans] were here to clean things up'.[4] These were National Guardsmen, not highly trained and, in many instances, with officers who were political appointees from the battalion's home town.[5] They didn't know much about leadership, and their charges didn't know much about battle.

The Americans made slow progress behind daily exchanges of mortar fire. In one exchange, US mortars dropped short on their allies in front of them. After nine days of probing, all the Americans had to show for their effort was a precarious roadblock. Units of their Baetcke Force under Captain John D. Shirley had managed to work their way around the western flank on 30 November and establish a toehold on the Sana-nanda track between Japanese sectors. With a fragile supply line, it was held in check by constant counter-attack on all sides. The Americans dug in on a fairly open space in the midst of swampy jungle surrounded by tall trees, vulnerable to sniping and surprise attacks.[6] After an early patrol was ambushed the unit kept within its perimeter, holding off repeated attacks.

The task force commander, Major Bernd Baetcke, was positioned west of the roadblock, poised to mount a rear attack on the Japanese if an attack on the front line succeeded. It didn't, and there was too high a risk of losing the supply line if he moved now into the roadblock. Supplies eventually got through under Captain Meredith Huggins after a particularly hard fight. Shortly after a concerted Japanese counter-attack reduced the roadblock perimeter, killing Shirley in the process. Huggins took command, and the roadblock bore his name for the next month. The name would outlast him there by a few weeks.

The Japanese repeatedly attacked the block but they couldn't remove it, and other US troops couldn't cut their way through to it.[7] Elsewhere, the Japanese were able to push back all attempts to break through their lines. The Australian diary that a few days before had been excited by the Americans' arrival was now reporting that, apart from Huggins roadblock, it was a 'dismal failure', with no significant advance made.[8]

The unit to which Private Yokoyama was attached was ordered to search out and destroy the enemy who had infiltrated their positions. He went out on the patrol with nine soldiers from a light-machine-gun squad. Three of them were in front of Yokoyama and the sergeant. The rest followed. Yokoyama heard a noise from the jungle, and immediately the machine-gunner at the front fell. The other two, trying to grab his gun, were shot in the head.

Yokoyama picks up the story: 'What I remember next is the sergeant screaming, "I'm moving forward!" and running on to fight, but he got shot in the arm and ran back to where I was. I immediately gave him first aid. I told him not to move but he didn't listen. I guess you will be afraid of bullets once you have been shot, no matter how brave and strong you are. While trying to move back, he was shot dead.'

By then all the front line had been killed, and a voice from behind said, 'Yokoyama, tell us what the heck is going on there.'

In shock, he screamed, 'The squad leader got killed.' His raised voice drew gunfire, so he stayed where he was in silence.

Soon after, he heard someone behind say, 'I think now Yokoyama is dead too. I can't hear his voice any more. Let's get out of here. It's getting dark. We'll come back for the bodies tomorrow.'

Yokoyama dared not let them know he was still alive or even move from his position. A few moments later, several Australian soldiers appeared and started digging a hole. At first, Yokoyama thought it was for the dead bodies, but then he realised they were digging a new foxhole. They didn't check the bodies they had just killed or their weapons.

Yokoyama stayed hidden behind the grass in front of the Australians, scarcely daring to breathe and trying to work out what they were up to. An eternity went by, with no opportunity for escape. Darkness came and he thought, 'I will be left alone in the middle of the enemy if I don't get away now.'

He grabbed the machine-gun and his rifle and 'ran like a rabbit'.

When he caught up with his squad, they were preparing to return to their bunker. One of them said in pretended off-handedness, 'Hey, you're still alive. We were about to go without you.'

Yokoyama found the sarcastic greeting strangely comforting. 'It felt good to come back even through all the struggle,' he says. 'I was really glad there was someone like him!'[9]

◆　◆　◆

On 7 December, with Australian positions ranged in a horseshoe around the front of the Japanese fortifications at the track junction, an Australian militia battalion arrived to relieve the battle-weary AIF troops. This unit was fresh—so much so that no real effort had been made to train its soldiers for battle. After the decisive victory at Oivi–Gorari the command had assumed that the militia would no longer be needed, so it was used instead as army labour, working on the wharves of Port Moresby. This would be its first battle.

The militia attacked Japanese positions without detailed briefing or preliminary reconnaissance, and with signal cable that was shorter than the distance to the Japanese line. The battalion in the field had to use runners to communicate with its command. The defenders in their hidden posts could see the troops advancing and opened fire. The Australians had no idea how to deal with a wall of enfilading machine-gun fire in thick jungle and scrub. Within five hours, 229 militiamen were killed or wounded. A second militia battalion that had been brought into the battlefield a few days before was sent forward in the afternoon with the vague order to 'attack enemy positions astride the road'. It was a second disaster for the day, resulting in 130 more Australians killed, wounded or missing.[10] The Australian command retreated to a policy of constant patrols to probe Japanese positions. It wouldn't attempt a major attack for another twelve days.

After several failed attempts, further supplies got through to the roadblock on 8 December, and a wounded Huggins was evacuated to the rear. He reported to his superiors on conditions at the block. The men were living in muddy foxholes in an area 200 metres square, he said. Fever raged, their feet were rotting, food, ammunition and medical supplies were low, and disposal of waste and burial of the dead were both extremely problematic. They drank chlorinated water from a hole dug a metre deep. The Japanese often cut their communications wire and frequently tapped the line, so they had to be careful what they said—when they were able to say anything.[11] By 13 December, they had lost all radio and telephone contact. No runners were able to get through.

If the state of the Americans at Huggins was dire, it was nothing compared with that of the Japanese they had cut off. Tsukamoto's men had been in their positions since 21 November without reinforcements or reliable supplies. They were short of food, weapons and ammunition, dependent on a trickle that came down the Killerton track from time to time. They too were ravaged by malaria. Diarrhoea was rife in a breeding ground created by their encirclement. Under continual rain by night and scorching sun by day, they were again close to starvation.

'We were all skin and bone,' says Yokoyama, 'as if our stomachs were stuck to the inside wall of our back. Our pelvic bones stuck out too. We all suffered non-stop diarrhoea. We dug holes to put our buttocks and pelvis over and lay down on them when sleeping at night. Any overnight excretion would drip into the hole.'[12]

The rice supply got so low, Yokoyama says, that they were counting it out by grains. They existed on a porridge of fern buds with a little rice floating in it. Soldiers stationed close to the sea could obtain salt, but those like him at inland defences had no opportunity to obtain it or clean water. They had no choice but to drink water seeping into a hole from the water table, contaminated by human faeces and corpses.

'We talked only about food every day, like how much we missed Japanese food and craved plain rice, pickles, miso soup, sushi and so on. Ironically, most of us starved to death.'[13]

Holed up with uncertain supplies, the men took to scavenging or worse. Private Tetsunosuke Miyashita was with the reinforcements of 144th Regiment that had landed with Colonel Yamamoto and been absorbed into Murase Unit of 41st Regiment, south of Giruwa. Following a remark by a friend and with covering fire standing by, he searched for enemy bodies in the jungle near their positions. He found one, took a bag from the dead man's shoulder and darted back. In the bag were two packets of dry bread, a can of beef and two cigarettes. The squad members ate the food that night. The cigarette tobacco was mixed with dry leaves and rolled in paper from *Infantry Drill Regulations*. The cigarette lasted a week, with everyone enjoying a puff from time to time.[14]

Some scavenged more dangerously. The Takasago Volunteers were particularly adept at finding food—and sometimes ammunition—in Allied encampments when the soldiers were out on patrol. The Formosans would slip fearlessly into their tents and out in quick time.[15] Some, in their desperation, went further. An Australian soldier was found garrotted at the side of the road with his kitbag emptied of food. It was assumed this had been done by a Japanese straggler making his way from Gorari to the beachheads.

Harassed by air, artillery and mortar bombardment, Tsukamoto's force fought off repeated infantry-unit and patrol attacks. Yokoyama wasn't in the front line of the South-West Sector but in a foxhole in the middle of it. The ground attacks hadn't penetrated to his part of the defences, although Huggins roadblock was established behind. Yokoyama's role was to endure whatever the Allies threw at him.

'They weren't really positions, because we didn't have proper weapons but just kept digging a hole to hide ourselves. They attacked us with sixty artillery shells in the morning and evening every day. During the day, Australian observation planes flew over us on patrol. If they saw us, they would contact artillery units and guide them to fire on us. We said to each other, "Here they are again! Put out the fire and don't make any smoke."'[16]

After the war, the sinister syncopations of artillery bombardment resonated for decades in Miyashita's memory: the rhythmical 'boooboom boooboom' of the shells rising, followed by a series of explosions with the sounds of 'shudadan shudadan'. 'With the artillery smoke covering the area and the sound of falling and shattering trees in the air, our base became a scene of hellish carnage.'[17]

Given a crash-course in firing a light machine-gun, Miyashita was assigned a position north of Huggins roadblock. Stricken with malaria, he had dozed off when he was woken by a shout: 'Enemy!'

There was loud gunfire all around. He looked out of his foxhole to see enemy soldiers moving through a jungle thicket led by an officer who was shooting wildly with a gun in one hand. Miyashita pulled the trigger on his machine-gun, but it only made a clicking sound. As he struggled to see what the problem was and rectify it, voices shouted all around him.

'Fire the machine-gun! Hurry up and shoot!'

He gave up, put the machine-gun to one side and grabbed a 38 carbine while an ammunition carrier in the trench beside him loaded other rifles. In ten minutes the exchange ended and the enemy was gone.

Finding out that a nearby 41st unit had machine-gun specialists, he took the gun to them and asked if they could repair it. They explained that he'd had the muzzle too close to the embankment, and sand had got in the gun. It was stripped down, repaired and cleaned, and Miyashita was shown how to operate it properly. A few days later in another Allied attack the machine-gun functioned without mishap. Miyashita had regained the trust of his platoon.

Units nearer the coast than where Miyashita was placed fared relatively well. Although they too came under regular air and artillery bombardment, they were not subjected to ground attacks until the establishment of Kano roadblock and, even then, only on its forward perimeter. These troops were better supplied. They had access to food that was landed by sea and supplemented the rationed handful of rice with roots, crabs, snakes and anything else that was edible.

At the Line of Communication Hospital at Giruwa, it was a different story. With heavy rain almost every night in the wet season the Giruwa River had flooded, leaving lavatories and drains filled with water and unusable. Wards were under water, and seepage and sewage from the lavatories left parts of the hospital smelling foul. Equipment deteriorated in the humid climate: panniers rotted, leather straps lost their pliability, metal edges of lids corroded and screws fell out, stretchers rusted and could not be used.

The hospital had little food or medicine. The grave shortage of food added to the difficulty of getting patients back to health. Provisions that had come were generally poorly packed and often short in weight. Powdered bean paste, soy sauce and dried fish had all rotted and had to be thrown out. There was a shortage of medicines because supplies were being diverted to Guadalcanal.[18]

The incidence of malaria had increased dramatically at the hospital as the epidemic struck, exacerbated by pre-dawn chill. Of the medical personnel who weren't dead, many were patients themselves.

◆　◆　◆

An Australian cavalry unit fought its way to Huggins roadblock on 18 December, crossing several swamps, some chest-deep, and passing the rotting casualties of previous encounters while militia groups continued to stall on Tsukamoto's perimeter. The cavalry unit fought its way around fierce opposition from Murase Unit to occupy another point on the Sanananda track 400 metres north of Huggins. Called Kano roadblock, it was a tenuous position: Murase Unit still occupied the track between it and Huggins.

On the back of the Kano advance, the Allied leadership tried to generate some battle momentum with Australian militia battalions on three fronts of Tsukamoto's defences. A few posts were taken early in the assault, but under intense fire from concealed bunkers it ground to a halt. Some militiamen were reluctant to advance once their officers were hit.[19] The attack was called off when the command became unnerved by the toll of casualties.

Australian reinforcements had started to arrive from Gona. On 22 December they relieved the debilitated Americans at Huggins, but the Japanese still had strong defences there in Murase's force, and even stronger defences north of Kano. Kano faced the Central Sector, now under the command of General Oda, with Yazawa's 41st, the rest of the 144th replacements and artillery units and reserve forces standing by in Sanananda and Giruwa. It was a formidable assembly.

To the south, where Tsukamoto's outer line had been breached, the defences behind were fighting as ferociously as those at Gona had done, but even more effectively. As the US military historian Samuel Milner has observed, 'Most of the Japanese at Gona had been service and construction troops with little combat experience; those defending the [Sanananda] track junction were battle-tested infantry troops, probably as good as the Japanese Army had.'[20]

On the 20th, another attack was attempted with the same outcome as the day before, and again on the 21st. The Allied command seemed bereft of new tactics: the only changes were to shuffle companies around the attack points. By late December, the Americans' strength was so reduced from battle casualties and disease that they could only maintain defences and patrol the flanks. They no longer had the numbers to mount attacks. The Allied generals, Herring and Vasey, conferred and decided against shuffling the pack for another frontal attack. They would wait instead to bring in tanks and fresh troops, but no tanks were possible before the 29th and the troops were still tied up in Buna.[21]

Chapter 16

Buna falls

After two weeks of fighting, with numbing loss of life and no discernible progress, General MacArthur sacked his field commander at Buna. General Harding was replaced with General Robert Eichelberger as leader of the American forces there. MacArthur told him, 'I want you to remove all officers who won't fight. Relieve regimental and battalion commanders if necessary, put sergeants in charge of battalions and corporals in charge of companies . . . I want you to take Buna, or not come back alive.'[1] Frustrated by the lack of progress, MacArthur placed such pressure on his command chain that it would trigger rash actions and waste more lives before the Buna fight was won.

Eichelberger shuffled his colonels and majors while the Japanese defences remained steadfast, waiting in their network of fortifications. Colonel Yamamoto's army troops were in the Outer Camp around Duropa Plantation and in the Eastern Sector around the two airstrips; Captain Yasuda's navy marines in the Western Sector around Buna village and the government station known as the Buna mission. The first action with the reorganised Allied force was an Australian plan to engage the Japanese defences with Bren-gun carriers, thin-skinned reconnaissance vehicles that were open at the top and unarmoured below.

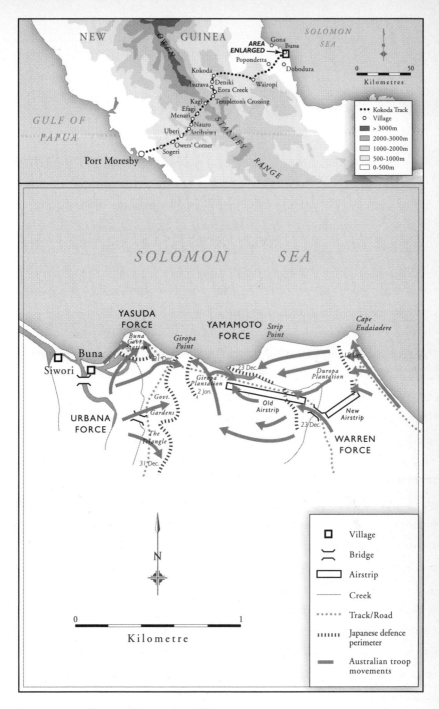

Japanese defensive lines and Allied troop movements around
Buna, December 1942/January 1943

Six A-20 bombers attacked Duropa Plantation with artillery support in the early morning of 5 December. Immediately after, the infantry and machine-gun crews of Warren Force attacked up the coast behind five Australian-crewed Bren-gun carriers. Having moved out of their bunkered shelters and back to their gun posts when the bombing stopped, the Japanese answered with heavy fire from their coastal barricade and concealed positions. In the debacle that followed the carriers' underbellies caught on stumps in the uneven ground, the vehicles rising in the air like startled animals. They made easy targets. Hand grenades were thrown into the carriers and adhesion mines attached to their sides by roaming Japanese. Some vehicles took direct hits from anti-tank guns.[2] Within twenty minutes all five Bren-gun carriers had been put out of action and their crews badly wounded. Heavy fire from the defenders and heat exhaustion prevented the Americans advancing more than forty metres.

The Buna defences were attacked on two fronts that day. Once the advance on Duropa Plantation was under way B-25 bombers attacked the mission, while the village nearby was subjected to artillery and mortar fire. Infantry of Urbana Force then moved up but couldn't advance. In the afternoon, they managed to push through swampy ooze to the main Japanese line just outside the village. The Americans attempted a rush on the village with fixed bayonets, but the charge was cut down by Japanese marines moving along their crawl trenches. One American platoon, however, pushed north across the village to the beach, where its troops dug in. Counter-attacks from the village and the mission on either side failed to dislodge this unwelcome development, which left the village effectively isolated.

Urbana Force's grip on the throat of Buna village seemed a small gain after more than two weeks of fierce fighting. But although the Japanese could shelter in their bunkers during bombardment, persistent mortar fire had worn down their resolve. They feared mortars and artillery more than aerial bombardment because there was less warning of them. The US troops may have advanced little, but their attacks had added to the Japanese casualties.

Japanese diaries found at Buna are full of complaints about promised or rumoured reinforcements failing to arrive. The diary of Corporal Okajima complained on 1 December they had been waiting for reinforcements for the past four days.[3] Another diary said there were reports all the time that reinforcements had landed but they never appeared, and later that 'somebody ate my whole day's rice ration and three other rations were stolen'.[4] Morale was slipping. It was unbearably hot, with the tall kunai grass shutting out the air and holding in the steaming heat. One unit had lost its original company and platoon commanders and their successors. 'Under such circumstances,' philosophised an unnamed soldier in his diary, 'my body will be buried in New Guinea and become fertiliser for the soil of Buna.'[5]

By early December food was in short supply, though not yet at starvation level. Lance-Corporal Uchiyama, in the Eastern Sector, noted, 'We are continuously short of rations. Eat only once a day and impossible to walk because of lack of strength. Suffering from attack of diarrhoea.' Thirty planes dropped rations and ammunition on 10 December, but these couldn't be distributed to all the troops. Food was dropped twice by parachute, records Uchiyama's 14 December entry, 'but did not come into our hands'.[6]

General Eichelberger decided to wait for tanks and fresh Australian troops to be brought up from Milne Bay. The tanks were light American M3 General Stuart tanks of the Australian 2/6th Armoured Regiment. By the night of 15 December, eight tanks had been landed at Oro Bay. Meanwhile, the Japanese were kept on their mettle with probes by patrols and artillery. The Allies brought in 105-mm howitzers using shells with a delay fuse. The Japanese called these 'earthquake bombs' because they lodged in the earth, and when they exploded the reverberations pounded bunker walls and often caught people moving across the ground.

Some of the Allied technology was still in the development stage. Two US flame-throwers were brought in to burn out a large Japanese bunker. The crew got undetected to within ten metres of the bunker and turned on the thrower. A dribble of flame got halfway to its target and set the grass on fire. The operational crew of four were all killed.[7] That evening, Yasuda sent a force of 100 men across the estuary island of

Musita to relieve the village. They attacked the Americans, yelling and screaming, but were driven back with mortars and machine-guns.

Many of the Kokoda Track battles had involved hand-to-hand fighting, but on the more open coastlands military technology was able to play a greater role, putting the Japanese at more disadvantage than in the mountains. The defenders of the village held their position tenaciously in the face of the onslaught. Groups of mortars were fired at them simultaneously like concentrated artillery in an improvised multiple 'hammer' bombing.

Their position had become untenable. By the night of 13 December, the defender force in the village had been reduced to 100 men whose supply line had been cut off for some days. Urbana Force had brought in fresh troops for a major assault. The Japanese evacuated the village and made their way along the coast to Giruwa. Americans entered the village in the morning and found it empty. Village huts were wrecked from the artillery, coconut palms splintered and broken. There were craters and shell holes everywhere, but bunkers still stood despite the artillery hits. Little food or equipment had been left behind.

◆　◆　◆

On the evening of 17 December, seven of the newly arrived Stuart tanks lumbered into line for an Allied push up the coast towards Cape Endaiadere. A mortar barrage was used to drown the roar of the motors and the clank of tracks. The Japanese in their bunkers, numbed after five weeks of regular bombardment, were unaware of this significant development. It was to prove decisive for the fate of the Buna beachhead.

Artillery and mortar fire did considerable damage to the front line of the Outer Camp in the morning. Then the tanks advanced in front of fresh Australian infantry, five Stuarts charging straight up the coast, two swinging around towards the airstrips. American troops moved in behind the Australians.

The Japanese in the Outer Camp were caught completely by surprise. The heavy fire and the curtain of flying debris—undergrowth and bark dislodged in the crossfire—meant they didn't see the tanks until it was too late. Within a few metres of the bunkers, the tanks began firing. Defenders ran desperately at the machines, leaping on top of them, but it was a suicidal gesture with Allied infantry just behind.[8] One tank was lost to a Molotov cocktail delivered in this manner and one halted with engine failure, but the Japanese positions were overrun. In a little over an hour, the attack moved briskly up to Cape Endaiadere and swung west along the coast from there.

Bunkers and blockhouses beyond the cape had mostly avoided the preliminary bombardment that day, and their occupants were by then aware of the approaching tanks. The Allied advance met stiff resistance and was stopped by a defence line 500 metres past Cape Endaiadere. By this stage, though, the attackers were in control of Duropa Plantation and clearing its remaining defensive positions. The Japanese had been resolute and immovable for weeks, but now the back of 229th Regiment's defence had been broken. Yamamoto ordered a fighting withdrawal back to the former government station where the Buna garrison operated its headquarters.

The push towards the airstrips in the Eastern Sector proved more difficult than the attack up the coast. The two tanks in front were stopped after a short distance, one of them put out of action with machine-gun damage to its turret. More tanks were brought down from the coast. After two hours of bitter fighting, the combination of tanks and infantry overcame a strong group of twenty blockhouses, many built of concrete and steel. The Japanese pulled back along the north side of the New Strip to bunkers near the wooden bridge over Simemi Creek and the foul swamp into which it merged.

The Japanese suffered severe losses in the fury of the day's onslaught, but they had ensured that the Allies' success was costly. One in three of the Australians participating in the operation were killed or wounded.[9] The defensive works had been nearly impregnable. Allied commanders viewing the ground gained in Duropa Plantation and by the New Strip concluded that these fortifications could not have been taken by infantry alone.[10] The tanks had made the crucial difference.

After a rest day Allied tanks and troops pushed on, overrunning Japanese positions east of Strip Point after a heavy fire-fight for most of the day. The terrain became quite marshy past Strip Point, and the fourteen-ton tanks got bogged. Yamamoto withdrew his troops across Simemi Creek over the bridge between the airstrips and through the shallows at the creek mouth, the only part of Simemi Creek that could easily be waded.

Once across the only obvious crossing points on the creek, Yamamoto set up his new positions to deny that convenience to Allied forces. Defending was made more difficult, with contact between garrison HQ and the withdrawing troops broken. Yamamoto could no longer communicate directly with his men, who now had to make many of the decisions themselves. Emplacements had been set up on an island at the mouth of the Simemi and on the west bank of the creek, positioned to fire across anyone foolhardy enough to wade through the shallows. Further upstream, the Japanese blew up a section of the bridge where it crossed the trench of the creek cutting through the swamp. New defensive positions were set up so the bridge and the gap in its middle were well covered.

The Americans tried to repair the bridge under a screen of smoke generated from mortars. They took a hastily built catwalk up to the gap, only to find it was shorter than the gap. With the Japanese now alerted to that plan, the Allies looked for another place to cross Simemi Creek. The creek was deep except at its mouth, with thick sago swamp on the approaches, and much of it covered by Japanese fire. Muddy and smelly, the Simemi was cluttered with broken timber and filled with rats and other vermin. It wasn't until the next day that an Australian patrol, wading neck-deep in places, found a way across the ooze at a big bend north of the bridge. Other troops followed them, moving south towards the Japanese defences on that side of the bridge.

Aware of the approaching force and knowing they risked encirclement, most of the 229th pulled back further west to a network of fire trenches connecting bunkers that had been built north of the Old Strip. They had strong mountain-gun and cannon support there, along with two anti-aircraft guns on concrete bases and surrounded by grass-covered earth embankments. Hidden in kunai, they would be difficult to pinpoint until close by. Meanwhile, engineers started repairing the bridge for US troops to cross that afternoon, then strengthened it for tanks to get across.

The Americans moved up the southern edge of the Old Strip, while the Australians swung around and pushed through skirmishes along the northern side. More GIs moved through the jungle south of the airfield. On Christmas Eve they were joined by tanks coming across the bridge. They advanced until late morning, when the anti-aircraft guns opened up on them. The Japanese hadn't fired them for some days, and the Allies had assumed they had run out of ammunition. In fact, they had held off to keep the last of their shells in reserve for an emergency. Warren Force's attack was just that. The anti-aircraft guns knocked out two tanks. A third turned over in a shell hole. The remaining tanks were held back until the guns could be silenced.

Japanese defensive positions were well placed to sight enemy troops' stealthy movement across the Old Strip and around the abandoned Zeros and transports. The airfield was cleared, and defenders were able to hold on to their foxholes forward of the bunkers. Allied troops tried to breach the Japanese lines for two days without success, finally finding a way unseen through an adjacent swamp to the two anti-aircraft guns, which they captured after hard, close-in fighting. Now that the Allies had broken through the rear of Eastern Sector's defence, a fighting rearguard was used to disguise the Japanese withdrawal to Giropa Plantation, like Duropa a prewar coconut palm enterprise.

The rearguard fought to the bitter end. Grenades were tossed back out of foxholes at the advancing Americans and Australians. Suicidal rushes with swords and bayonets were cut down. Many of the Japanese carried M-1 rifles and wore American helmets and fatigues acquired earlier in the campaign. At four in the morning on 29 December, twenty of Yamamoto's men infiltrated a US company command post and attacked with grenades and bayonets, yelling 'Medic, medic!' as if they were American wounded. In the scramble, several men were bayoneted in their sleep; others were killed in hand-to-hand fighting. All but five of the Japanese were driven off, but they left behind fifteen Americans killed and another twelve wounded.[11] It was a final gesture from an outnumbered force that had fought ferociously and now faced annihilation.

Some of the 229th were sustained by their belief in a cause. Others, like Lance-Corporal Uchiyama, found the air bombing at dawn and the mortar hammering all day sapping their spirit. 'We now only wait for the final moments to come,' he wrote nine days before his final diary entry. 'Every day one or two comrades are killed. I am disgusted with myself, only thinking when my end will come. As a L/Cpl I must encourage the soldiers, saying to the subordinates that war has just begun, fight to the end.'

By the 20th his desperation had turned almost elegiac. 'At dawn, enemy bombed the hell out of us. Observe only the sky with bitter regrettable tears rolling down ... Filled my stomach with dried bread and waited for my end to come. Oh remaining comrades, I shall depend on you for my revenge.' The next day, the tone became even darker. 'Oh, friendly troops, are you going to let us die like rats in a hole? ... Enemy bombing fiercely and our end is coming nearer and nearer.' The day before, there had been rumours of reinforcements on the way. Now they were revealed to be unfounded.

By the 22nd, after thirty-five days of fighting, Uchiyama was resigned to death, even welcomed it. 'No thoughts of returning home alive. Want to die like a soldier and go to Yasukuni Shrine.'[12] The regular evening barrage was exploding all around the Japanese trenches. 'Full moon shining through the trees in the jungle, hearing the cries of the birds and insects, the breeze blowing gently and peacefully,' Uchiyama wrote of a world imagined. 'Good news—friendly troops are near in the rear and friendly planes will fly tomorrow. How far is this true and how far an unfounded rumour? Whatever it is, it is happy news.'

His last entry, on 24 December: 'Enemy firing in front of us.'[13]

With the defences from the Outer Camp and Eastern Sector pulled back to the coastal strip between Giropa Point and the mouth of Simemi Creek, Allied tanks moved in on the afternoon of 29 December with infantry following behind. The four tanks advanced quickly—too quickly—ahead of the footsoldiers to the first line of defensive bunkers.

The Japanese had pulled back to a second line of bunkers, and when the tank troops realised they were shelling empty bunkers they moved on to the second line, still well in front of the infantry. While the tanks moved forward, Japanese filtered back to the front bunkers in time to subject advancing troops to intense fire when they arrived. By dusk, the tanks were out of ammunition and the attack halted.

The success of that resistance was short-lived. Three days later, with both American and Australian forces strengthened, six tanks cut quickly through Giropa Plantation and started clearing the beach down to the Simemi mouth with infantry mopping up behind. Allied casualties were high, but the Japanese positions were doomed.

The Australians had improvised a new bombing technique. A Mills bomb attached to a can of ammonal explosive was thrown into the bunker from the side. The explosion having rocked the bunker and stupefied its occupants, a can of avgas was tossed in and ignited by tracers, burning out the bunker and frying its occupants. By the morning of 2 January, Japanese emplacements on the island at the creek mouth had been overrun and tanks had cleared out other emplacements up to Giropa Point. Warren Force was poised to connect with Urbana Force, which had been working its way from the other end of the Buna defences although at a much slower pace.

◆　◆　◆

Having enclosed and pushed through Coconut Grove without much difficulty, Urbana Force had turned its attention to the Triangle, a well-fortified, jungle-covered tongue of land surrounded by swamp. On 19 December, an Allied attack up a bridge over Entrance Creek was stopped by crossfire. Another attack that afternoon under smoke cover had the same result. For the next two days the Americans tried repeated charges on the Triangle at its only practical approach, the bridge, without success. In one charge, they got to a line of bunkers only to find them vacated. The Americans were then caught in enfilading fire with severe casualties, sustaining more as they tried to evacuate their dead and wounded. Finally, Urbana Force settled for feigning an assault on the Triangle, its troops stopping after advancing a short distance and instead launching a mortar barrage on the Japanese, who'd come out of their bunkers to meet the infantry. After that piece of tit for tat, Urbana Force changed tactics and crossed Entrance Creek above Coconut Grove instead, establishing a bridgehead north of the Triangle and isolating it.

At the same time, US troops were attempting to take Musita Island, in the estuary of Entrance Creek, as a staging point for an assault on the mission. A footbridge to the island had been damaged, and the creek was tidal and unfordable. Captain Yasuda withdrew marines from the island to the mission to overlook and cover a second bridge on the north end of the island. American engineers repaired the damaged bridge on the 22nd, allowing troops to get onto the island and move up to the northern bridge, where they were stopped by heavy fire from across the creek. American artillery was brought onto Musita Island to pound the mission defences.

From the bridgehead across the creek from Coconut Grove the assault force attacked east into Government Gardens, overgrown with kunai and separated by swampland from the coconut-palm strip along the seashore. Foxholes and fire trenches hidden in the kunai enabled the Japanese to disorient the advancing troops with heavy fire, but it also distracted the defenders while the Americans on Musita crossed to the mission perimeter. A prompt Japanese response drove that force back over the bridge, but Yasuda was finding his force spread thin across two fronts. Taking advantage, a US platoon rushed through the kunai to the edge of the coconut-palm strip. It was a short-lived gain. With both Japanese defenders and US artillery firing on them—the latter unaware that their comrades had progressed that far—the Americans had to withdraw cautiously through the swamp, taking two days to get to safety.

On Christmas Day, 1942, two US companies crawled through the grass of Government Gardens. When they got to the coconut-palm strip, the Japanese attacked from the rear and isolated them. It took three days for Urbana Force to establish a corridor to its trapped forward companies, but once that was achieved Yasuda realised the Triangle was being outflanked and ordered its hasty evacuation. When US troops entered the Triangle on the evening of the 28th, they found empty bunkers and trenches strewn with abandoned arms and ammunition, signs of a defence force near the end of its tether.

Yasuda had received rations and ammunition by submarine on 25 December. The SNLP marines defended fiercely, although their command structure was starting to unravel. Reinforcements were still being talked of and failing to materialise. General Adachi had ordered General Yamagata, whose headquarters remained at Danawatu, on the other side of Gona, to move himself and his troops by sea to Giruwa. Their first task was to rescue the Buna garrison. Colonel Yazawa of 41st Regiment at Giruwa was ordered to lead a relief party by sea, unaware that the Buna defence was on the brink of collapse.

Two swimmers were dispatched from South Seas Force headquarters at Giruwa. One got through to Buna alive with the message that there was no fuel for barges to come to Buna. Yazawa's relief party would have to come on foot along the coast, and the garrison would have to break through enemy lines in a fighting withdrawal. It wasn't until the swimmer returned on 30 December that Giruwa became aware of the terminal state of Buna's defence. The messenger reported, 'Numbers are down to around 250 and food is scarce. They will be able to hold out for only a short time longer.'[14]

Yasuda telegraphed Eighth Fleet HQ in Rabaul on 28 December that the garrison was being gradually destroyed by enemy fire. His men were mounting counter-attacks with hand-to-hand fighting, but Yasuda's assessment was that they couldn't hold the garrison beyond the next morning. His message finished: '. . . all the men, whether navy personnel or labourers, have given all that could be asked of them. Our gratitude to our commanders and the support of navy air and surface forces is boundless. We pray for the prosperity of our imperial land far away and for lasting success in battle for all.'[15]

Yasuda's estimate was overly pessimistic. As the Allied attack at Buna entered its final stages, American troops set out to land in five assault boats east of the bridge from Musita Island to distract enemy attention from repair work on the bridge and to get troops to the mission side of

Entrance Creek. Through an error of navigation, they mistakenly landed on a finger west of the bridge where US troops were already in place. Under fire from both Japanese and Americans all five boats were sunk, and the bungled landing was lucky to incur no fatalities. The bridge was eventually repaired under fire anyway but its pilings were too weak, and the new planks fell into the river when troops started to cross.

The Allies now launched a three-front attack on the garrison headquarters. One company waded in the pre-dawn half-light of New Year's Eve across shallows between two spits at the creek mouth, having tested the route the previous day with no Japanese response. This time some GIs couldn't resist throwing grenades into Japanese landing craft pulled up on the beach. The sky came alive with flares and the noise of rifle and machine-gun fire. The Americans panicked into a running retreat until they were ordered back at gunpoint with another company in support.[16] They spent the day pushing slowly towards the bunkers north of the bridge.

On 1 January they attacked again from the spit, with a second thrust coming from Government Gardens, south-east of the mission, and tanks pushing through from Giropa Point. Defender resistance continued, but the garrison was reaching breaking point and starting to disintegrate. At nightfall, a general withdrawal was decided on.

About eighty army and naval staff from garrison HQ, half of them walking wounded, made a break for the beached landing craft on the spit—those not blown up by the Americans two days before. Carrying heavy packs of food, medicine and personal items, they were mown down by machine-gun fire. The few survivors returned to the bunkers, only about ten of them still fit to fight, and huddled around the last candle with those still there, discussing the coming final hours of the Buna garrison.

Yasuda ordered Ensign Suzuki of Yokosuka 5SNLP to steal through the encircling enemy and swim towards Giruwa with a final report. Suzuki set out at 2.30 a.m., reaching Giruwa after sunrise. Lieutenant Nakahashi, on the beach at Giruwa that morning, noted in his diary the arrival of a swimmer—a big naval man with a headband and a sword strapped to his back—with the news that Buna had fallen. Yasuda's report said, 'It is deeply regrettable that we have not been able to hold out for the arrival of the relief party.'[17]

◆　◆　◆

Captain Yasuda and Colonel Yamamoto had a high regard for each other despite the sometimes poisonous hostility between the services. Eighteenth Army had ordered a withdrawal from Buna, but Yamamoto had defied the order. He and his men remained with Yasuda and his troops, who had received no comparable naval order to withdraw. By the time the commander of South-Eastern Fleet, Vice-Admiral Kusaka, sent an order to withdraw to Giruwa, Yamamoto had received a new army order to remain at Buna until Yazawa's relief party arrived. Now it was Yasuda's turn to ignore his commander's instructions.

Ordnance was exploding around their bunker. They held off the approaching infantry for a while with machine-gun fire, waiting for the morning. Deep in the bunker, Yasuda joked, 'I hope we all survive tonight, because if we die our families will never be able to celebrate New Year's Day.'

Yamamoto added, 'I wish I could eat papaya before I die here.'

'Yes, sir. Fleshy papaya chilled in the refrigerator would be very nice,' the unit surgeon replied.[18]

By sunrise, Japanese were all along the beach that ran west from Buna village and in the water, some clinging to boxes and logs, a few in small boats and on rafts, some just swimming for dear life. It was pandemonium. Artillery and machine-gun fire were brought to bear on them, and they were strafed by Mitchells, Airacobras and Wirraways.

During the morning Yasuda charged from the bunker with ten men brandishing swords and bayonets, running at Allied soldiers approaching through the coconut palms. He shouted, 'Long live the Emperor and the Empire of Japan!', but the only word his assailants recognised before he fell was 'Banzai!'[19]

Soon after, Yamamoto emerged with his deputy commander and stood in front of the enemy soldiers. He shouted, 'Now you are crowing over us. You wasted a great deal of equipment and are about to over-power us. Now I will show you how Japanese soldiers end their lives. Shoot me!' His declamation wouldn't have meant much to his listeners, but someone obliged.[20]

Colonel Yamamoto had landed in Papua to take command of 144th Regiment after the repatriation of Colonel Kusunose. Diverted to the desperate defence of Buna for his seven weeks of fighting in this campaign, he had never led or even met the men of his regiment.

Yazawa finally left Giruwa on the evening of 2 January with 250 men of 170th Regiment and advanced on foot towards Buna. His troops drove a small US force away from a spit near Tarakena, two kilometres from Buna, and used it as a point to pick up survivors from the Buna garrison who had swum by night and hidden on shore during the day. A total of 370 men—180 army and 190 navy—were taken back to Giruwa, the northern end of the last remaining beachhead in the Japanese campaign to capture Port Moresby.[21]

Chapter 17

Evacuation

Private Nishimura was in a bunker towards the southern end of the Giruwa–Sanananda defences, only a short distance from where American soldiers were dug in. He and his comrades had eaten little in the previous few days. Hunger gnawed at their very souls. Nishimura has a vivid memory of a bizarre incident that took place in the midst of the savagery and squalor of the northern beachhead battles.

'I remember it was Christmas Eve,' he recalls, 'and the American soldiers were cooking something. Some nice smell was wafting towards us, making us even hungrier.'

After they had been tortured for some time by the sweet aroma, probably something special for Christmas like canned turkey, one of the Japanese, a man who spoke quite good English, stood up, saying, 'I've had enough.'

He stripped down to his underpants and staggered out towards the American position, pretending to be drunk. He was clearly unarmed. For some time his comrades could make out only a few muffled voices and occasional muted laughter. There was no gunfire. They waited in apprehension and some curiosity. What was going on out there, out of sight and on the edge of earshot? Would they ever see their mate again?

A few hours later, the soldier returned with an armful of food. Asked what had happened, he said, 'We were having a good time eating and drinking, whether we were enemies or not. I got something for you guys, too, so share this around.'[1] The Japanese then celebrated Christmas on the track to Sanananda.

◆ ◆ ◆

As their capture of the Buna government station was drawing to a conclusion, the Allied command made plans to reinforce its assault force at Soputa for a major drive down the Sanananda track. Fresh American troops relieved those manning the two roadblocks halfway down the track. Two 25-pounder cannons were redeployed from Buna to Soputa. Four tanks were brought there on 5 January, but heavy rain prevented any more vehicles getting up to Soputa for several days. The tracks were so muddy that jeeps couldn't bring in supplies, and the airstrips at Dobodura and Popondetta were unserviceable for a few days.[2]

This was not going to be a reprise of the Allied tactics in Buna, where superiority of numbers was used in repeated futile attacks with disproportionate loss of good men. This time heavy artillery fire would be followed by infiltration of enemy lines by small units. While General Vasey planned a multi-pronged attack, Allied patrols conducted a series of probes on Japanese positions, keeping the defenders on constant alert, testing their lines for weak points.

Patrols were nerve-racking exercises in which failing to see the enemy before he saw you could be fatal. The fear of weapon malfunctions added to the tension. Guns could be rendered useless in so many ways: by rain, by being dropped in putrid swamp water, by getting tangled in the twisting jungle foliage.

One time, Sergeant Imanishi was out on patrol in the mangroves with two of his men when they ambushed a group of five or six Americans. Ordering his machine-gunner to fire, Imanishi heard only the dry crunch of a jammed mechanism. The Americans heard the same sound and leapt back to temporary safety.

'What happened?' Imanishi growled to the machine-gunner.

'The gun's jammed. I can't take it out. It got caught in the root.'

They could hear the Americans moving cautiously towards their position. Imanishi crawled forward on his belly to extricate the gun from the gnarled mangrove root. Retreating quickly a short distance, the Japanese lay waiting for the Americans to reappear, but they didn't. Instead, they sent several rounds into the position just vacated by the Japanese, then moved rapidly away.[3]

Every day, the Japanese defences had to endure Allied artillery bombardment. Defenders in their bunkers or foxholes could hear the shells being fired, then exploding. The sounds of shattering vegetation and the moaning of the wounded combined with the ominous drift of artillery smoke and the stench of death. After a routine barrage, the soldiers would call out to each other from their foxholes, 'Hey! Are you OK?' There were fewer voices each day.[4]

Private Yokoyama, with Takenaka Unit in among Colonel Tsukamoto's defences in South-West Sector, has a more droll take on the unrelenting daily barrage. Every morning the Allies would shoot off eighty rounds, he says. He would count them, because he knew that when they were all fired he could go to the toilet.

In one artillery raid a shell hit a tree alongside Private Miyashita's foxhole, giving him what felt like an electric shock to the head before he went blank. When he came to, he touched his head to find part of his scalp ripped off. Two squad members were dead in the foxholes on either side. Miyashita's skull bone was exposed and his head felt slippery with blood. Later, the wound would fester and become fly-blown, with maggots dropping on his back, but Miyashita survived the war. For the rest of his life he sported a scar on a bald patch where the wound had been.[5]

Although the Japanese defended grimly and effectively, giving ground only after inflicting heavy losses, their physical condition was declining drastically. Illness was rife, and hunger sharpened into starvation. Japanese casualties were mounting. At the end of December, Lieutenant Ogawa of Asai Unit reported to the newly arrived General Oda that they were under daily mortar shelling. Lieutenant Misasue was ill, Ogawa wrote,

but would continue to command unless his condition got worse. Lieutenant Munenaga had 'a malignant fever'. He continued to command
from within his bunker, but slept a good deal. All officers and men were
patients of some sort, and an increasing number were going mad. Food
was becoming scarce, but even without rations, the lieutenant assured
Oda, 'we will defend the front line'.[6]

Through December and January, food deliveries became more and
more sporadic; the further down Sanananda track the troops were positioned, the worse it was. Miyashita noted that initially they were allocated
a mess-tin of rice to last five days. Later the allocation was half a mess-tin,
expected to last seven days. By January, his unit had no supplied food.
With a little of what rice they still had, they would simmer plant shoots
and fern-like soft weeds, which they foraged for in the pallid light just
before dawn. Salt was obtained from the powdered soy sauce they managed to eke out over the month. A handful of rice, a sardine and a small
amount of powdered miso made a special treat for New Year's Day. By
mixing the rice with edible greens, they were able to stretch one day's
ration into three.[7]

A Japanese soldier recorded that the new year had been welcomed
with rice and captured canned meat. Seven men shared a *Kinshi* (cigarette) and a can of sardines. The next day they made a soup from a bird
they shot and, with nothing else available, cooked some bananas for sup-
per. Over the following days the soldier recorded a succession of mortar
attacks, rumours of reinforcements that never came and meagre supplies
of rice. If the men moved, he wrote, they got hungry. His last entry, on
10 January, was: 'Ate some meat captured from the enemy. Enemy penetrated our position.'[8]

The Japanese furthest inland on the Sanananda track were drifting
towards starvation. Once again, almost by accident, some began eating
human flesh. It was the most readily available food. If one could overcome one's revulsion, it was a means of staying alive.

The corpses of soldiers who'd been shot near Japanese positions stank
after a few days in the sweltering Papuan sun. The stench got so bad that
Japanese would crawl out of their foxholes, cut open the dead men's

bellies, take out the innards and bury them. To someone on the edge of starvation, slicing off a piece of raw liver was tempting. It could be surprisingly tasty, and the soft meat was easy to chew and swallow. Once the hump of social taboo had been crossed, eating human flesh ceased to be morally problematic for these starving men. 'No one who was at Giruwa could have survived that siege without eating human flesh,' claims Nishimura, 'and that was the truth of it. Nobody wanted to do it, but it was their last resort. It was eat, or die.'[9]

Because this practice was more prevalent inland, where lack of supply was chronic, and because these positions were overrun first, the Allies became aware early of the resumption of cannibalism. Yokoyama recalls an American calling out from behind Allied lines on a crackly megaphone (in English, translated by a comrade), 'Don't take any of those bodies back!'[10] The Allied soldiers, often hungry but not starving, were naturally revolted. Some used their outrage as an excuse for not taking prisoners, but until then neither side had bothered much with the burden of looking after prisoners anyway.

Lieutenant Riichi Inagaki, a paymaster with the construction unit 15th Pioneers, was an exception—he was captured at Giruwa. Interrogated about the prevalence of cannibalism, Inagaki said he had spoken to people who had eaten human flesh, but that he had not witnessed the practice or done it himself. He had only eaten horse flesh from the abandoned packhorses. That's plausible, since he was stationed near the coast where small amounts of food did irregularly arrive.

Inagaki defended cannibalism to his interrogators, however, saying it was unsurprising given the conditions in which many of the Japanese soldiers were existing: often up to their armpits in swamp ooze, smitten by malaria and fevers, desperately short of food. Some of the men suffered such serious vitamin B deficiency, causing night blindness and deafness, that they couldn't see plain objects except in broad daylight and in their delirium would fire in the general direction of any sound.[11]

By now nearly every combat soldier on both sides sported a bandage of some sort around a wound somewhere on his body. Yokoyama had led a relatively charmed war, but it wasn't to last. One day, he was sitting in his foxhole, dreaming about food and his home town, Fukuyama. Sensing he was being watched, he looked around and spotted an Australian peeking from behind a tree. Yokoyama had beside him a gun he'd picked up along the way. He'd been trained to shoot a rifle back in Japan and had turned out to be a good shot, but as a medical corpsman he'd not been issued with a rifle. Up to that point he had never had to fire the gun he'd acquired, using it just to brand himself as a soldier.

Trying to remember his training of over a year before, Yokoyama put his rifle to his shoulder and fired, but by then the Australian had ducked behind the tree. When he appeared again with rifle at the ready, Yokoyama dropped down into his foxhole; the bullet flew over his head. This exchange was repeated a few times, then Yokoyama saw a huge flash. 'Suddenly, it felt like someone from the back had punched me in the head and I put my hand onto my cheek. Nothing was there, but four of my fingers went into my mouth.'

He slumped onto the floor of his foxhole and drifted into semiconsciousness.

'I vacantly thought my life was going to end at Giruwa. In the meantime, the wound kept bleeding and I had nothing to stop it. Intimate memories just flashed through my mind, floating up and melting away. I was thinking if today was payday at my old work and when I should say "*Banzai!*" without humiliating myself.'

Then he heard a distant voice saying, 'Yokoyama is dead, shot in the face.' He wanted to say, 'I'm still alive,' but he couldn't.

The voice was that of a soldier from another foxhole looking in to see what had happened. The Australian had been killed when he stepped out to shoot at the medic.

When he recovered his bearings, Yokoyama realised he had to patch his wound quickly but couldn't find anything suitable. Looking around, he saw the body of the dead Australian, whose head had a bandage around it. He removed the bandage and wrapped it around his own wound.

'That saved my life,' says Yokoyama. 'I was supposed to hate the Australian who shot me, but I felt thankful to him for leaving me his bandage.'

Later, maggots started to crawl in the wound because he didn't have any way to clean it. Yokoyama tried to get rid of the maggots until a veteran told him they would actually cure his wound by eating the rotten flesh. Yokoyama says, 'He always said to me, "Because of the maggots and the dead Australian soldier, you are still alive talking to us now."'[12]

◆　◆　◆

On 8 January, the Allies resumed their attack. Two defensive perimeters occupied by Murase Force between the two roadblocks were subjected to fifteen minutes of delayed-fuse shelling at noon, followed by infantry attacks on both the eastern and western flanks, to no significant effect. One American company was forced to dig in overnight thirty metres from the defenders' front line. The other waded into a swamp waist deep after heavy rain the day before. Coming under intense Japanese fire, this group soon found the swamp closing over their heads and were forced to withdraw. Two days later, they found that the smaller perimeter east of the track had been abandoned. In occupying it, the Allies found their first evidence of cannibalism in the Giruwa area.

What the Allied command failed to discern in its outrage were the signs of a defensive force close to collapse. By January many of the Japanese soldiers were criticising and disobeying their officers, but their defiance of their military indoctrination didn't manifest itself in mutiny or desertion to any significant extent. They remained steadfastly loyal to their emperor and struggled on as duty and their training demanded, in sullen obedience.[13]

Unaware of the state of the opposition, Vasey pressed on with a four-stage attack on the Sanananda–Giruwa defences. On the 9th, US troops established themselves across the Killerton track to prevent any Japanese escape down that path and to launch a flanking attack on Sanananda from the west. On the 12th, the main thrust began with an attack on Tsukamoto's positions at the junction of the two tracks. The Japanese hadn't fired field or anti-tank guns since 23 December, and the Allies assumed they had run out of that ammunition. The arrowhead of Vasey's attack was made up of three Stuart tanks brought up from Buna, but the only path for them was along the track. It was too marshy elsewhere.

The attack was a serious misjudgment. Not only had Tsukamoto mined the path, he had been holding his anti-tank shells for just such an emergency. Kawamoto Force, the Regimental Artillery Company, was ready, armed and waiting. The leading tank was pierced by a shell and its radio destroyed, so it was unable to warn the two tanks behind. They rumbled on blithely.[14]

The second tank was hit by Kawamoto's men, and the advance crashed to a halt. Under cover of Japanese fire, a suicide squad called *Nikuko-han*[15] jumped on the stricken tanks, opened their turrets and dropped in hand grenades and Molotov cocktails. The *Nikukohan* were killed in the explosion. It was impressive enough to inspire Shimada to poetry: 'These brave men,' he wrote later, 'thoroughbreds all, soaked the ground with their blood and fell to earth like the cherry blossom.'[16]

The Allied infantry fought on doggedly without tank support for a small patch of ground, but for an attack intended as decisive this one had been remarkably unproductive. The commanders concluded that evening that more all-out attacks were likely to be ineffectual and expensive. They decided instead to surround the Japanese positions, cut their supply lines and harass them with repeated mortar bombardment. If the Allies couldn't drive the Japanese out, they would starve them out. What Vasey didn't know as he reformulated his strategy was that Colonel Tsukamoto had already given the order to evacuate South-West Sector.

◆　◆　◆

Because South-West Sector had lost all communication with General Oda and the rest of South Seas Force on the 9th, Colonel Tsukamoto had received no order to withdraw. He could not seek approval for any planned action, either, but he was operating fairly autonomously by then anyway. Tsukamoto's force was reduced to 240 men, including the sick and wounded. With no rations or ammunition, he realised, his troops faced starvation or annihilation if they remained at the track junction.

The evacuation was ordered for 8 p.m. The colonel issued instructions for the handling of equipment, the movement of the sick and wounded, the packing of personal effects of the dead and the posting of a rearguard. Lieutenant Susumu Fukukawa's company, down to forty men, would lead the evacuation, attempting to break through two lines of Allied troops in sufficient time under cover of dark to be well away by sunrise. They would be unable to carry anyone, so it was up to each group to decide how to deal with those too ill or injured to walk.[17]

The first Private Yokoyama knew of the evacuation decision was when an orderly came back from battalion headquarters saying, 'We've got to get out of here quickly! Other units are already evacuating.'

A number of his corps were too sick to move. Some of the soldiers told them, 'We are going to attack the enemy,' but few were fooled by that lie. Those who were willing to kill themselves silently received grenades left alongside them with feigned casualness. Some of the wounded asked the relatively fit to help them kill themselves. After the war, one of the men who got away would hold a service annually in memory of comrades he helped to commit suicide. Others, without the wherewithal to kill themselves, pleaded and tried to follow their departing comrades. Yokoyama too tried to fake indifference, but they'd shared a waterlogged hell-hole too long for that.

'It was hell for real,' he remembers. 'I don't know any more appropriate expression for it. It was so hard leaving your wounded mates behind to run away.'[18]

Nishimura's group concocted a mutual deceit. The mobile told the immobile they were going on a sortie to pilfer food from the enemy camp. The sick and wounded, told to protect the precinct while the raiding party was away, asked the others to leave them a couple of machine-guns.

'Leave it to us. We will resist the enemy,' they assured their departing comrades. There is no doubt in Nishimura's mind they knew exactly what was happening, but no one was prepared to articulate it.[19]

The fit moved out of the camp. Fukukawa's men inched down a path recognisable only because it had been flattened over time by villagers walking along it. Using a luminous compass to assist, their only light was from the moon glimmering through gaps in the forest canopy. They advanced stealthily, dropping to the ground when they smelt smoke from a nearby outpost. Five or six grenades exploded close by, and Private Ishikawa groaned when a fragment hit him. Silence was paramount. If they used their rifles they would reveal their presence and their positions.

Tsukamoto ordered a left turn, and the men obeyed after some hesitation. Immediately they came under machine-gun fire from above. As with the grenades, this seemed to come in response to a suspicious noise rather than knowledge that there were troops in the vicinity; in any case, none of it was directed at the evacuating soldiers. Deciding to drop down to a stream, the party waded down the rushing watercourse in the dark. From time to time they heard distant voices and footsteps, but there was no telling if they belonged to friends or foes.[20]

The Kumusi River could be heard in the distance. The decision was made to cross it and follow the opposite bank. Scouts sent down the river found a suitably narrow point for crossing. Now sufficiently out of earshot of Allied front lines, they were able to chop bridge supports and string a line at chest height so the men could grope their way over the river in the pre-dawn half-light.

It was hard enough for the relatively fit to get across the makeshift bridge. Some with foot or leg wounds were virtually one-legged; others were barely able to support their own body weight; a few were almost blind, and some with arm wounds simply couldn't grip the line. Moving gingerly along the logs, many were unable to complete the crossing. They toppled the two or three metres to the rushing torrent below, with a receding cry or in resigned silence, never to be seen again. Those on the bridge could only watch helplessly as a fellow soldier dropped away in front of them, or hear the last cry and splash behind them above the roar of the river. To Fukukawa, 'the sight of these pitiful deaths remains a painful and graphic memory'.[21]

Those who got across continued through trackless jungle, pushing through dense vegetation, chest-deep in swamps, 'our main concern being survival, our one hope that if and when we reached the assembly area, there would be food'.[22] The retreating troops tended to stay in small groups from the same unit. Yokoyama walked behind a mate from

Takenaka Unit. One morning, while they were taking a break, he felt uneasy, worrying about their slow pace and wanting to push on.

He said to Danjo, his friend, 'I feel I need to get to the assembly point as soon as possible.'

Danjo replied, 'Hey, we usually don't get to have a break like this, so why go and ruin it?'

Yokoyama stayed but became restless again. He said he would go on ahead for a while, then rest and wait for the others. He crossed the road into the jungle and walked on, but soon he heard gunfire behind him. Yokoyama never saw his friend again.[23]

As he got closer to the assembly area, Yokoyama came across soldiers who no longer had the stamina to continue. He remembers, 'I found some dying soldiers on the ground, surrounded by flies and crawling with maggots, but still holding on to a cooking utensil as if they'd never let it go until they died.'

He came across a familiar face among those falling by the wayside, 'a lieutenant from my neighbouring village, such a dignified man'. The man was lying on his back, barely moving, holding a sword across his chest.

Yokoyama came up to him and said, 'I am Yokoyama from the next village. Would you walk with me, sir? I could help you out.'

The lieutenant replied, 'No, just go on without me. I am tired. Besides, it feels good lying on the warm grass like this, so I don't mind dying here.'[24]

Miraculously, 120 totally exhausted men reached the assembly area at Barumbari, near the mouth of the Kumusi. There, engineers of 15th Independent Regiment provided small boats to move them in short hops up the coast to Lae. They were not to know that they wouldn't reach there for another three months.

◆　◆　◆

When he arrived at Giruwa on 22 December, General Oda had told his new troops they would be reinforced and that Japan would never let Giruwa fall—which only fuelled more reinforcement rumours and disappointments. Tokyo had different ideas. Imperial General HQ decided on 4 January that because of Japan's lack of shipping and inability to deliver supplies, its forces in Guadalcanal would be evacuated incrementally by night to the north Solomons, and its troops around Giruwa would be moved to Lae and Salamaua after those two bases had been reinforced. The order was transmitted to General Imamura of Eighth Area Army at Rabaul, and 102nd Regiment was dispatched to Lae by General Adachi, but it wasn't until the 13th that the order to withdraw was passed on to Yamagata, perhaps prompted by a plea for reinforcements from Oda.

On 12 January, a desperate Oda had sent a message to Adachi, saying in part:

> Most of the men are stricken with dysentery. Those not in bed with illness are without food and too weak for hand-to-hand fighting. Starvation is taking many lives and it is weakening our already extended lines. We are doomed. In several days, we are bound to meet the same fate that overtook Basabua and Buna. Our duty will have been accomplished if we fight and lay down our lives here in the field. However, this would mean that our foothold in New Guinea would be lost and the sacrifices of our fellow soldiers during the past six months will have been in vain. I urge that reinforcements be landed near Gona at once.[25]

The next day, Adachi instructed Yamagata to evacuate Sanananda and Giruwa. They were to withdraw to the mouths of the Kumusi and the Mambare and go by sea from there to Lae. As many sick and wounded as possible were to be evacuated by barge from Giruwa. The rest would have to break through the Allied lines and make their way overland to the Japanese-held area beyond Gona and on to the Kumusi mouth. The whole operation was to be delayed until 25 January, when there would be moonlight to assist.

Yamagata was unaware that Tsukamoto's force had already gone, but the Allies were equally in the dark. On the 14th, a patrol was sent south from the roadblock to locate the current northern perimeter of Japanese defences there. They found a sick soldier lying in the bushes. Interrogated, he told them all able-bodied men had left the sector. He'd been too sick and had collapsed on the track. Vasey ordered immediate pursuit of the departed troops. The Allies pushed through the Japanese perimeters and after a few brief fire-fights killed the troops who had been too weak to evacuate.

General Oda moved his headquarters nearer to the coast and gave command of Central Sector to Colonel Fuchiyama of the Anti-aircraft Artillery Battalion. Still in the sector were 2nd Battalions of the 41st (under Major Koiwai) and the 144th (now under Major Kato).

During their push on the remnants of South-West Sector Australian troops moved up the Killerton track, reaching Killerton village the next day without opposition. Back on the track to Sanananda, a US platoon had infiltrated the defences of Murase Force, which then moved its positions up the track forward of Central Sector. With fierce resistance holding off the Americans for the day, it was decided to resume the attack in the morning with mortar and artillery bombardment. Major Murase's men could hear the sounds of two more M3 tanks being brought in overnight. Discretion now seeming the better part of valour, the force withdrew in the dark back to the western end of Central Sector.

The Allies launched an all-out attack on several fronts on the 16th. Australians pushed easily through from Killerton village to Cape Killerton and down the coast towards Wye Point, where they encountered stiff resistance from Coastal Sector defences under Colonels Tomita and Yazawa, the latter returned from his rescue mission to Buna and now suffering from the malaria he'd picked up there. The beach between Wye Point and Sanananda was still in Japanese hands.

Another Australian company made its way across from Killerton to Sanananda, wading through a swamp to get to the track at the rear of Central Sector while Americans drove north from the roadblock. Japanese casualties were high, with the encirclement cutting off their main escape routes. Although those in the main strongholds resisted fiercely, fighting hand to hand, their prospects were grim.

Fifteenth Independent Engineers' Colonel Yokoyama, whose advance party had commenced MO Operation, had been in command of all army units in the Buna area until General Oda took up those duties in late December. By that time, the Japanese command structure was starting to fall apart. Staff officer Tanaka (of Buna Detachment, not the Colonel Tanaka who drowned with General Horii) recalled that the situation was 'worsening day by day, and being commander of the detachment just prior to its descent into chaos must have had a great psychological impact'.[26]

Among Yokoyama's responsibilities on his return to the engineers was to evacuate casualties from the coastal areas west of Sanananda Point. With increased pressure from the major Allied attack on 16 January, the sick and wounded were assembled on a narrow strip of jungle-fringed beach only about four metres wide. Vulnerable to the constant shelling, they had few defensive emplacements and no tools to dig trenches. The waiting evacuees lay down, heads among the roots on the edge of the jungle, waves lapping almost at their feet. The intensity of the attack increased overnight and escalated again the next morning, but all the Japanese could do was endure it. Many were killed or suffered further injuries while they waited.

On the evening of the 17th, as the Allies got closer, contact with Detachment headquarters was lost, thunderstorms drenched the wait-ing men and the few foxholes filled with water. At that time, Yokoyama had a high fever of 40°C. He was injecting morphine and camphor and periodically crawled into the sea to relieve himself of diarrhoea for half an hour at a time.

After nightfall, Yokoyama saw two barges silently approach the beach out of the wild roar of the storm, lightning revealing them as they neared. Everyone was ordered to get aboard. In a mad, undignified scramble, those who couldn't board unassisted were dragged on by others.

When Yokoyama got to Barumbari, General Yamagata demanded his return to Giruwa. The boats he had commandeered for his patients had been intended for Yamagata's use. Yokoyama cabled back that a medical examination had diagnosed high fever and severe diarrhoea and he would not be able to return. The general was furious, his dignity affronted, and he telegraphed army headquarters to initiate a court-martial. Eighteenth Army investigated the facts and much later advised Yamagata that the matter would be dealt with in an appropriate manner, but no official inquiry was ever held.

Years later, in a 1958 statement to the War History Office, Yokoyama would explain his position. With communications so difficult in the jungle, he said, orders seldom reached relevant officers in time. Often, an officer had to decide for himself how to deal with circumstances as they arose.

By the time General Oda arrived at Giruwa he was racked with malaria, and he said to Yokoyama, 'As you are familiar with the area [he'd been there since July], please do what needs to be done.'

Yokoyama added that debilitating health and long-term malnutrition dulled both his own judgment and fighting spirit and those of his troops.[27]

◆ ◆ ◆

Pressed from all sides and with no order to withdraw, Central Sector under Colonel Fuchiyama was facing the prospect of a fight to the finish. Coastal defences were subjected to intense artillery fire, and the Allied forces were making inroads into their lines. Yamagata decided the situation at Giruwa was too dire to wait until the 25th to withdraw. He still had eight serviceable barges at his disposal from Mambare, even if the first two had been appropriated by Colonel Yokoyama. Patients who were not trapped behind the Allied advance had been moved to the hospital staging area at Giruwa by the 18th.

Yamagata drafted an order that day. Buna Detachment would withdraw to the mouth of the Kumusi from 8 p.m. on 20 January. South Seas Force would follow a line four kilometres inland. The 170th infantrymen of Nojiri Battalion and Colonel Hozumi's mountain-gun battalion would break through to Gona and move up the coast to Barumbari. Casualties and designated units would be evacuated on barges on the 19th and 20th. Buna Detachment HQ, including Yamagata, would depart on the first of these.

The new orders were passed to General Oda only, with instructions not to distribute them until 4 p.m. the next day. They were sent on to Nojiri and Hozumi in sealed envelopes that were not to be opened before that hour. Five messengers were sent separately to the besieged Fuchiyama force, each with the same orders, written on signals paper in Japanese phonetic characters in case they were caught. One of the messengers got through in the morning.

Fuchiyama, who was with Major Koiwai at the time, read the orders and commented, 'This is not possible.' His force didn't have the strength to break through the surrounding enemy and extricate casualties. The two commanders decided they would stay, burn the regimental colours of the 41st in their charge and prepare themselves for an honourable death.

Koiwai returned to his unit to find that rumours of the withdrawal had got there first. He was sure he could persuade his own troops to fight to an honourable death, but engineers and supply troops were also milling around, looking to pick up crumbs of information. If the visitors asked, 'If they are military orders, shouldn't we withdraw?', Koiwai was not sure he could answer them. He had earlier put a case to Fuchiyama for withdrawal, and his own arguments were bound to be raised again.

The upshot was a decision to withdraw as instructed. Fuchiyama put the infantryman Koiwai in charge of planning a break through the Allied perimeter.

Koiwai asked, 'What about transport of casualties?'

The colonel bowed his head in silence, an expression of intense pain on his face. 'Living is certainly harder than dying,' he sighed.

Company commanders had already been told they must decide how best to tell immobile casualties of the withdrawal, when another messenger came through from Oda with the order that the wounded were to be left at the camp when the withdrawal began. Responsibility for that decision no longer rested at company level.[28]

The line of withdrawal would be through one part of their perimeter that had so far received little Allied attention. Torrential rain began to fall on the afternoon of the 20th and continued into the evening. For once the constant downpours that had dogged the Japanese throughout this

campaign would be to their benefit. Moving out was more likely to succeed under cover of pouring rain, for some Allied positions were only
thirty metres away from the Japanese departure line.

At 8 p.m. in drenching rain, the men assembled on the road in the
centre of camp. Bidding farewell to stretcher-bound casualties with
instructions to 'take their lives before the Allies arrived the next morning', they moved off into the darkness, Murase Battalion of 100 men
leading. Major Koiwai explained the position of those left behind in his
memoir: 'They did not know surrender and the shame of being captured
was considered worse than death. To take one's life with the weapons
used to attack the enemy protected the country and avoided disgrace to
one's family—in other words, it was considered to be an act of loyalty to
the emperor and of filial piety to one's parents. Further, it was believed
that such an act would ensure the everlasting repose of one's soul as a
deity in Yasukuni Shrine.'[29]

By dawn, the withdrawal had moved past Allied front lines and by
noon it reached what they thought would be a well-patrolled track to
Basabua with a line of Allied positions. The party was broken into small
sections and filtered through gaps between those positions under cover
of night. Major Koiwai, with Major Murase and Lieutenant Hayashi,
was designated to guard the 41st regimental colours. The flag was to be
protected with the colour party's lives. It should be destroyed rather than
be allowed to fall into enemy hands.

◆ ◆ ◆

On the 19th Buna Detachment was under heavy artillery fire, having
just received the order to withdraw the next day. General Yamagata and
his headquarters staff, selected units and 140 casualties boarded two
barges that had arrived that afternoon. The malaria-stricken Colonel
Yazawa was among those casualties. The barges left that night for the
Kumusi mouth and arrived before dawn.[30]

That day, Sergeant Imanishi had seen a senior officer walking towards
the beach with soldiers following. The officer yelled at them, 'The boats
won't come tonight. Don't follow me.'

He turned back, but soon afterwards Imanishi noticed him returning to the beach and thought, 'Well, the rescue boats will come tonight.'

He went back to his company and told the wounded men there, 'The rescue boats are coming tonight. You get down to the boats and evacuate from here.'

They did so. After a while, one of the soldiers came back to tell Imanishi there was a place for him on the boat, but he refused to go without an order to retreat.[31] The next day, the order came to withdraw at 10 p.m.

That following evening, four more barges arrived. Allied artillery fire was directed on the embarking men as they tried to board, causing confusion and mayhem as men pushed to get on the departing barges. They sailed to Barumbari with their communications gear aboard, but only part of their designated human cargo. Two of the barges returned the following night, but by then the Allies had occupied the coast around Giruwa and it was not possible to get anyone on board. Those left behind stayed behind.

The coastal units divided into platoons at the appointed time on the 20th to commence their overland withdrawal. As Imanishi's platoon prepared to leave in the pouring rain, wondering how they would find a way through the surrounding enemy, Warrant Officer Matsuo said, 'They don't hold hands with each other to surround us. There is always a way to break through.'

Each was able to follow the man in front thanks to frequent lightning flashes illuminating the backs of soldiers walking in front. Imanishi's group walked through enemy positions for three nights before finding a path that followed the coast. Like Yokoyama retreating down the Kumusi, Imanishi found the way lined with soldiers and officers lying alongside the track. Some were just sitting quietly. Some were already dead. Sometimes Imanishi would hear gunfire, sometimes dogs barking. He wondered if these were military dogs used to chase the retreating Japanese, but if so he never saw them.

On the way, an ill and vomiting Imanishi broke the taboo and ate human flesh. His group stopped at a village where Japanese soldiers had earlier killed and buried five villagers. The starving men in Imanishi's unit dug up the bodies and cooked and ate them. One of his soldiers cooked up a liver and gave some to the sergeant, telling him to suck the juice, not eat the flesh. Imanishi ate some anyway and sucked the juice as well, to live another day.[32]

Oda, on hearing that the commander of Buna Detachment had left on the first barge, declared, 'I have been betrayed by Yamagata.' In Japanese military tradition, the commander of a defeated force does not retreat but remains in position and commits suicide. That principle, it seemed, no longer applied.

Oda oversaw the withdrawal of the last of the units, then turned to the duty soldier and said, 'That's done then. I wish to smoke a last cigarette. Go on ahead.'

One version of events—Major Koiwai's memoirs—has Oda's staff unable to penetrate the Allied lines before daybreak and returning. Thinking escape was impossible, the general resolved to stay and share the fate of the sick and wounded. He gave his papers, food and tobacco to his comrades. After Colonel Tomita declared that he too would stay the headquarters staff made another attempt to escape, but without success. They returned to the camp to find Oda and Tomita had laid out a cloak and together committed suicide.[33]

The alternative version, in General Yoshihara's memoirs, is briefer, with the duty soldier hearing gunshots and returning to find the bodies of the two senior officers.[34] The duty soldier was Private Fukuoka, who had paddled the canoe from which General Horii lost his life. If this scenario is accurate, Fukuoka had been present at the deaths of both commanders of South Seas Force.

The withdrawing units had mixed fortunes. Some of Oda's headquarters staff found their way through Allied lines, although most were never seen again. Nojiri Battalion came under heavy attack trying to break through and the majority were killed in repeated encounters. The rest got through to Gona and beyond.

The Mountain Artillery Battalion penetrated the Allied front lines but its own commander, Colonel Hozumi, was so weakened by diarrhoea he was scarcely able to move. He eventually shot himself with his pistol, but here too there are conflicting accounts of how he reached that end. One version, the more official one, has it that Hozumi told his subordinates to go on without him but they refused, saying they would carry him on their backs. Knowing that to do so would compromise their chances of survival, he pushed them away and settled the issue with his pistol.[35] The other version has Hozumi begging to be carried, and his men refusing on the grounds that other casualties had been denied that choice. Out of humiliation and despondency, Hozumi resorted to suicide.[36] Almost all of this group were subsequently overtaken by Allied pursuers and only a few got to the Kumusi.

Among the retreating troops who did get to the river was Sergeant Imanishi, although he arrived in dreadful health. Months before, in the Owen Stanleys, he had found an American-made pistol loaded with eight or nine rounds. He kept the pistol with him, treasuring it as a sort of talisman for his last battle, if and when that was to happen. He would take out as many of the enemy as he could with the bullets he had, keeping the last one for himself. It would be a noble and patriotic death. Now, as he reached the Kumusi, he knew he was safe for the time being. He saw some parrots in a tree and decided to take a shot at them with his prized American pistol. He lined up one bird and pulled the trigger. It jammed.

He thought, 'What if I had needed to use this against the enemy?'[37]

Chapter 18

The long journey home

The men of South Seas Force and the other units with them had been in Papua for up to six months. They had pursued an audacious but ill-conceived and improperly authorised enterprise to swoop on Port Moresby from the direction its defenders would least expect. The venture that had seemed so promising had come to nothing. For the troops, it had been a descent into hell in a deceptively majestic land. Each survivor would have Kokoda and the beachheads of Buna and Gona etched into his soul for the rest of his life. But their war was not yet over. Inescapable as Japan's doom now seemed, the residue of MO Operation would fight to the bitter end.

As the ragtag soldiers arrive at the mouths of the Kumusi and Mambare rivers our story is coming to its end, but nothing is ever absolutely concluded. Even a dead Japanese soldier doesn't cease to be; his spirit moves on to the netherworld through the portal of Yasukuni Shrine. For the survivors their story stutters on, agony turning to anecdote, their new lives filled until the mortal conclusion that precedes timelessness.

◆　◆　◆

Colonel Tsukamoto, having withdrawn his force on 12 January, arrived at Barumbari near the mouth of the Kumusi on the 23rd and was placed under the command of the newly appointed Colonel Akio Yoshida. The previous commander of 144th Regiment, Colonel Yamamoto, had been killed in the Allied assault on Buna. Although Tsukamoto's unauthorised withdrawal had shaken the crumbling operational command at Giruwa there was no inquiry into the colonel's actions in the rapidly deteriorating war effort, not least because the officers affected lay dead at Giruwa camp.[1]

In a misunderstanding of orders, the regimental colours of the 144th, in the care of Warrant Officer Shimada, had been taken to Rabaul but were returned to Mambare by submarine on 2 February. The colour party, in tattered uniforms and no shoes, eventually brought them back to Rabaul.[2]

The 41st colour party, led by Major Koiwai, arrived at Barumbari with the regimental flag intact on the 28th. Settling in a camp set up by Miyamoto (1st) Battalion, they joined the forty-five surviving men of Takenaka Unit, including medical corpsman Yokoyama. The unit had made its way along the Kumusi to its mouth, but Lieutenant Takenaka was no longer among them.[3]

Four thousand men had broken out from Giruwa. Of these, 850 had not made it to Barumbari, either killed in fighting during the retreat or dropping out through illness or sheer exhaustion. Casualties left behind at the Giruwa camp numbered 300. The three Buna-area beachheads had been defended by 11,000 men, including reinforcements.[4]

While survivors of Giruwa arrived individually or in groups—some barely able to walk, some still remarkably fit—the men were ferried up to Mambare. The entire remaining strength of Buna Detachment, about 1900 men, had assembled there by 7 February, including seventy navy personnel who had escaped from Buna itself. In addition, 1200 sick and wounded had reached Barumbari and been transferred to Mambere. With landing vessels brought down from Lae, there were now twenty barges to carry them north to that town.

Two companies of Okabe Detachment came from Lae with the

barges. One carried out clearing operations up the Mambare River; the other established a holding camp by the Ampolo River, beyond the Kumusi, for units withdrawing overland. This latter company held off several attacks by Allied pursuit parties at the mouth of the Ampolo.

Beginning on 11 February, evacuated soldiers were transported from Mambare to Salamaua, in the case of 41st Regiment, and to Lae for the 144th. Barges could move with safety only at night. Progress was agonisingly slow. With unhygienic conditions causing widespread gastric disorders, waiting soldiers were moved to Mambare village, but a new phase of the war was opening in other parts of New Guinea. Transport barges were diverted to supply that operation. The withdrawal did not recommence until March.

◆　◆　◆

Yokoyama was the junior member of a three-man clinic set up in a hut in Salamaua by the remnants of his corps. With new medical supplies shipped in from Rabaul, they treated local people as well as soldiers. New Guineans would come from up to ten kilometres away and queue in front of the clinic.

Yokoyama eventually moved with his regiment to Rabaul, travelling in short hops by barge at night, hiding the boats and themselves by day. When they got to Rabaul they were just skin and bone, dressed in tatters and wandering aimlessly. He recalls, 'Some officer who'd just arrived from Japan complained. "Why are they all looking so shabby and don't even salute me?" Well, we were no longer soldiers, just skeletons disguised as humans.'[5]

Forty-first Regiment was reduced to just over 200 men by the time it reached Rabaul. It was dissolved on 2 September and transferred to Korea under the command of the Demobilisation Duty Officer. The 41st's commander, Colonel Yazawa, had been killed in action after the evacuation from Mambare River.[6] His antagonist, Major Koiwai, would survive to write a memoir with philosophical musings after the war.

Commander Tsukioka of Sasebo 5SNLP, who had survived both Goodenough Island and Buna, was one of the few navy men to be evacuated from Papua, but he didn't get much further. He was killed in action at Salamaua in June 1943.

◆　◆　◆

The handful of men who emerged alive from the long and punishing journey to hell and back were leaving the land that had held them prisoner, comprehensively defeating them in a way that a determined, better-equipped enemy or the flawed calculations of their own leaders could not have achieved unaided. It should have been a transcendent moment of enormous relief, but it wasn't. The New Guinea leg of their war might be over, but the war itself was far from resolved. It was lurching towards inevitable defeat somewhere in an unimaginable future. In their mental numbness those still fit to fight were required to do their duty, either in the pretence that victory was possible or just to lay their lives on the line—for what? Only the seriously ill were spared the demand to fight on.

South Seas Force was evacuated to Hopoi, east of Lae, by 11 March, then to Rabaul by late April. On 17 June, an order of battle of Eighteenth Army dissolved Nankai Shitai and absorbed it into 55th Division, at that time fighting in Burma. Nishimura arrived in Rabaul on 20 June, two months after most of South Seas Force, and came down with a virulent strain of malaria. Sergeant Imanishi was so sick by the time he got to Rabaul that he was returned to Japan for treatment. He had recovered sufficiently to be serving in southern China when the war ended.[7]

In August the remnants of 144th Regiment boarded a troop-ship to Formosa, on their way to join up with 55th Division. The ship was sunk by an American submarine near Kaohsiung Harbour in Formosa. Most of the troops on board, who included Warrant Officer Shimada and Private Nishimura, were picked up by Formosan fishing boats.

The survivors of the 144th joined their new division in October, fighting in Burma near the Indian border. In May 1944, in a lull in the fighting against the British caused by the onset of the wet season, Nishimura was assigned to a group to be sent back to Japan with the remains of comrades killed in battle.[8]

Colonel Kusunose had been repatriated and was recovering in hospital in Kochi in December 1943 when a regimental party arrived at Asakura railway station carrying the ashes of dead soldiers in boxes held in a white sling. Kusunose made his way from hospital and stood silently in a corner of the station, a sad and dejected figure, watching each wooden box as it passed by.[9]

Officers in the Japanese military were often transferred to different units. Colonel Tsukamoto became a commander in Third Air Command after New Guinea and was stationed in Phnom Penh in Indochina at war's end. Major Koiwai was attached to Staff HQ in Tokyo, but by the end of the war was on Jeju Island in Korea with 96th Division. The commander of Buna Detachment, General Yamagata, was transferred to headquarters of the garrison division in Kyoto, but his escape from the line of fire was short-lived. He became commander of 26th Division in the Philippines and died on Leyte Island fighting the Americans in February 1945.

In Korea, Private Yokoyama was promoted to corporal and given a choice of joining with forces in the Philippines or returning to Japan. His friends said, 'Let's stay together. There's nothing good waiting for us back in Japan, so why don't we leave here together?'

Yokoyama told the commander he had decided to stay with the division, but was told, 'The deadline was yesterday.' He was returned to Japan, and his friends went on to Leyte.

Yokoyama had worked with Sergeant Tamura in the Salamaua clinic. Hearing he was leaving them, Tamura told the medical corpsman he would be missed.

'Well, you too will get to go home soon, Sergeant,' said Yokoyama. But it was not to be. At about the time Yokoyama was getting on his ferry to go home, Tamura committed suicide. None of Yokoyama's friends survived Leyte.[10]

Sergeant Tsunoda, the Zero pilot who had been stationed at Buna for the brief period it operated as an airfield, ended the war with a kamikaze unit in the battle for Iwo Jima. Tsunoda's mission was to escort the kamikaze planes to the enemy fleet and confirm the results.

'I believe those who died by kamikaze attack didn't want to die,' he says, 'but they still took off with beaming smiles. Those young boys [they were mostly teenagers] looked so anguished on the evening before they left. But when they gathered on the airfield the next morning, they were all smiling as if they'd changed into someone else. I cannot explain what was in their minds.'[11]

After returning from the war Yokoyama started working again at the Mihara textile factory in Hiroshima, as he had before the war. He left the city in the week before 6 August 1945, a good day not to be in Hiroshima.

'Luck,' says Yori-ichi Yokoyama, 'was the only difference between being alive and being dead.'[12]

Chapter 19

Out of the ashes

On 15 August 1945, most Japanese heard the voice of their emperor for the first time. On state-run radio, through crackling static, Hirohito's words were difficult to grasp. His voice was surprisingly high-pitched and his enunciation stilted, his language florid and ambiguous. 'The war has developed not necessarily to Japan's advantage,' he said with considerable understatement. 'In order to avoid further bloodshed we shall have to endure the unendurable, to suffer the insufferable.' He stressed the enemy's 'cruel bombs' and expressed regret for the people who'd worked with Japan 'for liberation of east Asia'. When he finished, a radio announcer re-read the entire speech in everyday language.[1]

Japan was destitute at the end of the war. Its infrastructure, cities and industrial base had been destroyed. Its people were starving; close to nine million were homeless. Unemployment was high and the return of demobilised soldiers would make it worse. About 1.7 million service-men had been killed in the war, along with one million civilians, mostly in air raids. Over 3 per cent of Japan's population had been sacrificed in pursuit of its dream of empire.[2]

Effective power in Japan was assumed by General Douglas MacArthur, appointed Supreme Commander of the Allied Powers. Since few Allied personnel spoke good Japanese or understood the Japanese system of government, the occupation had to operate through the existing Japanese bureaucracy. Provided with an opportunity for change, Japan grabbed it with both hands.[3]

Among the first problems to be dealt with were those of feeding a starving nation and ensuring the orderly return of Japanese soldiers and civilians marooned overseas at the end of hostilities. When Hirohito made his radio announcement 6.5 million of his subjects were overseas as part of the war effort, three million of them civilians sent out to help administer occupied territories.[4] Among the soldiers awaiting demobilisation and repatriation were survivors of South Seas Force's failed campaign to capture Port Moresby, who'd since been deployed to other battlefields.

The return to Japan of all those overseas at the end of the war took years. By mid 1946 over two million Japanese remained unrepatriated, and the location of another half million was unknown. Many surrendered Japanese servicemen were used as prison labour by Allied authorities, who were happy to delay the repatriation process. The British and the Dutch used Japanese postwar prisoners to reimpose colonial authority in Malaya, Burma and the Dutch East Indies. Others were forced to work for one side or the other in China's civil war, and large numbers perished in Siberia as a result of the slow repatriation of those troops who came under Russian control.[5]

The American occupation personnel arrived expecting a confrontation with the nation of fanatics with which they had been at war. Instead, they found 'a populace sick of war, contemptuous of the militarists who had led them to disaster, and all but overwhelmed by the difficulties of their present circumstances in a ruined land'.[6] The wartime demonisation of Anglo-Americans was now redirected at the militarists and ultra-nationalists in an instance of *tenko*, the almost untranslatable Japanese word that describes a radical mass turnaround.[7] The same spirit insinuated itself into the ranks of the disbanding military. Many soldiers returned to accuse the officers who'd led them in battle of cowardice, greed, abuse of privilege and cruelty.[8] Some exacted revenge on particular individuals.

Late in 1945, as the Allies were setting up their war crimes tribunals, the newspaper *Asahi* proposed that the Japanese should compile their own lists of possible war criminals and perhaps conduct their own trials.[9] There was surprising public support for this idea. As it turned out, there was no Japanese participation in the judgments. Of the eleven judges on the Tokyo tribunal, some represented countries that, by the end of the two years of hearings, were embroiled in civil or colonial wars and on the verge of collapse. Justice Pal, the Indian appointee and author of one of the three dissenting judgments, was the only judge with significant experience in international law.[10] Derided by many Western commentators as a naïve, anti-Western opinion, Pal's judgment is the one most embraced by present-day Japanese.[11]

Although the procedures generally followed those of Anglo-American law, there were striking anomalies. The emperor was not indicted, nor were the implications of his role as supreme leader allowed as evidence. Many civilians involved in planning and promoting the war were not tried. Instead, the trials focused on mid-level officers. The behaviour of Allied soldiers was not admitted as defence evidence; the atomic bombs dropped on Hiroshima and Nagasaki were certainly not to be examined as war crimes. The war trials were widely perceived in Japan as 'victors' justice' and may have influenced the subsequent reluctance of the Japanese to examine more closely the actions of some of their compatriots in the war.

Colonel Tsuji, the maverick from Imperial HQ who 'authorised' the overland invasion of Port Moresby, was implicated in atrocities against civilians in Malaya and Singapore and against POWs in the Philippines and Burma. He escaped from the Allies at the end of the war, avoiding prosecution as a war criminal.

After the Occupation ended, Masanobu Tsuji resurfaced and was elected to the Japanese parliament. The popularity of his best-selling accounts of his escape from the Allies and his role in the Malaya campaign helped his election. He disappeared in Laos in 1961 after a 'turbulent political career from which the shadow of his military past was never fully erased'.[12] He never reappeared and in 1968 was formally declared dead.

Colonel Kusunose was also in the sights of the inquisitors. In December 1945, as material was being gathered for the coming trials, he was called before the Allied Occupation Forces to give unsworn testimony. The interest was in Kusunose's role as commander of the regiment responsible for the Tol plantation massacre in New Britain. Kusunose refused to comply with the order and instead went deep into a forest on the side of Mt Fuji. He took no food or warm clothing, and eventually died of starvation and exposure to the Japanese winter. He left behind a letter of explanation. As an Imperial military officer, Kusunose wrote, he could not accept victors' justice.[13]

The story of the other repatriated survivors of Kokoda is mostly a happier one. Many of the men enjoyed their resumed family life and the economic miracle of postwar Japan. In May 1947 a new US-designed constitution came into force, based on the British model of government. Japan was fashioned into a peaceful, pro-Western democracy, but the balance of global power was moving dramatically. The Communists had won the civil war in China, and in 1949 the People's Republic of China came into existence. The Cold War with the Soviet Union and by extension China changed Allied economic policy in Japan. The US Undersecretary of the Army was sent to Japan and came back recommending a build-up of industry and trade. Japan was to be a bulwark against Communism. In 1947 it was given $US400 million to underwrite an economic plan similar to its wartime plan but without the military component. A proposed purge of the *zaibatsu*, the business conglomerates, was shelved.[14]

With the outbreak of the Korean War in 1950 came $4 billion of orders for Japanese supplies. Prime Minister Yoshida called this war 'a gift from the gods'. Japan's industry surged, restoring its people's income to near-prewar levels.[15] Out of the disaster of the Pacific War and the ashes of Hiroshima and Nagasaki, Japan was able to become the global economic and trading power it had tried to become through conquest.

It is in this milieu of economic recovery that returned soldiers like Sadashige Imanishi, the platoon leader from Tsukamoto Battalion, rebuilt their lives. Imanishi settled back in Motoyama in the mountains behind Kochi, working for the regional authority there. Soon after his return, he married a woman from the next village. Overlooking Yoshino River, the playground of his boyhood, their house was down the road from that of Shigeji Fukuoka, the soldier who had paddled the fatal canoe for General Horii and Colonel Tanaka. Enthusiastic to educate himself, Imanishi studied administration and construction and eventually became mayor of Motoyama.[16] He returned to Papua New Guinea in 1969 with an official delegation from the Ministry of Health. They recovered and cremated a large number of bodies and brought them back to Tokyo's Chidorigafuchi cemetery for the unknown war dead.

Having avoided incineration at Hiroshima, Yori-ichi Yokoyama continued working in the Teijin group's fibre factory. He soon settled into family life. He moved up from the production line and into the company's public relations section, then to a newly opened factory in the city of Tokuyama, further west.[17] Life and the war experience had taught him enough to make up for his lack of formal education.

Yuki Shimada, the warrant officer entrusted with the regimental colours of the 144th, returned to Tosa City, a fishing port adjacent to Kochi, where he lived a peaceful life as a family man and a rice retailer.

Yukiharu Yamasaki, the sergeant who lost part of his hand at Isurava, worked for a trucking company after the war. In 1947 Allied war crimes investigators ordered him to Tokyo for questioning, but nothing came of it and he was soon released. He returned to his job and the family he had started in Kochi.

After demobilisation, Kokichi Nishimura drifted around the country working odd jobs, convinced the Americans wanted to interrogate him about the Tol plantation massacre. In fact, he'd been nowhere near Tol when the massacre occurred, having been with Horie Battalion on the other side of New Britain. His delusions of persecution may well have arisen from post-traumatic stress disorder from his experience at Mission Ridge on the Kokoda Track.

During this period, Nishimura married. By 1955, he'd calmed down and set up a factory–laboratory outside Tokyo turning out ultralight steel beams. By the 1970s, he was making up detailed lists of comrades fallen in battle and planning a return to New Guinea. His eldest son was killed in a traffic accident at this time, adding to his psychological stress and seeming to cement his determination to recover the remains of comrades left behind in the Kokoda campaign. When he announced his intention, a family argument erupted. He transferred all his assets to his wife and two remaining sons and never saw them again. Only his daughter took his side.

Nishimura returned to New Guinea in 1980 and set up base there, building a house near Popondetta, on the northern coastlands. A year later, he began searching the overgrown area that had once been the Sanananda track junction, using a metal detector, shovel and hoe. He unearthed large numbers of bones, some with 'dog-tag' identity discs. The Allies had removed most of the bodies of their dead from the battlefield in 1942 and 1943, so any bodies found were most likely to be Japanese. Nishimura moved on to Gona and Buna, then further afield to Waju, near Gorari.

Following his success in the lowland regions, he began making bone recovery trips along the Kokoda Track. He was particularly interested in searching the section of Mission Ridge where he says the rest of his platoon was wiped out, but searching the foxholes brought only disappointment. There were no bones to be found there. One day, elsewhere in the area, Nishimura found five leg bones wearing Japanese army boots. They were found in black soil. Nishimura persuaded himself that Australians had recovered the bodies of his dead comrades and burnt them on a mass funeral pyre. He cremated the leg bones and kept the ash and some of the black soil in his house at Popondetta.[18]

Though the evidence suggests otherwise, it's nonetheless possible that Nishimura's platoon was wiped out at Mission Ridge as he describes, but if this version of events is a figment of his imagination, we need to bear in mind that it arose in a young man facing his first intense battle. The landings at Guam, Rabaul and Salamaua had all been relatively benign, and at Isurava Nishimura was on the fringe with Horie Unit. At Mission Ridge the enemy was close for the first time, hidden, but with a reputation for fierce, relentless fighting. A Juki rat-tatting behind and enemy fire in front can be a terrifying and traumatising introduction to the reality of battle, especially for a young soldier overestimating his ability to cope. The depiction of the Omaha Beach landing in the movie *Saving Private Ryan* perhaps gives some sense of what the young Nishimura was experiencing. The scars of such catastrophic stress can be deep and permanent.

◆　◆　◆

The Kochi–New Guinea Association represents all New Guinea veterans resident in Kochi Prefecture. It is not restricted to 144th Regiment, although the vast majority of members are from that unit. The association gathers formally once a year on the third Sunday of October to hold a remembrance service, always at Gokoku Shrine in Kochi City and followed by a reunion dinner at a restaurant nearby.

Like its equivalents in Australia, the association has not been without controversy. Its second president, Masura Moriki, was captured at Oivi and spent the rest of his war in the POW camp at Cowra in New South Wales. Moriki wrote a book about his experiences in Cowra. Some of his fellow veterans think he should have taken the path of suicide rather than return to Japan as a former prisoner of war.

'He should have killed himself before the war ended,' says Imanishi. 'He must have had many chances to do it. He's shameless.' Imanishi boycotted the annual ceremony while Moriki was president.

Yamasaki was also active in the Kochi–New Guinea Association. Vice-president to Moriki, he was more sanguine about the president's past. Questioned about it, he replies with an enigmatic smile, 'I'm sure he had many chances to kill himself.' Yamasaki took over the presidency when Moriki died in 2002, and Imanishi resumed his involvement with the association.

Nishimura grew increasingly eccentric and fractious over the years. In his periodic returns to Japan he would stay with his daughter in Tokyo, but otherwise he slept in the back of his car when travelling around the country. While many of the relics he collected ended up with the association, Nishimura was suspended for breaking its rules, most flagrantly building a memorial at Efogi without association permission. He was still allowed to attend the annual Shinto ceremony as a private individual, which was all the unsociable Nishimura was interested in doing anyway. In later years he became friendly with Imanishi, who viewed him with a bemused tolerance he had been unable to muster for Moriki.

'We don't tolerate unique people very well in Japan,' Imanishi says.[19]

There was a similar association in Fukuyama for veterans of 41st Regiment, but most of the survivors of the Papuan campaign had been killed at Leyte, and with its small membership the group had become inactive by the turn of the century. Yokoyama, now living in Tokuyama, maintains a collection in memory of his wartime comrades, and in Fukuyama there is a memorial and a shrine in honour of the wartime dead, but the veterans' association has run its course.

An overarching association, the East New Guinea Veterans Association, covered the entire New Guinea campaign. Its annual memorial ceremony at Tokyo's Yasukuni Shrine was discontinued after the 25 April 2005 service owing to dwindling membership. It's the same problem that has confronted Australian organisers of Anzac Day, and is exacerbated by the fact that Japan has been involved in no war since 1945.

◆　◆　◆

'You never recognised the enemy as a human being,' recollects Imanishi in the twilight of his life. 'It was like a hunter with a rabbit in front of him. If you didn't kill the enemy, you would get killed.'[20]

The men of South Seas Force always recognised the fire power and technological superiority of the Americans, but they didn't have such high regard for their fighting ability. On the other hand, they respected the skills of the Australian soldier in close combat. After the war, many Japanese felt a strong bond with Australia and Australians, whether they met any or not.

Imanishi says he felt a particular connection with Australian athletes competing at the Tokyo Olympic Games in 1964, and would barrack for them when no Japanese were competing. It's an attitude to a former enemy that most Australian veterans of Kokoda would find extremely difficult to comprehend, but it seems to emanate from a sense of having shared the experience of utmost horror. Perhaps it's a variant of Stockholm syndrome.

Reflecting on his 1969 visit to Cairns, Imanishi says, 'I thought what a beautiful place [Australia] was. So big and wide. I never imagined there was such a country as this.'

The Kokoda veterans we spoke to were unanimous in their view that war should always be the last resort in solving any international dispute. 'I often say to my wife and children that it is so sad that there are always people fighting somewhere in the world,' Yamasaki says. 'We say to each other, "Why do we have to fight? We are all human beings."'[21]

To Yokoyama, it's ironic that people can't see what can be done to prevent war until they've actually gone to war. Imanishi notes that Japan has learnt the misery of war from its defeat. He hopes Australians have learnt the same thing from their victory.

'War is beyond our imagination,' he says. 'It is something tough, dirty and horrible. It simply turns human beings into madmen. Both sides became crazy.'

'By submerging the terrible experience of war under a bright future, we survivors can finally explain to the war dead what we achieved out of their death,' concludes the former sergeant. 'Then, their spirits would be saved also.'[22]

Survivors don't survive forever, not even the garrulous Sadashige Imanishi. He died in May 2007. Of the veterans we have followed in this account, only the providentially lucky Yori-ichi Yokoyama of the 41st and the irascible Kokichi Nishimura of the 144th were still alive when we completed the book.

Chapter 20

The path of infinite sorrow

Sadashige Imanishi has a recurring dream. He is swimming in a river in which hundreds of dead bodies float by. The river's current is strong, but in his dream Imanishi is able to swim against it. He has to navigate between the bodies gliding slowly past him, heavy, lifeless and wrapped in brown tattered cloth. It is hard work. His tired arms push through the water's bulk, but with a supreme effort he is able to make progress against the force of the current. He passes more bodies and knows that no matter how many float by, more will follow. At no time in his dream is there a break in the steady stream of human driftwood.[1] Death, it seems, is inexhaustible.

◆ ◆ ◆

Yori-ichi Yokoyama, the former medical corpsman with a lucky streak, decided to return to Papua New Guinea in November 2005 for the first time since 1943. In preparation for the visit he made 250 pairs of miniature straw sandals.

'The Japanese soldiers were walking the long Kokoda Track in bare feet,' he said. 'I'm making these sandals after wondering if their shoes would have worn out by now.'[2]

His plan was to offer the sandals to the spirits of his fallen comrades to ease their long walk in the afterlife. He kept them in small wooden boxes reminiscent of the boxes in which soldiers carried home the ashes of the dead.

An old man now, Yokoyama flew to Port Moresby with a party of Japanese, accompanied by his daughter and son-in-law and a neighbour from Shunan City. After more than sixty-three years, he had finally reached the objective South Seas Force had been aiming for when it landed in New Guinea in August 1942. That fact seemed of little significance to him, but then he hadn't been a front-line infantryman. In any case, he had more important things in mind than achieving the military goal of a long-gone regime.

Yokoyama's party went to Rabaul, where they danced a prayer for the spirits of the war dead, then on to Kokoda and down to Giruwa village. These were the two places where he spent much of his Papuan wartime sojourn. The Kokoda he saw bore some resemblance to the one of his memory—with the flat projecting tongue of land, the plantations behind, even the airstrip in the same position—but the Giruwa of 2005 was not the one he knew.

Papuans move their villages around periodically. After nearby Mt Lamington erupted in 1951, Giruwa was moved. Its present-day site was under water during the war. Now it is just behind Sanananda instead of down the coast. Much of the countryside was also unrecognisable to Yokoyama, except for the mangrove swamps. They brought back disturbing memories of the bodies of Japanese soldiers floating between raised roots. Shocking images from the past hacked their way to the front of Yokoyama's thoughts.

Villagers welcomed the party to Giruwa. The Japanese went into a small hut in which bones and pieces of equipment left behind from the war were on display. Seeing soldiers' equipment with their names inscribed was heartbreaking for the old soldier, but the most profound moment was still to come. He was shown a skull said to be that of Colonel Yamamoto, the erstwhile commander of 144th Regiment, who had perished in the last days of the Buna garrison.

Yokoyama ran his palms over the surface of the skull like a blind man trying to identify something. He lifted it up to the light, staring at it and trembling. Tears streamed down the eighty-year-old's cheeks. His family tried to console him, but nothing could stop the flow of sorrow that poured out of him. Yori-ichi Yokoyama kept saying, 'Forgive me for leaving you all behind. Now I have come back. I have come back.'

The visitors dedicated incense to the soldiers who had not survived that terrible campaign and prayed for their spirits.

◆　◆　◆

The road between Giruwa and Kokoda still crosses the Kumusi River at the point where the wartime Wairopi bridge had been erected, bombed and reerected several times until the Japanese gave up. In 2005 a permanent bridge crossed the river, permanent until the floods that followed Cyclone Guba swept it away in 2007.

Yokoyama stopped at the modern-day Wairopi bridge, went to the railing and leant out over the river with one of his boxes of straw sandals. The Kumusi flowed strongly and serenely below the bridge and on to the Solomon Sea further north. The old soldier's frail hands were made more frail by the emotion of the moment. He held the box over the water, paused as if undecided what to do next, then let go. It fell to the river like a leaf from a tree, to be swallowed in an instant by the Kumusi's strong flow. Yokoyama had given the remaining sandals to one of the authors to distribute along the Track.

The demons in the far reaches of Private Yokoyama's imaginings had been chased away. By his gesture, the spirits of men of 41st and 144th Infantry Regiments of the Imperial Japanese Army were now able to march freely back up the path of infinite sorrow to a better world.

Shadows of fallen soldiers left their water-logged dugouts and trudged up the Kokoda Track to Ioribaiwa Ridge, fleeting figures on a ghostly, jungle-walled path. Their steps grew lighter as they approached the ridge, where they waited and turned back, their confidence growing through each valley and razorback of the return journey, until they got to the Solomon Sea. There they waded out to barges for waiting merchant ships to take them, abuzz with excitement inside cramped holds, to the land of their birth, to railway stations at Asakura and Fukuyama.

The spirits paused in their odyssey, marching up and down, running with weighted packs between the soulless brick buildings that marked out square parade grounds in their two regimental headquarters until it was time to go back out the imposing iron- and brick-columned entrances, back to the towns and villages of their childhood. The veterans of the Kokoda campaign were finally at peaceful rest in the luminous fields of Yasukuni Shrine. In the innocence of young boys, everything is joyful and the world is full of hope.

Appendix I

Japanese soldiers appearing in this book

Soldiers listed are those who appear more than once.
*Major characters' names are in **bold**.*

ADACHI Hatazo	Lt–Gen	Cdr, Eighteenth Army
FUCHIYAMA Sadahide	Lt–Col	Cdr, 47th Field Anti-aircraft Artillery Bn
FUKUKAWA Susumu	Lt	3rd Bn 144th Regiment
FUKUOKA Shigeji	Pte	South Seas Force HQ
FUTAMI Akisaburo	Maj–Gen	Seventeenth Army
HAYASHI Shojiro	Cdr	Cdr, Kure 5SNLP
HIRANO Kogoro	**Lt**	**1st Bn 144th Regiment**
HORIE Tadashi	Maj	Cdr, 2nd Bn 144th Regiment
HORII Tomitaro	**Maj–Gen**	**Cdr, South Seas Force**
HOZUMI Shizuo	Lt–Col	Cdr, 55th Mountain Artillery Regiment
HYAKUTAKE Haruyoshi	Lt–Gen	Cdr, Seventeenth Army
IMAMURA Hitoshi	Gen	Cdr, Southern Area Army
IMANISHI Sadashige	**S–Sgt**	**1st Bn 144th Regiment**
INAGAKI Riichi	Lt	Paymaster, 15th Pioneers
INOUE Kiyomichi	Lt	2nd Bn 144th Regiment
KANEMOTO Rinzo	Lt	55th Supply Regiment

KATO Kokichi	Maj	Cdr, 2nd Bn 144th Regiment
KOBAYASHI Asao	Maj	Cdr, 3rd Bn 41st Regiment
KOIWAI Mitsuo	**Maj**	**Cdr, 2nd Bn 41st Regiment**
KUSUNOSE Masao	**Col**	**Cdr, 144th Regiment**
KUWADA Gen'ichiro	Lt-Col	Cdr, 3rd Bn 144th Regiment
MATSUYAMA Mitsuharu	R. Adm	Cdr, 18th Squadron
MIKAWA Gun-ichi	V-Adm	Cdr, Eighth Fleet
MIYAMOTO Kikumatsu	Maj	Cdr, 1st Bn 41st Regiment
MIYASHITA Tetsunosuke	Pte	144th Regiment
MURASE Gohei	Maj	Cdr, 3rd Bn 41st Regiment
NAKAHASHI Kokichi	Lt	55th Mountain Artillery Regiment
NISHIMURA Kokichi	**Pte**	**2nd Bn 144th Regiment**
ODA Kensaku	Maj-Gen	Cdr, South Seas Force
OKINO Jiro	Pte	144th Regiment
SAKAMOTO Atsushi	Lt	1st Bn 144th Regiment
SHIMADA Yuki	WO	144th Regiment
TAKAGI Yoshifumi	Lt	1st Bn 55th Mountain Artillery Regiment
TAKENAKA Hideta	Lt	3rd Bn 41st Regiment
TANAKA Toyonari	**Lt-Col**	**South Seas Force**
TOMITA Yoshinobu	Lt-Col	South Seas Force
TSUJI Masanobu	**Lt-Col**	**Imperial HQ**
TSUKAMOTO Hatsuo	**Lt-Col**	**Cdr, 1st Bn, 144th Regiment**
TSUKIOKA Torashige	Cdr	Cdr, Sasebo 5SNLP
TSUNODA Kazuo	S-Sgt	Second Air Corps
UCHIYAMA Seiichi	L-Cpl	3rd Bn 229th Regiment
YAMAGATA Tsuyuo	Maj-Gen	Cdr, Buna Detachment
YAMAMOTO Shigemi	Col	Cdr, 144th Regiment
YAMAMOTO Tsuneichi	Maj	Cdr, Basabua Garrison
YAMASAKI Yukiharu	**Sgt**	**3rd Bn 144th Regiment**
YANO Minoru	Cdr	Cdr, Kure 3SNLP
YASUDA Yoshitatsu	Capt	Cdr, Yokosuka 5SNLP
YAZAWA Kiyoshi	**Col**	**Cdr, 41st Regiment**
YOKOYAMA Yori-ichi	**Pte**	**3rd Bn 41st Regiment**
YOKOYAMA Yosuke	**Col**	**Cdr, 15th Independent Engineer Regiment**

Appendix II

The Japanese military hierarchy

Names in brackets were subsequent occupants of the position.

Southern Area Army   Gen Hitoshi IMAMURA

Seventeenth Army   Lt-Gen Haruyoshi HYAKUTAKE
Chief of Staff   Maj-Gen Akisaburo FUTAMI
Staff Officer   Lt-Col Hiroshi MATSUMOTO

Eighteenth Army   Lt-Gen Hatazo ADACHI
Chief of Staff   Maj-Gen Kane YOSHIHARA
Chief of Operations   Col Joichiro SANADA
Staff Officers   Lt-Col Kumao IMOTO
Lt-Col Shigeru SUGIYAMA

Buna Detachment   Maj-Gen Tsuyuo YAMAGATA
Staff Officers   Col Kikutaro AOTSU
Lt-Col Gozo KITA
Maj Kengoro TANAKA

South Seas Force   Maj-Gen Tomitaro HORII (Maj-Gen Kensaku ODA)
Staff Officers   Lt-Col Toyonari TANAKA (Maj Yoshikuni TAJIMA)
Lt-Col Yoshinobu TOMITA
Guards Officer   Lt Hausukichi INOUE

144th Reg	Col Masao KUSUNOSE (Col Shigemi YAMAMOTO) (Col Akio YOSHIDA)
1st Bn	Lt-Col Hatsuo TSUKAMOTO
	1st Coy Lt Sadao HAMADA
	2nd Coy Lt Taneshige TAKIISHI
	3rd Coy Lt Munekichi NOSE
2nd Bn	Maj Tadashi HORIE (Maj Kokichi KATO)
	4th Coy Lt Masao OKAZAKI
	5th Coy Lt Tokushige KIHARA
	6th Coy Lt Ugashige UEMURA
3rd Bn	Lt-Col Gen'ichiro KUWADA
	7th Coy Capt Sumiyoshi KAMIYA
	8th Coy Lt Yoshie YANAGISE
	9th Coy Lt Masahide HAMAGUCHI
55th Mtn Art'y Bn	Lt-Col Shizuo HOZUMI
47th Field Anti-aircraft Art'y Bn	Lt-Col Sadahide FUCHIYAMA
41st Reg	Col Kiyoshi YAZAWA
1st Bn	Maj Kikumatsu MIYAMOTO
2nd Bn	Maj Mitsuo KOIWAI
3rd Bn	Maj Asao KOBAYASHI (Maj Gohei MURASE)
15th Ind Engineer Reg	Col Yosuke YOKOYAMA
42nd Anchorage Cmd	Lt-Col Shiseto RYUTO
Fourth Fleet	V-Adm Shigeyoshi INOUE
Eighth Fleet	V-Adm Gun-ichi MIKAWA
Chief of Staff	R-Adm Shinzo ONISHI
Snr Staff Officer	Capt Shigenori KAMI
Staff Officer	Cdr Toshikazu OMAE
18th Squadron	R-Adm Mitsuharu MATSUYAMA
Sasebo 5SNLP	Cdr Torashige TSUKIOKA
Kure 3SNLP	Cdr Minoru YANO
Kure 5SNLP	Cdr Shojiro HAYASHI
Yokosuka 5SNLP	Capt Yoshitatsu YASUDA

Notes

Chapter 1   On Ioribaiwa Ridge
1   Okada, *Lost Troops*, p. 14
2   Ham, *Kokoda*, p. 255
3   Bullard, *Japanese Army Operations in the South Pacific Area*, p. 142
4   Jorgensen, *War History of South Seas Force,* p. 13
5   Shimada, interview 2004
6   Bullard, p. 143

Chapter 2   Empire and emperor
1   Gordon, *A Modern History of Japan,* p. 49
2   Although Japanese personal names are conventionally set out with family name first and given name second, in this book we have used the reverse order familiar to Western readers
3   Gordon, p. 116
4   *Ibid.*, p. 93
5   *Ibid.*, p. 118. Andressen, *A Short History of Japan*, p. 93
6   Gordon, p. 119
7   Andressen, p. 94. Beasley, *The Japanese Experience*, p. 234
8   Beasley, p. 235. Gordon, p. 121. Andressen, p. 96
9   Choucri, North and Yamakage, *The Challenge of Japan Before World War II and After*, p. 123
10   *Ibid.*, p. 119
11   Gordon, p. 162
12   Reischauer and Craig, *Japan: Tradition and Transformation,* p. 204

13   Gordon, p. 145
14   *Ibid.*, p. 150
15   Reischauer and Craig, p. 206
16   Beasley, p. 238. Gordon, p. 175. Choucri, North and Yamakage, p. 118. Reischauer and Craig, p. 235

Chapter 3   *The road to total war*
1   Gordon, *A Modern History of Japan*, p. 187. Reischauer and Craig, *Japan: Tradition and Transformation*, p. 242. Choucri, North and Yamakage, *The Challenge of Japan Before World War II and After*, p. 126
2   Gordon, p. 182. Reischauer and Craig, p. 195
3   Gordon, p. 188
4   Reischauer and Craig, pp. 249-250. Gordon, p. 188
5   Coincidentally, the Japanese often describe their behaviour in Asia during the war as *mewaku kakeru* (to cause bother): Buruma, *A Japanese Mirror*, p. 60
6   Gordon, p. 190
7   Choucri, North and Yamakage, p. 140
8   Gordon, p. 196
9   Choucri, North and Yamakage, p. 141
10   Gordon, p. 198
11   Hata, 'The Marco Polo Bridge Incident', p. 248
12   Yanaga, *Japan Since Perry,* p. 574
13   See Gerster, *Travels in Atomic Sunshine*, pp. 109-118
14   Gordon, p. 206
15   Gordon, pp. 204-206. Andressen, *A Short History of Japan*, p. 107
16   Gordon, p. 206. Andressen, p. 107
17   Reischauer and Craig, p. 260
18   Hunsberger, *Japan and the United States in World Trade*, p. 20
19   Choucri, North and Yamakage, p. 160
20   *Ibid.*, p. 166
21   *Ibid.*, p. 160
22   Andressen, p. 111. Choucri, North and Yamakage, p. 175
23   Choucri, North and Yamakage, p. 172
24   A well-known expression in Japanese, this has an English equivalent in 'take the plunge' or 'cross the Rubicon'. The temple's verandah jutted out over a deep ravine.
25   Butow, *Tojo and the Coming of War*, p. 267
26   Choucri, North and Yamakage, p. 180
27   Stinnett, *Day of Deceit*, pp. 248-250
28   Choucri, North and Yamakage, p. 181. Beasley, *The Japanese Experience*, p. 246
29   Choucri, North and Yamakage, p. 167
30   Reischauer and Craig, p. 269
31   *Ibid.*
32   FitzSimons, *Kokoda,* pp. 81-82

Chapter 4   From the mountains to the sea
1   Kochi is now a city, the only city on the southern side of Shikoku, although not big by Japanese standards. It is about the size of Canberra.
2   Imanishi Yumi, interview 2008
3   Happell, *The Bone Man of Kokoda*, pp. 20–21
4   Imanishi, interview 2004
5   The Fukuyama that raised 41st Regiment is not the city we see today. That Fukuyama was an Atlantis, sunk under waves of concentrated American bombing two days after the atomic bomb was dropped on nearby Hiroshima (Gerster, *Travels in Atomic Sunshine*, p. 274). Eighty per cent of Fukuyama was flattened. From the rubble has risen a new Fukuyama, like so many of today's Japanese cities a bustling, anonymous metropolis of undistinguished functional architecture. There is little visual sign of an enduring ancient culture. It's all in the people, in their politeness and gentility.
6   Yokoyama, interview 2008
7   Yokoyama, interview 2005
8   Shimada, interview 2004
9   ATIS Interrogation Report 6/1 #9
10   *Ibid.* #10
11   Happell, pp. 14–15
12   Yamasaki, interview 2004
13   *Ibid.*
14   ATIS Research Report #122, p. 10
15   Nishimura, interview 2005
16   Some translations call the force South Seas Detachment, *shitai* being translatable as either 'force' or 'detachment'. It was a detachment because it was not part of any division, but we have used 'force' (as have others) for simplicity's sake. *Shitai* is also used for smaller units detached from a larger force, and we translate it as 'detachment' in these instances.
17   Chen, 'Tomitaro Horii'
18   *Ibid.*
19   Imanishi
20   Nishimura. Happell, pp. 24–26

Chapter 5   Forward base Rabaul
1   Stone, *Hostages to Freedom*, p. 42
2   Imanishi, interview 2004
3   Nishimura, interview 2005. Happell, *The Bone Man of Kokoda*, p. 27
4   Yamasaki, interview 2004
5   Stone, p. 47
6   *Ibid.*, p. 69. Chen, 'Battle of Rabaul'. Moremon, 'Japanese Perspective: Rabaul 1942' in Australia-Japan Research Project, 'Campaign History'
7   Okada, *Lost Troops*, p. 6
8   Stone, p. 91

9   Nishimura

10 Stone, p. 96

11 *Ibid.*, p. 89

12 *Ibid.*, pp. 89–90

13 See Aida, *Prisoner of the British*, p. 2

14 *Ibid.*, p. 90

15 Ham, *Kokoda*, p. 112

16 Stone, p. 112. FitzSimons, *Kokoda*, p. 74

17 Stone, pp. 91–92

18 *Ibid.*, p. 91

19 Gamble, *Darkest Hour,* p. 157

20 Nishimura. Happell, p. 28

21 Bullard, *Japanese Army Operations in the South Pacific Area*, p. 28

22 Chen

23 Moremon

24 Stone, p. 39

25 Moremon

26 *Ibid.*

27 Moji, *At the End of Sky and Sea,* p. 91

28 Iwamoto, 'Case Study: Rabaul: Japanese and New Guinean memories of wartime experiences at Rabaul'

29 *Ibid.*

30 *Ibid.*

31 Kanemoto, *Chronicle of the War in New Guinea*, p. 90

32 Imanishi

33 Happell, p. 34

34 Bullard, p. 41

35 FitzSimons, p. 98

36 Bullard, pp. 66–69

37 Stanley, 'He's (not) coming south: The invasion that wasn't' in Bullard and Tamura (eds), *From a Hostile Shore*

38 Stone, p. 168

39 Lewis, 'The Battle of the Coral Sea'

40 Bullard, p. 64

41 *Ibid.*, pp. 96–97. 'Reconnaissance by Kanemoto Rinzo' in Australia-Japan Research Project, 'The Human Face of War'

42 Kanemoto, pp. 92–101

43 Bullard, p. 98. Bullard, 'Horii supply proposal' in 'The Human Face of War'

44 Bullard, p. 100

45 *Ibid.*

Chapter 6   The taking of Kokoda

1   Barrell and Tanaka, *Higher than Heaven.* p. 27. The pamphlet was called *Read This and the War Is Already Won.*

2   Bullard, *Japanese Army Operations in the South Pacific Area*, p. 101
3   Futami, *Record of a Beating Heart and Recollections*
4   Bullard, p. 104
5   Day X is the Japanese military's equivalent of the Allies' D-day
6   Imanishi, interview 2005
7   Ham, *Kokoda*, pp. 4–5
8   Bullard, p. 107. Ham, p. 45
9   ATIS Current Translations 3/2 #266
10   Bullard, 'Atrocities' in Australia-Japan Research Project, 'The Human Face of War'
11   James, *Field Guide to the Kokoda Track*, p. 38
12   Ham, p. 45
13   *Beyond Kokoda* (Episode 1), SGSS Productions
14   Yanagisawa, interview 2005
15   Imanishi
16   Bullard, p. 101
17   *Ibid.*, p. 110
18   Imanishi
19   Brune, *A Bastard of a Place*, p. 103
20   Imanishi
21   ATIS Current Translations 3/2 #218
22   *Ibid.* #266
23   *Ibid.* #218
24   *Ibid.*
25   *Ibid.*
26   Bullard, p. 138

Chapter 7   *The fateful delay*
1   Ham, *Kokoda,* p. 145
2   Bullard, *Japanese Army Operations in the South Pacific Area*, p. 112
3   Ham, p. 138
4   Okada, *Lost Troops*, p. 4
5   *Ibid.*, p. 10
6   ATIS Current Translations 3/2 #218
7   Imanishi, interview 2005
8   Okada, p. 10
9   Yamasaki, interview 2004
10   Yokoyama, interview 2008
11   Imanishi
12   ATIS Current Translations 3/2 #218
13   This was 53rd Battalion, which had been pressed into active service in New Guinea with minimal training.
14   *Beyond Kokoda* (Episode 1), SGSS Productions
15   Honner, 'The 39th at Isurava'
16   Okada, p. 10

17 *Ibid.*, pp. 10–11
18 ATIS Private Records 3DRL/4005
19 Imanishi, interviews 2004 and 2005
20 144th Infantry Regiment Official Record, pp. 209–211
21 Okada, p. 11

Chapter 8   Milne Bay

1 These days, it's promoted as an ecotourism destination
2 Bullard, *Japanese Army Operations in the South Pacific Area*, p. 126
3 Brune, *A Bastard of a Place*, p. 302
4 *Ibid.*, pp. 303–305
5 Moji, *At the End of Sky and Sea*
6 Brune, pp. 301–302
7 *Ibid.*, pp. 329–331
8 Moji
9 Bullard, p. 147
10 Brune, p. 356
11 *Ibid.*, p. 361
12 Bullard, p. 149
13 Brune, pp. 371–374
14 Bullard, p. 150
15 *Ibid.*, p. 152
16 Rolleston, *Not a Conquering Hero*, p. 88
17 Bullard, p. 153
18 ATIS Current Translations 3/2 #248
19 *Ibid.*
20 ATIS Spot Report 4
21 Bullard, p. 154
22 ATIS Spot Report 4
23 Unit diary, 2/12th AIF Battalion
24 Bullard, p. 154
25 Brune, p. 379

Chapter 9   To the end of the line

1 Bullard, *Japanese Army Operations in the South Pacific Area*, p. 134
2 Okada, *Lost Troops*, p. 13
3 James, *Field Guide to the Kokoda Track*, p. 298
4 Imanishi, interview 2004
5 James, p. 283
6 Shigetaka, *Human Chronicle*, p. 181
7 ATIS Bulletin #358
8 Bullard, pp. 141–142
9 Shigetaka, p. 187
10 James, p. 248

11 *Ibid.*
12 Unit diaries, 2/14th Bn, 2/16th Bn and 2/27th Bn AIF
13 Brune, *A Bastard of a Place*, pp. 206–207
14 *Ibid.*, pp. 208–209. James, p. 227
15 Nishimura, interview 2005. James, p. 250. Happell, *The Bone Man of Kokoda*, pp. 54–56
16 Happell, p. 59
17 ATIS Bulletin #358
18 Nishimura. James, p. 251. A minor variant of the story has three bullets, one in the wound on initial inspection, a second found by a 'doctor' a few days later and the third found years after: Happell, p. 59.
19 ATIS Current Translations 3/2 #218
20 ATIS Bulletin #358
21 Ham, *Kokoda*, pp. 240–241
22 Okada, pp. 13–14
23 Radio Australia, 'Malaria found in PNG Highlands'
24 Centers for Disease Control (USA), www.cdc.gov/malaria
25 Bullard, 'Malaria' in Australia-Japan Research Project, 'The Human Face of War'
26 Dengue Fever Information Sheet, WHO
27 'Scrub Typhus', NT Centre for Disease Control Fact Sheet, via http://www.health.nt.gov.au/Centre_for_Disease_Control/Publications/CDC_Factsheets/index.aspx
28 Bullard, p. 142
29 ATIS Enemy Publications #24
30 Yokoyama, interview 2008
31 Yokoyama, interview 2005
32 Moreman, 'Kokoda 1942: Japanese advance' in Australia-Japan Research Project, 'Campaign History'
33 Bullard, 'Atrocities' in Australia-Japan Research Project, 'The Human Face of War'
34 Ham, p. 64
35 ATIS Information Request Report [12/26]
36 ATIS Spot Report 15
37 Tsunoda, interview 2005
38 Bullard, p. 157
39 *Ibid.*
40 *Ibid.*, p. 158
41 James, p. 198
42 Porter papers
43 Jorgensen, *War History of South Seas Force*, p. 13
44 Brune, p. 241
45 ATIS Enemy Publications #33
46 Bullard, p. 158
47 Ham, p. 252
48 ATIS Spot Report #2
49 Bullard, p. 142

Chapter 10 'Change the marching direction'

1   Okada, *Lost Troops*, p. 16
2   Bullard, *Japanese Army Operations in the South Pacific Area*, p. 159
3   Okada, p. 17
4   *Ibid.*
5   ATIS Current Translations 3/2 #218
6   Jorgensen, *War History of South Seas Force*, p. 14
7   Imanishi, interview 2005
8   *Ibid.*
9   Okada, pp. 17–18
10   Bullard, p. 159
11   Ham, *Kokoda*, p. 314
12   Jorgensen, p. 14
13   Koiwai, *Recollections of Major Mitsuo Kowai*
14   *Ibid.*
15   Unit diary, 2/25th Bn AIF, 27/9/42
16   *Ibid.*, 28/9/42
17   Moremon, 'Kokoda 1942: Australian counter-attack' in Australia-Japan Research Project, 'Campaign History'
18   FitzSimons, *Kokoda*, p. 398
19   Ham, p. 315
20   ATIS Interrogation Report 6/1 #10
21   Okada, p. 19
22   Happell, *The Bone Man of Kokoda*, p. 65
23   Jorgensen, p. 39
24   Bullard, p. 166
25   Okada, p. 18
26   ATIS Current Translations 3/2 #218
27   ATIS Bulletin #358
28   ATIS Interrogation Report 6/1 #9
29   Okada, p. 18
30   *Ibid.*, p. 20
31   *Ibid.*, p. 21
32   Crooks, *The Footsoldiers*, pp. 192–193

Chapter 11 Buying time

1   Bullard, *Japanese Army Operations in the South Pacific Area*, p. 160
2   ATIS Current Translations 3/2 #218
3   Bullard, p. 167
4   Unit diary, 2/25th AIF Battalion, 8/10/42 and 9/10/42
5   Crooks, *The Footsoldiers*, p. 197
6   Unit diary, 2/33rd AIF Battalion, 12/10/42
7   Ham, *Kokoda*, pp. 350–351
8   Unit diary, 2/25th Bn, 15/10/42

9   ATIS Current Translations 3/2 #218
10 Bullard, 'Atrocities' in Australia–Japan Research Project, 'The Human Face of War'
11 A plane carrying a Uruguayan rugby team crashed in the Andes in 1972 and the survivors were not found for eleven weeks. They stayed alive by eating the flesh of those killed in the crash
12 Ham, p. 347
13 Bullard, 'Atrocities'
14 Unit diary, 2/1st AIF Battalion, 23/10/42
15 Crooks, p. 191
16 Imanishi interview, 2005
17 Imanishi interview, 2004
18 Koiwai, *Recollections of Major Misuo Koiwai*
19 Jorgensen, *War History of South Seas Force*, p. 20
20 Ham, p. 380

Chapter 12   General Horii's last stand

1   Okada, *Lost Troops*, p. 24
2   *Ibid.*
3   Imanishi interview, 2005
4   Tsunoda interview, 2005
5   Kanemoto, *Chronicle of the War in New Guinea*, pp. 120–123
6   Imanishi
7   *Ibid.*
8   Ham, *Kokoda*, p. 382
9   Bullard, *Japanese Army Operations in the South Pacific Area*, p. 171
10 *Ibid.* p. 170
11 Ham, p. 394
12 Crooks, *The Footsoldiers*, p. 219
13 Unit diaries, 2/2nd AIF Battalion, 9/11/42 and 10/11/42 and 2/3rd AIF Battalion, 9/11/42
14 Unit diary, 2/2nd Bn, 11/11/42
15 Crooks, p. 226
16 Bullard, p. 172
17 Imanishi
18 *Ibid.*
19 Jorgensen, *War History of South Seas Force*, p. 24
20 Koiwai, *Recollections of Major Misuo Koiwai*
21 Jorgensen, p. 28
22 Koiwai
23 Happell, *The Bone Man of Kokoda*, pp. 67–69
24 Ham, p. 398
25 Imanishi
26 Bullard, p. 173

27   *Ibid.*

28   The story of Horii's death was told by Fukuoka to Koiwai, who wrote it up in *Recollections of Major Misuo Koiwai*. It is retold in: Bullard, p. 173; Tamira, 'Death of Horii' in Australia–Japan Research Project, 'The Human Face of War'; Ham, p. 398; Jorgensen, p. 41

Chapter 13   Dug in on swampland
1   Okada, *Lost Troops*, p. 23
2   ATIS Enemy Publications #24
3   Okada, p. 25
4   *Ibid.*, p. 32
5   Horner, 'Strategy and command in Australia's New Guinea campaigns' in Australia–Japan Research Project, 'Higher Strategy'
6   Ham, *Kokoda*, p. 414
7   McCarthy, *South-West Pacific Area—First Year, Kokoda to Wau*, p. 531
8   ATIS Current Translations 3/2 #221
9   ATIS Bulletin #47
10   *Ibid.*
11   Nishimura, interview 2005
12   ATIS Interrogation Report #54
13   Tamura, 'Takasago Giyutai' in Australia–Japan Research Project, 'The Human Face of War'
14   Suzuki, *A military doctor's New Guinea war report*, p. 44
15   ATIS Interrogation Report #55
16   Imanishi, interview 2005
17   Milner, *Victory in Papua*, p. 169
18   *Ibid.*, p. 175
19   ATIS Bulletin #80
20   Horner, *Blamey*, p. 360
21   Ham, pp. 450–451
22   Milner, p. 184
23   *Ibid.*, p. 187
24   ATIS Current Translations 3/2 #249
25   Bullard, *Japanese Army Operations in the South Pacific Area*, p. 191

Chapter 14   Madness and desperation
1   Okada, *Lost Troops*, p. 25
2   *Ibid.*, p. 26
3   *Ibid.*, pp. 29–30
4   Yokoyama, interview 2008
5   Brune, *A Bastard of a Place*, p. 443
6   *Ibid.*, p. 432
7   *Ibid.*, p. 434
8   ATIS Current Translations 3/2 #243

9   Bullard, *Japanese Army Operations in the South Pacific Area*, p. 187
10 Unit diary, 2/14th AIF Battalion, 28/11/42
11 Bullard, p. 190
12 Unit diary, 39th CMF Battalion, 5/12/42
13 Milner, *Victory in Papua*, p. 213
14 Bullard, p. 181
15 Milner, p. 214
16 Unit diary, 2/16th AIF Battalion, 30/11/42
17 Brune, p. 455
18 Unit diary, 39th Bn, 3/12/42
19 Brune, pp. 476–478
20 Unit diary, 2/16th Bn, 9/12/42
21 Brune, p. 484
22 Bullard, p. 186
23 British anti-tank rifle grenade designed to penetrate armour
24 Milner, p. 218
25 *Ibid.*
26 Yoshihara, *Southern Cross*

Chapter 15   *On the track to Sanananda*
1   Brune, *A Bastard of a Place*, p. 557
2   Imanishi, interview 2005
3   Unit diary, 2/1st AIF Battalion, 22/11/42
4   Unit diary, 2/2nd AIF Battalion, 20/11/42
5   Perret, *Old Soldiers Never Die*, p. 310
6   Milner, *Victory in Papua*, p. 219
7   *Ibid.*, p. 221
8   Unit diary, 2/1st Bn, 30/11/42
9   Yokoyama, interview 2005
10 Brune, pp. 563–568
11 Milner, pp. 224–225
12 Yokoyama
13 *Ibid.*
14 Miyashita/Haruki, 'Desperate battle of the "crash-course light-machine-gun squad"' in Australia-Japan Research Project, 'Campaign History'
15 Nishimura, interview 2005
16 Yokoyama
17 Miyashita/Haruki
18 ATIS Enemy Publications #24
19 Brune, p. 570
20 Milner, p. 227
21 Brune, p. 577

Chapter 16   Buna falls
1   Horner, *Crisis of Command*, p. 232
2   Milner, *Victory in Papua*, p. 2238
3   ATIS Current Translations 3/2 #283
4   *Ibid.* #254
5   *Ibid.* #249
6   ATIS Bulletin #80
7   Milner, p. 250
8   Ham, *Kokoda*, pp. 467–468
9   Center of Military History, *Papuan Campaign*, p. 48
10   Milner, p. 264
11   *Ibid.*, p. 280
12   Shinto shrine in Tokyo dedicated to the spirits of soldiers who died fighting for the Emperor
13   ATIS Bulletin #80
14   Bullard, *Japanese Army Operations in the South Pacific Area*, p. 195
15   *Ibid.*
16   Milner, p. 313
17   Bullard, p. 196
18   Yamamoto, *Yokosuka 5th SNLP*, pp. 185–186
19   *Ibid.*, p. 405
20   *Ibid.*, pp. 162–163
21   Bullard, p. 196

Chapter 17   Evacuation
1   Nishimura, interview 2005
2   Milner, *Victory in Papua*, p. 332
3   Imanishi, interview 2005
4   Miyashita/Haruki, 'Desperate battle of the "crash-course light machine-gun squad"' in Australia-Japan Research Project, 'Campaign History'
5   *Ibid.*
6   Bullard, *Japanese Army Operations in the South Pacific Area*, p. 198
7   Miyashita/Haruki
8   ATIS Current Translations 3/2 #254
9   Happell, *The Bone Man of Kokoda*, pp. 78–79
10   Yokoyama, interview 2008
11   ATIS Interrogation Spot Report #11
12   Yokoyama, interview 2005
13   Ham, *Kokoda*, p. 490
14   Milner, p. 345
15   A diminutive of *Nikudan Kogeki Han*, or Body Attack Squad
16   Jorgensen, *War History of South Seas Force*, p. 37
17   *Ibid.*, p. 42
18   Yokoyama, 2005

19 Nishimura
20 Jorgensen, p. 42
21 *Ibid.*
22 *Ibid.*
23 Yokoyama, 2005 and 2008
24 *Ibid.*, 2005
25 Milner, p. 347
26 Bullard, p. 207
27 *Ibid.*, pp. 207–208
28 *Ibid.*, pp. 202–203
29 Koiwai, *Recollections of Major Misuo Koiwai*
30 Milner, p. 362
31 Imanishi
32 Happell, pp. 79–80
33 Koiwai
34 Yoshihara, *Southern Cross*
35 Bullard, p. 204
36 Jorgensen, p. 59
37 Imanishi

Chapter 18   The long journey home
1 Bullard, *Japanese Army Operations in the South Pacific Area*, p. 209
2 *Ibid.*, p. 205
3 *Ibid.*, p. 204
4 *Ibid.*, pp. 205–206
5 Yokoyama, interview 2005
6 Bullard, p. 210
7 Yumi Imanishi, interview 2008
8 Nishimura, interview 2005
9 144th Infantry Regiment Official Record, p. 209
10 Yokoyama, interviews 2005 and 2008
11 Tsunoda, interview 2005
12 Yokoyama 2008

Chapter 19   Out of the ashes
1 Gerster, *Travels in Atomic Sunshine*, p. 25
2 Dower, *Embracing Defeat*, p. 45
3 Andressen, *A Short History of Japan*, p. 119
4 Dower, p. 48
5 *Ibid.*, p. 51
6 *Ibid.*, p. 24
7 Tsurumi, *An Intellectual History of Wartime Japan 1931–1945*, pp. 5–13
8 See research in ATIS Research Report #122
9 Dower, p. 59

10   *Ibid.*, p. 466
11   Justice Radhabinod Pal produced a 1235-page judgment dismissing the legiti-
      macy of the war trial as victor's justice, although he conceded that atrocities were
      carried out by the Japanese armed forces.
12   Bullard, 'Tsuji Masanobu' in Australia-Japan Research Project, 'The Human Face
      of War'
13   144th Infantry Regiment Official Record, pp. 209–211
14   Andressen, pp. 123–124
15   *Ibid.*, p. 125
16   Yumi Imanishi, interview 2008
17   Yokoyama, interview 2008
18   A detailed account of Nishimura's postwar activities can be found in Happell,
      The Bone Man of Kokoda
19   Happell, p. 223
20   Imanishi, interview 2005
21   Yamasaki, interview 2004
22   Imanishi

Chapter 20   *The path of infinite sorrow*
  1   Imanishi, interview 2004
  2   Yokoyama, interview 2005

Bibliography

Books

Aida Yugi, *Prisoner of the British* (transl. Hide Ishigaro & Louis Allen), Cresset Press, London, 1966

Andressen, Curtis, *A Short History of Japan*, Allen & Unwin, Sydney, 2002

Barrell, Tony and Rick Tanaka, *Higher Than Heaven: Japan, war and everything*, Private Guy International, Sydney, 1995

Beasley, WG, *The Japanese Experience*, Weidenfeld & Nicholson, London, 1999

Borton, Hugh, *Japan's Modern Century*, Ronald Press, New York, 1970

Brune, Peter, *A Bastard of a Place*, Allen & Unwin, Sydney, 2003

—— *Gona's Gone!: The battle for the beach-head 1942*, Allen & Unwin, Sydney, 1994

Bullard, Steven (ed. & transl.), *Japanese Army Operations in the South Pacific Area: New Britain and Papua campaigns, 1942–43*, Australian War Memorial, Canberra, 2007

—— and Keiko Tamura (eds), *From a Hostile Shore*, Australian War Memorial, Canberra, 2004

Buruma, Ian, *A Japanese Mirror: Heroes and villains of Japanese culture*, Jonathan Cape, London, 1984

Butow, Robert J, *Tojo and the Coming of the War*, Princeton University Press, Princeton, NJ, 1961

Choucri, Nazli, Robert C North and Susumu Yamakage, *The Challenge of Japan Before World War II and After*, Routledge, London, 1992

Crooks, William, *The Footsoldiers*, Printcraft Press, Sydney, 1971

Dilley, Roy, *Japanese Army Uniforms and Equipment, 1939–1945*, Almark, London, 1970

Dower, John, *Embracing Defeat: Japan in the aftermath of World War II*, Penguin Books, London, 1999

FitzSimons, Peter, *Kokoda*, Hodder & Stoughton, Sydney, 2004

Gamble, Bruce, *Darkest Hour*, (2006) Zenith Press, St Paul, Minn., 2006

Gerster, Robin, *Travels in Atomic Sunshine*, Scribe, Melbourne, 2008

Gordon, Andrew, *A Modern History of Japan*, Oxford University Press, New York, 2003

Ham, Paul, *Kokoda*, HarperCollins, Sydney, 2004

Happell, Charles, *The Bone Man of Kokoda*, Macmillan, Sydney, 2008

Hata Ikuhiko, 'The Marco Polo Bridge Incident' in James W Morley (ed.), *The China Quagmire: Japan's expansion on the Asian continent, 1933–1941*, Columbia University Press, New York, 1983

Horner, David, *Blamey: Commander-in-Chief*, Allen & Unwin, Sydney, 1998

—— *Crisis of Command: Australian generalship and the Japanese threat, 1941–1943*, Australian War Memorial, Canberra, 1978

Hunsberger, Warren S, *Japan and the United States in World Trade*, Harper & Row, New York, 1964

James, Bill, *Field Guide to the Kokoda Track: An historical guide to the lost battlefields*, Kokoda Press, Sydney, 2006

Jowett, Philip, *The Japanese Army 1931–45*, Osprey, Oxford, 2002

Kanemoto Rinzo, *Nyuginia senki (Chronicle of the War in New Guinea)*, Kawade Shobo, Tokyo, 1968

McCarthy, Dudley, *South-West Pacific Area—First Year, Kokoda to Wau*, Australian War Memorial, Canberra, 1959

Milner, Samuel, *Victory in Papua*, Office of The Chief of Military History, Dept of Army, Washington DC, 1957 (ibiblio.org/hyperwar)

Moji Chikamori, *Sora to umi no hate de: Dai 1 koku kantai fuku-kan no kaiso (At the End of Sky and Sea: Recollections by an adjutant of the 1st Air Fleet)*, Mainichi Shimbun-sha, Tokyo, 1978

Perret, Geoffrey, *Old Soldiers Never Die: The life of Douglas MacArthur*, Random House, New York, 1996

Reischauer, Edwin O and Albert M Craig, *Japan: Tradition and transformation*, Allen & Unwin, Sydney, 1989

Rolleston, Frank, *Not a Conquering Hero*, self-published, Eton, Qld, 1984

Shigetaka Onda, *Ningen no Kiroku: Nyuginia Jigoku no Senjo (Human Chronicle: New Guinea, battle field of hell)*, Tokuma Shoten, Tokyo, 1994

Stinnett, Robert B, *Day of Deceit: The truth about FDR and Pearl Harbor*, Touchstone, New York, 2000

Stone, Peter, *Hostages to Freedom: The fall of Rabaul*, Oceans Enterprises, Yarram, Vic., 1995

Takida Kenji, *Taiyo wa moeru (The Pacific Burns)*, Kachoo Shuppan, Tokyo, 1995

Tanaka Hiromi, 'Japan in the Pacific War and New Guinea' in Bullard and Tamura (eds), *From a Hostile Shore*, Australian War Memorial, Canberra, 2004

Tanaka Kengoro, *Operations of the Imperial Japanese Armed Forces in the Papua New Guinea Theatre During World War II* (transl. Nobuo Kojima), Japan Papua New Guinea Goodwill Society, Tokyo, 1980

Tsurumi Shunsuke, *An Intellectual History of Wartime Japan 1931–1945*, KPI, London, 1986

Yamamoto Kiyoshi, *Yokogotoku; Kaigun Yasuda Butai Buna gyokusai no tenmatsu* (*Yoko-suka 5th SNLP:The glorious sacrifice of theYasuda Naval Unit at Buna*), Seiunsha, Tokyo, 1985

Yanaga Chitoshi, *Japan Since Perry*, McGraw-Hill, NewYork, 1949

Yoshihara Kane, *Southern Cross* (transl. Doris Heath), Australian War Memorial, Canberra, 2006

Papers, articles, websites, diaries

ATIS Bulletin #47 (Yokoyama Force orders)

ATIS Bulletin #50 (diary, unknown soldier,Yamamoto Bn)

ATIS Bulletin #80 (diary, L/Cpl Uchiyama, 3rd Bn, 229th Reg)

ATIS Bulletin #358 (diary, Lt. Sakamoto, 2nd Bn, 144th Reg)

ATIS Current Translations 3/2 #204 (diary, Lt Kamio, 3rd Bn 170th Reg)

ATIS Current Translations 3/2 #206 (diary, Sasebo, 5th, SNLP)

ATIS Current Translations 3/2 #218 (diary, Lt Hirano, 1st Bn, 144th Reg)

ATIS Current Translations 3/2 #221 (daily log of 47th Field A/A Artillery Bn)

ATIS Current Translations 3/2 #243 (diary, unknown soldier, Gona)

ATIS Current Translations 3/2 #248 (diary, Sei Tatemachi, 14th Pioneers)

ATIS Current Translations 3/2 #249 (diary, unknown soldier, Buna)

ATIS Current Translations 3/2 #254 (diary, unknown soldier, Buna)

ATIS Current Translations 3/2 #266 (diary, Infantry Signals Unit)

ATIS Current Translations 3/2 #283 (diary, Cpl Okajima, 3rd Bn, 229th Reg)

ATIS Enemy Publications #24 (report by Lt Okubo,Army Medical Officer)

ATIS Enemy Publications #33

ATIS Information Request Report [12/26]

ATIS Interrogation Report 6/1 #9 (Pte Jiro Okino, Muriye unit, 144th Reg)

ATIS Interrogation Report 6/1 #10 (Pte Taro Yamamoto, 3rd Bn, 144th Reg)

ATIS Interrogation Spot Report #11 (Lt Inagaki, 15th Pioneers)

ATIS Interrogation Report #54 (Lt Inagaki, 15th Pioneers)

ATIS Interrogation Report #55 (Iwataro Fusei, 15th Pioneers)

ATIS Private Records 3DRL/4005

ATIS Research Report #122, 'Antagonism between officers and men in the Japanese armed forces (1945)'

ATIS Spot Report #2

ATIS Spot Report #4 (notebook of Sasebo 5th SNLP)

ATIS Spot Report #15 (notebook of Toshio Sato, Rabaul interpreter)

ATIS Spot Report #37 (diary, A/cdr 2nd MG Coy)

Australia-Japan Research Project, 'Campaign History', Australian War Memorial, Canberra, 1997 (ajrp.awm.gov.au/ajrp)

—— 'Higher Strategy', Australian War Memorial, Canberra, 1997 (ajrp.awm.gov.au/ajrp)

—— 'Rabaul', Australian War Memorial, Canberra, 1997 (ajrp.awm.gov.au/ajrp)

—— 'The Human Face of War', Australian War Memorial, Canberra, 1997 (ajrp.awm.gov.au/ajrp)

Axis History Forum (forum.axishistory.com)

'Battle of Isurava' at 'Australian Military Units' (www.awm.gov.au/units)

'Battle of the Coral Sea', *Sea Power Centre Australia*, 2006 *(*www.navy.gov.au/spc/history/general/coralsea)

Bowen, James, 'The Battle of Isurava—Australia's Thermopylae', 2006 (www.users.bigpond.com/battleforaustralia/battaust/kokodacampaign/isurava)

Centers for Disease Control, US Dept of Health and Human Services (www.cdc.gov)

Chen, C Peter, 'Battle of Rabaul' and 'Tomitaro Horii', at 'World War II Database', 2008 (ww2db.com)

Futami Akisaburo, *Kodoki oyobi kaisoroku (Record of a Beating Heart and Recollections)*, unpublished MS

Honner, Ralph, 'The 39th at Isurava', *Stand To*, July–August 1956

Koiwai Mitsuo, *Koiwai Mitsuo Shosa no kaiso (Recollections of Major Mitsuo Koiwai)*, unpublished MS

Jorgensen, FC (transl.), *War History of South Seas Force*, unpublished MS, attributed to Lt Kokichi Nakahashi, 1969

Lewis, Robert, 'The Battle of the Coral Sea', 1998 (www.anzacday.org.au/history/ww2/bfa/coralsea)

Nelson, Hank, '*Taim bilong pait*: The impact of the Second World War on Papua and New Guinea' in *Southeast Asia under Japanese Occupation*, ed. Alfred W McCoy, Yale University South East Asia Studies, New Haven, Conn., 1980

Okada Seizo, *Lost Troops* (transl. Seiichi Shiojiri), unpublished MS, 1948

Papuan Campaign: The Buna-Sanananda Operation, Centre of Military History, United States Army, Washington DC, 1990 (www.history.army.mil/books/wwii/papuancamp/papcpn-fm)

Porter, Major-General Selwyn, papers, AWM PR00527 Box 10

Radio Australia, 'Malaria found in PNG highlands', news report, 8 April 2008

Shindo Hiroyuki, 'Japanese air operations over New Guinea during the Second World War', *Journal of Australian War Memorial*, no. 34: June 2001

Suzuki Masami, *Nyuginia gun'i senki (A military doctor's New Guinea war report)*, Kojinsha, Tokyo, 2001

Yoshihara Kane, *Southern Cross* (transl. Doris Heath), Australian War Memorial, Canberra (ajrp.awm.gov.au/ajrp)

Interviews

October 2004
Imanishi Sadashige (144th Infantry Regiment)
Shimada Yuki (144th Infantry Regiment)
Yamasaki Yukiharu (144th Infantry Regiment)

April 2005
Imanishi Sadashige (144th Infantry Regiment)
Nishimura Kokichi (144th Infantry Regiment)
Tsunoda Kazuo (2nd Air Corps)
Yanagisawa Teruko (widow of Yanagisawa Hiroshi, 15th Independent Engineers Regiment)

Yokoyama Yori-ichi (41st Infantry Regiment)

April 2008
Yokoyama Yori-ichi (41st Infantry Regiment)
Imanishi Yumi (daughter of Imanishi Sadashige)

Acknowledgements

The authors gratefully acknowledge the invaluable assistance of several people in producing this book. First and foremost, we thank the six veterans of MO Operation who spoke to us extensively about their experience of the Pacific War for both this book and the documentary *Beyond Kokoda*, which preceded it. We would also like to thank Stig Schnell and Shaun Gibbons of SGSS Productions for their initiative in starting the chain of events that produced the TV show and the book.

Our knowledge of the Japanese side of the war and specific information about the Kokoda Track and adjacent regions would be less without the mentoring, advice and assistance of Professor Tanaka Hiromi, Kondo Shinji, Dr Steven Bullard, Bill James and Clive Baker. We are also grateful to the archives of the Australian War Memorial for providing such a valuable source of information. We thank Douglas Papi, Russell Kukuna and Michael Tutuana for their assistance in our 'sampling' of the Kokoda Track, and the Ichikawa brothers, Yosuke, Shuzo and Sadamu, Abe Kazuhiko and Kimura Daisuke for their assistance and guidance in Fukuyama and Kochi.

The manuscript would have been less accurate and readable but for the scrutiny it received from Peter Williams, Jan Stretton and Judy Herbert.

Finally, we would like to thank the folk at Allen & Unwin for their input into the book in its final published form, particularly Richard Walsh and Ian Bowring for believing in it from the outset, Liz Keenan, the copy editor, for chasing out tautologies and other unnecessary verbiage lurking in the manuscript, and Rebecca Kaiser for guiding the journey from manuscript to bookshop.

Index